"Keith Krance is one of the smartest Facebook ads experts I've ever worked with. Thanks to him we were able to set up our first profitable Facebook ad campaign to our Podcaster's Paradise webinar campaign, which was getting a 6 to 1 ROI, AND helped us ignite our entire new webinar sales funnel!"

—JOHN LEE DUMAS, HOST OF THE #1 BUSINESS PODCAST "ENTREPRENEUR ON FIRE"

"Since becoming a member of Keith and Perry's 80/20 Facebook Express program, I've added over $500,000 in revenue to my company by managing clients' Facebook accounts AND generated over $2,200,000 in sales for my clients in less than six months!"

—SETH GREENE, FOUNDER, MARKET DOMINATION, LLC

"After taking Keith's advice, within just a few days I cut my cost per click and CPM (cost per thousand impressions) by half! If you have a chance to learn from Keith, or work with Keith, DO IT."

—BRIAN BAGNALL, CEO, BAGNALL & ASSOCIATES

"When it comes to Facebook Advertising experts Keith Krance is the best of the best. Over the past few years Keith and his team have helped us generate tens of thousands of quality leads and millions in sales directly from Facebook. His stuff works!"

—BILL HARRISON, BestsellerBlueprint.com

"Keith Krance and his team are incredible! In the short time we've been working together, I have experienced an increase of more than $100,000 in sales for a new service offering on just over $19,000 in ad spend. We expect to reach $200,000 a month very soon (starting from zero). In a world where there seems to be quasi experts on every corner, these guys can actually deliver on their promise. I highly recommend Keith and his team."

—TRAVIS LANE JENKINS, CONSULTANT TO DOCTORS, AND HOST OF "THE ENTREPRENEUR'S RADIO SHOW"

"I'm a believer! Not only did Keith Krance take the guesswork out of running Facebook ads, his strategies brought us a flood of new qualified traffic that is now converting straight into the top of our funnel. Thanks to Keith, we're now running promotions regularly with great success."

—Lisa Williams, Marketing Director, The Jack Canfield Training Group

"Keith Krance continues to enlighten our community of digital marketers with intelligent and creative traffic advice. As one of the top Facebook advertising experts, Keith is the contact you want to have when setting up, scaling, and simply making money on Facebook."

—Molly Pittman, Social Marketing and Facebook Ads Manager at Ryan Deiss's Digital Marketer

"Perry Marshall has done more to de-mystify Google AdWords for business owners than any person on earth. With this book, he's done the same for Facebook. If you want to cut through the smoke quickly and make money advertising on Facebook, this is the book to read."

—Ken McCarthy, The System Seminar, Tivoli NY

"The irony of living in the Information Age is that good info has gotten harder to come by. The lame stuff still manages to clog the pipes, causing chaos and preventing you from discovering the legit specifics that can actually help you in your quest for business success and a bigger bottom line. Perry Marshall has been a first-stop, one-stop resource for the best possible advice on making AdWords work since Google unleashed it on the marketing community . . . and now, Perry's new tome on Facebook's astonishing (and yet-to-be-fully-tapped) power to reach gazillions of targeted, eager prospects (most of whom you'd never even know existed, otherwise) is the first and probably the only book you need to be one of those early adopters who score fastest. Perry's books are always essential. This one is perhaps more so than usual."

—John Carlton, the most respected and ripped-off veteran copywriter on the web

"Aw, the whole thing makes my head hurt. But other than puffery about 600-million customers, Perry's an honest man in a field rife with charlatans. If anybody can make practical sense of Facebook for marketers, it's Perry. He has his finger on its truth—as advertising media not social media. He also realizes there is a short window of time during which it offers greatest opportunity. He identified this with Google AdWords. Now this book shows how to capitalize on ideal timing with this media. Finally, he is a well-disciplined direct-response practitioner who holds this accountable for ROI. I bestow my 'No B.S. blessing.'"

—Dan S. Kennedy, legendary direct marketing advisor
and author of the *NO B.S.* book series, www.NoBSBooks.com

"Perry Marshall is amazing! He reinvented himself from engineer to white paper expert to become the world's leading expert in Google Adwords. Now with his secret weapon, Tom Meloche, he's reinvented himself again, this time as the guru in Facebook advertising . . . through which, he points out, you can access 600 million customers in 10 minutes."

—Bob Bly, author of over 60 books including *Complete Idiot's Guide to Direct Marketing*, *The Online Copywriter's Handbook*, and *Public Relations Kit for Dummies*

"Perry Marshall is a terrific writer who makes wonderful use of stories and analogies to illustrate a concept. He does this exceptionally well in the chapter on ad copy writing, 'The Power of Hidden Psychological Triggers.' That chapter alone is worth the price of this book.

"Many companies have tried Facebook ads and failed for one simple reason: they treated Facebook advertising like search advertising.

"Facebook is social advertising. Social advertising is about understanding and reaching the user. Not the user's behavior; but the actual person. This is where the book shines. It walks you through strategies of reaching your target audience based upon the person's social profile so that you aren't just accumulating 'Likes,' but actually gaining new customers.

"I'd recommend this book to anyone who is advertising, or wants to advertise, on Facebook. Social advertising is unique from most other types of advertising, and this book will teach you the concepts and how-tos you must understand so that your Facebook ads increase your overall profits."

—Brad Geddes, author of *Advanced Google AdWords*

"One of the things I love about Perry is that he always shoot from the hip. *Ultimate Guide to Facebook Advertising* is written with no holds barred, which means that all the 'juicy' tips that might get left out of other, similar books are all in this book. It's more than just a tactical 'how to.' It goes into the psychological aspects of ad writing specifically suited for Facebook and gives all kinds of practical advice for fan pages. So for anyone who really wants to get serious about Facebook advertising, this book is definitely a must read."

—SHELLEY ELLIS, CONTEXTUAL ADVERTISING EXPERT, WWW.CONTENTNETWORKINSIDER.COM

"Perry Marshall led the pack with Google AdWords back in 2006. He's still leading the pack today with Ultimate Guide to Facebook Advertising. Perry and Tom Meloche combine 'insider' knowledge of marketing on Facebook with proven marketing fundamentals for a powerful one-two punch that delivers results. Perry doesn't just theorize about how Facebook marketing works, he does it himself, and he's worked with thousands of others to hone his knowledge of this emerging landscape. If you're thinking of marketing on Facebook, or if you're already doing it, you'd be crazy to not get *Ultimate Guide to Facebook Advertising*."

—CLATE MASK, PRESIDENT, INFUSIONSOFT

"Hands down, I have never seen a more comprehensive in-depth study of successful Facebook advertising than what you are holding in your hands. Perry has done it again, he's extracted the 'gold' within this amazing system of advertising that every astute marketer should devour and implement."

—ARI GALPER, FOUNDER AND CEO, UNLOCK THE GAME, WWW.UNLOCKTHEGAME.COM

"Perry and Tom not only understand every nuance of the technical aspects of getting Facebook ads to work for your business, they also understand the psychology behind what works and what doesn't when it comes to advertising online. If you're looking for an über-effective way to master the art of driving traffic to your offers through paid advertising, get this book—it truly is the ultimate guide!"

—MARI SMITH, CO-AUTHOR OF *FACEBOOK MARKETING: AN HOUR A DAY*

"*Ultimate Guide to Facebook Advertising* just might be your ultimate guide to earning a ton of money with this social media phenomenon. What you don't know about Facebook could hurt you and what you will learn about Facebook from this book definitely will help you. It's a fun and easy read and a surefire way to seriously increase your income."

—[THE LATE] JAY CONRAD LEVINSON, THE FATHER OF GUERRILLA MARKETING,
AUTHOR OF *GUERRILLA MARKETING* SERIES OF BOOKS—OVER 21 MILLION SOLD; NOW IN 62 LANGUAGES

"Facebook advertising appears simple, but it's trickier than search engine marketing. In this book, Perry Marshall and Tom Meloche teach you secret of "Right Angle Marketing"—selling based on who people are and what they identify with. This is entirely different from Yahoo! or Google. They help you determine how to prioritize Facebook within your particular marketing mix. Then they take you by the hand and lead you through the minefield, showing you the tools, bidding techniques, and sales cycles of Facebook ads. Without their help, the odds are stacked against you. With their help, your chances of success are excellent."

—ALEX MANDOSSIAN, HERITAGE HOUSE PUBLISHING, AUTHOR OF *THE BUSINESS PODCASTING BIBLE*

"You're getting the *Ultimate Guide to Facebook Advertising* from the ultimate expert in Facebook ads. Keith Krance is a bonafide genius when it comes to advertising on Facebook. Don't walk—run to get a copy of this book."

—RUSS HENNEBERRY, EDITORIAL DIRECTOR AT RYAN DEISS'S DIGITAL MARKETER

"Perry Marshall delivers a huge amount of advertising experience and Keith Krance brings dynamic innovation. Together, they are well established as the leading Facebook marketers on the planet."

—JAMES SCHRAMKO, SUPERFASTBUSINESS.COM

Entrepreneur
MAGAZINE'S

ULTIMATE
GUIDE TO
facebook
ADVERTISING
Second Edition

- Access more than a billion potential customers in 10 minutes
- Leverage the latest game-changers to **pinpoint your most profitable audiences**
- Master strategies and techniques of successful Facebook advertisers

PERRY MARSHALL KEITH KRANCE THOMAS MELOCHE

EP
Entrepreneur
PRESS®

Entrepreneur Press, Publisher
Cover Design: Andrew Welyczko
Production and Composition: Eliot House Productions

This publication is designed to provide accurate and authoritative information in regard to the
subject matter covered. It is sold with the understanding that the publisher is not engaged in
rendering legal, accounting or other professional services. If legal advice or other expert assistance is
required, the services of a competent professional person should be sought.

Library of Congress Cataloging-in-Publication Data
Marshall, Perry S.
      Ultimate guide to facebook advertising: how to access more than a billion potential
customers in 10 minutes/ by Perry Marshall, Keith Krance, and Thomas Meloche
      p. cm.
      ISBN-13: 978-1-59918-546-0 (paperback)
      ISBN-10: 1-59918-546-6 (paperback)
      1. 1. Facebook (Electronic resource) 2. Internet advertising. I. Krance, Keith. II. Meloche,
Thomas. III. Title.
HF6146.I58M364 2014
659.14'4—dc23   2014025082

Printed in the United States of America

18 17   10 9 8 7 6

Contents

Chapter 1

Facebook's Move to Rule the World

IT ALL STARTED IN A COLLEGE DORM ROOM, AND WHY IT MATTERS TO YOU

Facebook was founded in Mark Zuckerberg's Harvard University dorm room by Zuck, his roommates, and friends. It was not built for you, the advertiser. They did not have you in mind. They were not trying to meet your needs. They were not interested in providing you "clicks."

Instead, they were simply making a cool, digital place for Harvard students to see and connect to other Harvard students. Real connections. Real names, real people, real pictures, and real Harvard email addresses required to register.

It was a place to connect with the college version of "friends"—the studious guy sitting next to you in physics or the slender girl in calculus. A place to really connect, without anonymous, fake user names that had come to dominate most use of the internet. A place to meet without the expectation of committing to a "date."

It grew.

> "*When you give everyone a voice and give people power, the system usually ends up in a really good place. So, what we view our role as, is giving people that power.*"
>
> —MARK ZUCKERBERG

Within 30 days, more than half of Harvard's undergrads had become members. It grew some more.

First to other Boston colleges, the Ivy League, and Stanford. Then to other universities across the country and around the world. Then to high school networks and a few select companies.

Two and a half years after it was launched, in September 2006, Facebook finally opened the floodgates when it opened service to anyone over the age of 13 with a valid email address. Facebook has far surpassed its original goal of one billion members, and the company is valued at over a hundred billion dollars.

The founders of Facebook created history. They redefined what it means to interact on a global scale. They created a massive social graph of how the world is connected: whose friends, parents, brothers, cousins are friends with whom, and on and on.

Facebook knows what its members look like, think, enjoy, and visit because they are the world's largest:

- Photo-sharing site;
- Thought-sharing site;
- Liking site;
- Linking site.

Even with Google's gargantuan lead, Facebook possibly will become the world's largest advertising site, especially as the internet continues its trajectory toward easy mobile device access.

FACEBOOK IS THE ONLY COMPANY THAT OWNS THE MOBILE PHONE!

The majority of internet use is now via smartphones and tablets. This is bad news for all the old-school internet companies. But it's good news for Facebook. Why?

Because Facebook is the only company that is putting FULL-SCREEN DISPLAY ADS in front of mobile phones users and getting away with it on a daily basis.

All the other online ads are either in apps or tiny, inconsequential banner ads. Facebook puts display ads and videos right in the middle of the news feed, and many people see dozens every day. *Plus, many times those ads don't really seem like ads.* Above the ad, the post says "Suzy Smith likes ACME corporation" so the ad has implied endorsement.

This *works*. On a massive scale.

As exciting as all this is, it is important for advertisers to remember that Facebook did not build the site for us, the advertisers. They built it for themselves.

The hottest young college grads Facebook hires from the world's top universities don't say, "I want to work at Facebook to help them maximize ad revenue." Please know that even despite Facebook's massive gains in the ad department, the company doesn't exist simply to send you customers.

Regardless of why Zuckerberg built Facebook or what high ideals his staffers may hold, the personal demographic information Facebook collects is tremendously valuable to us advertisers.

Facebook is not stupid.

It is more closely connected with its advertisers than any other platform on the planet. Facebook visionaries already have years' worth of additional ideas to implement. How do we know this? We see the ideas publicly volunteered every day on Facebook pages by Facebook advertisers.

Adult supervision at Facebook is minimal, which is probably why it is so absolutely brilliant. The company almost exclusively hires fresh, college graduates. The brightest college grads on the planet, but still fresh, college graduates.

These are the smart kids, smarter than you, smarter than us. They have never had a "real" job outside of Facebook.

They have never tried to live off revenue generated by an ad. They do not feel your pain.

Remember that. It is really important.

To use Facebook's paid advertising tools effectively, it is important to understand just how much its creators and designers *are not* really trying to help you. Fortunately, they do need cash, and we do need clicks, so we can get some great work done together. We focus on the clicks, and they focus on changing the world.

Facebook has the potential, the real potential, to be highly relevant for decades to come. Our rule of thumb is the founder's rule: When you have a dynamic and visionary founder running a business, better to bet on that business continuing to be a success for as long as you see that founder at the helm.

We suggest that as long as you see Mark Zuckerberg engaged at Facebook, you should plan on Facebook being a dynamic and growing, competitive place to advertise.

Oh, Mark was born in 1984.

He will probably be around for a long, long time.

1984? It turns out that *Little* Brother is the one who's watching you.

ONE TOOL TO RULE THEM ALL, AND IN THE FACEBOOK BIND THEM

One Tool to rule them all,
One Tool to find them,
One Tool to bring them all
And in the Facebook bind them.

The poem should haunt Google. Facebook is actively creating one tool to bind the entire internet together. And Facebook, not Google, is in charge.

But wait, there's more!

Facebook built Facebook Mobile and smartphone users log in an average of 14 times a day. These users are connected to Facebook nearly 24/7. *The Guardian* reports that four out of five users log in via mobile. Facebook reports that mobile users are more than twice as active as non-mobile users. No one owns the phone like Facebook. Facebook is the only way to reach some of your customers. "Come on over for a 10 percent special discount. Good for the next 30 minutes!"

Facebook Places lets Facebook users announce where they are and see where their friends are. Friday nights in the big city need never be lonely again. Friends share where they have been, what they have liked, and where they will be, so you can meet up while the night is young.

But wait, there's more.

Facebook is extending the social graph even deeper into their partners' websites, so your website pages can be "liked" like a Facebook page. These likes automatically enter the news feed of your Facebook community.

Not at all obvious to most people is the fact that Facebook is now a major source of search engine optimization (SEO). Social media likes and tweets are a major influence on search engine rankings.

One tool to rule them all, and in the Facebook bind them.

YOUR MISSION, SHOULD YOU CHOOSE TO ACCEPT IT, MOVES TO FACEBOOK

So what do you do with all of this information about Facebook? Simple. Your mission is to buy a click for $1, turn it into $2, and then make more profit than your competitors from your $2. This is your mission, and it has moved to Facebook. It is a new platform but a very old mission.

The rest is just strategy and tactics. Many existing strategies and tactics that we have taught to over 100,000 Google advertisers work directly in Facebook. You need to understand your sales funnel, craft a compelling ad, have a focused goal for your landing page, and track and follow up with your leads and your customers. More important, you want to do this automatically.

We will teach you the strategy and tactics required to fulfill your mission: to get those clicks, and to turn them into customers.

Some tactics, especially those built around keywords and bidding strategies, have changed dramatically for Facebook. Don't worry, we will show you the secrets we have found to be successful in Facebook.

Your Mission, a Penny at a Time

Those who like numbers will appreciate how powerful your fundamental mission is. Depending on the size of your market, your mission may also be stated as, "Your mission is to buy a click for $1 and to reliably and repeatedly turn it into $.01 worth of pure profit."

This is how pro gamblers think. If they can find a game where betting a dollar nets them a penny, they are in heaven. They sit there for hours and hours playing round after round trying to bet as much as possible to earn that 1 percent net.

They even have a name for it. They call it "grinding." The best part about grinding when you're a digital marketer is that you do not have to actually sit at a table in a smoke-filled room. Digital grinding happens in that area of the web now called the "cloud," and clouds are much nicer than smoke-filled rooms.

Also, you do not have to live in Vegas. In the online world, the game comes to you.

Think about this for a moment: a 1 percent net ROI that may be achieved within a matter of minutes from when the investment was made. What is the return on a dollar, on an annual basis, that can bring 1 percent every three minutes? The figure is so large it makes even Goldman Sachs blush. A penny, if enough clicks are available, is a fortune. Empires are built on a 1 percent net profit.

Don't despise making a penny, especially if you can make it reliably and repeatedly. Instead, focus on how to make a lot more pennies. Focus on how to get a lot more clicks.

Perhaps it is on Facebook?

For your sake, we hope so. Because advertising on Facebook is actually a lot of fun.

For some advertisers, using Facebook paid advertising to find new customers is also stunningly easy. Take the quiz in Chapter 2 to find out if you are one of the lucky ones. Facebook advertising may be a great fit that will cause new customers to fall into your lap.

Go to www.perrymarshall.com/fbtools for the latest updates and to get valuable resources for more clicks from Facebook for less money.

Is Facebook for Me?

CAN EVERY BUSINESS BENEFIT FROM ADVERTISING ON FACEBOOK?

The truthful answer is: Not really.

Facebook may not be for you. This book might be a waste of your time. Facebook ads might be a waste of your money.

So you might as well find out right now.

This chapter will answer the question for you.

Facebook offers so many opportunities to reach customers with specialized advertising that almost every business can benefit from some form of paid advertising on Facebook, even if it spends only a few dollars a week.

However, it is one thing to use paid Facebook advertising sparingly—for example, to tell your fans about an event—and quite another to commit to making Facebook a significant new source of leads or traffic for your business. This chapter will determine if Facebook ads can be a significant source of leads for your business. Or not.

> *"If you find a path with no obstacles, it probably doesn't lead anywhere."*
>
> —FRANK HOWARD CLARK

ARE YOU A LOCAL BUSINESS WITH A PHYSICAL LOCATION WHERE CONSUMERS REGULARLY COME TO PURCHASE YOUR GOODS AND SERVICES?

Does your business have a doorknob that customers turn? If so, then **Facebook is for you**. Dentists, doctors, lawyers, veterinarians, physical trainers, gyms, specialty shops, cupcake stores, specialty groceries, beer and wine shops, restaurants, mechanics, theaters, and music venues are highly likely to benefit from locally targeted Facebook campaigns, which may cost as little as $100 to $200 a month.

Facebook allows you to advertise to people who live within a few miles of your location, to advertise directly to your known customers, and to advertise directly to your customers' friends who live nearby. These features, and the nature of Facebook, make Facebook a great candidate to fill your advertising needs.

Facebook is amazing for selling locally because Facebook makes it easy to get your message in front of your local market demographic even before your target audience has begun searching for your particular product or service.

HOW TO FIND OUT IF YOU CAN REALLY SELL ON FACEBOOK

I (Perry) suspect it is possible to successfully sell almost any product or service on Facebook. However, it is clear that some products sell on Facebook like magic and others are really, really difficult to sell there. The interesting question for your business is "How easy will it be to sell on Facebook?"

Some types of products or services are a natural fit for selling on Facebook. So natural, you can set up a campaign and start finding new customers in a few short minutes. Other types of products and services will be a harder sale. And, quite frankly, Facebook may not be a good channel for purchasing clicks until you have exhausted easier channels.

Where does your business fall? I've created an entire website, *IsFBforME.com*, to help you answer that question. The site asks you ten short questions about your business and results in a score from 1 to 10 that you can use to better understand how your business fits with Facebook.

Take a nonscored version of the test here. The more the following statements describe your product or service, the more **Facebook is for you.**

Our Stuff Is Unique

Facebook is for you if you sell unique or personalized products. Facebook is the worldwide capital of individual expression. It's the perfect place for customized and personalized products, items that express a person's own tastes and preferences or engage potential customers on a human-to-human level.

You will not maximize Facebook's marketing potential if you are selling products that could be listed in the "commodity" category or if your customer can easily find your product at big-box retailers and national chains. If people can easily buy your product elsewhere or can compare prices easily online, then selling your product profitably on Facebook will be difficult. When you advertise on Facebook, always lead with those products that are most unusual, unique, and eye-catching.

Facebook is the place to sell products that don't carry an expected price. If your customers know exactly what your product should cost, you probably should not be selling it on Facebook. Sell unique products, where the value is determined by the customer's desire to have something interesting, not by the price.

We Sell to Consumers

Facebook is for you if you sell to consumers, not businesses. Facebook is a place for individuals to connect with friends and family. It is best used by businesses as a place to find and connect to individuals and individual consumers. It is not a good place to sell to other businesses. Although corporations have pages on Facebook, their presence there is as a sales presence to market to consumers, not as a purchasing presence to buy from your business.

Facebook can be effective in selling to buyers at small companies with only a few employees because most of those companies blend business and personal life. But the larger the client you are seeking to sell to, the harder it will be to use Facebook. Many larger companies actively block Facebook use within the company. These companies might even punish or dismiss employees for spending time on Facebook at work. This is not exactly the location to try to close a deal.

Can Facebook Sell to Businesses? Does It Work for B2B?

Certainly it can, especially small businesses and "SOHO" (Small Office / Home Office). But in general, the more corporate and the more "work and production" oriented your offer is, the less simpatico it is with Facebook. People go to Facebook to *escape* work.

We Sell Fun Products

Facebook is for you if your products are fun. It is a great place to sell events, memberships, experiences, personal improvement, travel, and entertainment. Facebook is fun! It is a place where people go to connect, to play, and to socialize. It is a place to feel, express opinions, and display emotions.

Facebook is a great place to advertise products that are fun and appeal to a person's core identity, which is why a membership in a group or a club is a great sales opportunity on Facebook. Events, travel, and entertainment are full of fun and positive emotions. These subjects are naturally social, and people love to ask "Where have you been?" "What have you seen?" and "Where do you want to go?"

If you provide personal improvement products, especially anything that's new, trendy, hip, or cool, Facebook is also a great fit. If your product involves some form of training, accent the social advantages more than the academic aspects, such as how learning a new language can make travel more fun.

On the flip side, if your product is technical, academic, complex, or requires deep thought, it may be hard to sell on Facebook. It can be done, but you will need to create additional materials *outside* of Facebook to get your buyer educated on the benefits of your product. You will likely need to create videos, tutorials, and automated emails and have a formal plan to deliver them.

We Harmonize with Identity, Personal Beliefs, and Convictions

Facebook is for you if your business harmonizes with a person's identity—political affiliations, religious convictions, beliefs, or social movements. On Facebook, it's a significant advantage if your company and your target customer lean in a particular direction religiously, politically, or socially.

Regardless of whether your company leans right or left or whatever, there are lots of people who may be predisposed to do business with you for that particular leaning. And you should take advantage of it. There are very simple ways you can target your customers on Facebook and communicate with them so that you connect to the things they care about.

If you appeal to a variety of such backgrounds, then you can design specific marketing campaigns to cater to each of those preferences. You may have different pockets of people within your customer database, and the better you understand those pockets, the more you can target your ads and the more you can sell.

If this isn't immediately obvious, don't give up. You might want to survey your customers and see if you can identify any political, social, or religious preferences. Better yet, get your customers to "like" your Facebook page, and then review their profiles for "likes and interests" and the summary reports that Facebook provides.

Many business owners find beliefs and convictions are held by their customers after they close the first sale. These factors may well shape what you say to your customers so you can deepen the emotional bond they share with you.

PERRY MARSHALL'S FACEBOOK QUIZ

To make it easier for you to understand how well Facebook paid advertising may work for your business, take the following ten-question quiz. It will give you a score from 1 to 10, with the higher score representing a better potential outcome for Facebook advertising.

Take the quiz now at *IsFBforMe.com* and record your score below.

Scan QR Code to Go To IsFBforMe.com.

My Score: What It Means

1: *Danger.* See if you can get your money back for this book.

2–3: *Caution.* If your final score is 2 or 3, then finding new leads and customers through paid advertising on Facebook is likely to be difficult, time-consuming, and expensive. If you are a small company or a startup, it may be a losing proposition, and you should focus your advertising dollars elsewhere to find new leads and customers.

However, you should probably still use some Facebook paid advertising to feature events, market to existing customers, and collect customer and lead demographics. Facebook is an amazing tool simply for what it can teach you about your own customers, such as their age, gender, location, affiliations, favorite books, favorite music, favorite movies, political affiliations, and other likes and interests. Buying some Facebook advertising may be useful just to help you collect this data.

4–5: *Helpful.* If your final score is 4 or 5, then paid advertising on Facebook has the potential to bring you more customers, but it will take a bit of work, and it probably should not be your primary source of traffic. The biggest benefit of being on Facebook is to provide you another channel to connect to existing customers and to collect detailed customer demographics.

6–7: *Significant.* If your final score is 6 or 7, then you are definitely in the Facebook sweet spot. Facebook paid advertising may be a new way for you to attract significantly more traffic to your website. In addition, at least for the next few years, you may be able to get this traffic very affordably.

8–10: *Jackpot.* If your final score is 8 to 10, then you have hit the Facebook jackpot. It is possible that Facebook paid advertising may even become your number-one traffic source.

If you scored 6 or above, you should devour every word of this book.

If you scored 5 or lower, there is still a lot of useful content for you here, but some chapters will be less important because you likely will be spending only tens of dollars, not tens of thousands of dollars, on Facebook ads. Read extra carefully Chapters 17, 18, and 19.

Sample Scores

At the beginning of the chapter, we suggested some types of local businesses that might do well selling themselves or their products on Facebook. Now you know why we were able to make that statement. We score these business types at 7.5 or higher every time: dentists, doctors, personal lawyers, veterinarians, physical trainers, gyms, specialty shops, restaurants, mechanics, theaters, and music venues.

- Dentist: Score 8
- Vinyl Records-Only Store: Score 8.4
- Musical Venue That Hosts Events: Score 9.2
- Summer Day Camp with Religious Affiliations: Score 9.6
- Selling Industrial Network Cards: Score 3.6 (Perry's previous job)

IS GOOGLE ADWORDS FOR YOU?

Hey, while you're trying to decide about Facebook, you might as well score yourself for Google, too. Which is better for your business? "Google Search" or "Google Display"? Find out in just 60 seconds at www.IsAWforMe.com.

Take the short quiz and get an instant ScoreCard on how appropriate your business is for 1) Google AdWords for keyword search and 2) Google's Display Network. You can compare your score to the www.IsFBforMe.com quiz and prioritize the three major ad networks on the internet.

www.IsAWforMe.com

- Selling Automated Tutors to Home-Schooling Families: Score 8.4 (Tom's education business)
- Selling Hipster T-Shirts: 6

SHOULD YOU ADVERTISE ON FACEBOOK FIRST? NEW RULES FOR THE NEW WORLD ORDER

Facebook is changing the texture of online advertising. For the first time in more than a decade, I (Perry) actually advise some of our clients to start paying for advertising on Facebook before—or even instead of—using Google AdWords.

Is this sacrilegious?

Not at all. If you have been following our advice, you know we are not Google fanatics, we are pragmatic marketers. We will take a cost-effective click from wherever we can get it. If Facebook makes it easier than Google, then bless 'em. I will use their tool until the next guy comes along. There is always a next guy. So if you are starting a new venture or just starting digital marketing, should you consider using Facebook first as your initial source of traffic?

Are you a local business and did you score above 9 on the "Is Facebook for Me" quiz? YES—start first with paid ads on Facebook.

Are you a national online business, did you score an 8 or higher on the quiz, and do you have a strong affiliation with a belief or movement that people identify themselves with on Facebook? YES—start first with paid ads on Facebook.

Are you a local professional with finite capacity and did you score an 8 or higher on the quiz? YES—start first with paid ads on Facebook. You may be able to generate all of your business just with Facebook advertising, and you will save yourself the learning curve of Google AdWords tools.

Please understand, "starting" is simply a matter of building a Facebook page and running ads for a week or two. I am not advising you to never use other advertising channels. In fact, except for the case of the professional who may get fully booked and not be interested in adding more business, I expect everyone to develop multiple sources of clicks and leads. TO NOT DO SO IS STUPID.

If starting first on Facebook is recommended, that's because it will probably be easier for you to hone your message, build your funnel, and capture your market's demographics on Facebook than anywhere else. So take advantage of it.

It took ten years, but the world finally has an advertising channel that will be a better place for some businesses to start than Google AdWords.

Congratulations, Facebook.

FACEBOOK WAS FOR ME—TOM'S STORY

I am a Facebook fanatic. I've built an entire software company from the ground up using Facebook ads to sell our product. The ads are simple, powerful, and affordable. However, I didn't start my advertising with Facebook in mind.

I designed a software tool for accelerated learning called HomeSchoolAdvantage. It was ready for beta users, and I needed to drive a few hundred of them to the site to kick the tires and see if they would take it out for a spin. I created an awesome landing page to convert leads to trial users, and I was ready for clicks.

Because I had prior success driving traffic with Google AdWords, I started there. Google, however, was doing all sorts of snaky things, "Oh, you want a click? That's $2 to $3." After a time, of course, that comes down to $1, then $0.50, but by then they've given me an amazingly low "Quality Score."

I was a homeschool tutoring service selling to homeschoolers by advertising on the keyword *homeschool*; my URL is HomeSchoolAdvantage.com. You would think it would be a good match.

Not so, said the great and mighty Google.

Now, I was willing to arm-wrestle with Google bots to convince them I was a good advertising fit and should receive cheaper clicks and a higher score. I could have tried to convince Google bots I was "quality" by placing articles, blog posts, and content outside of the paywall—all my hard work was behind the paywall. I could have done some tricks with my keywords, I could have done all these things, but they all require a lot of work.

Or.

I had been on Facebook, so I thought perhaps I could try this new Facebook advertising thingy and see how it worked. I put up my first ad.

Magic.

Facebook immediately drove clicks to my existing landing page and never stopped. No weird quality score. No exorbitant pricing scheme. No struggle.

I was hooked. I immediately saw all sorts of conversions coming in, coming in for 40 percent less than I was paying on Google, and I wasn't arm-wrestling the system to drive the clicks.

FACEBOOK WAS FOR ME—TOM'S STORY, continued

Awesome.

I was an entrepreneur launching a highly speculative software venture where the typical failure rate is over 90 percent. I was already spending all of my time, creative energy, and money trying to change the world. I needed to put my energy into listening to my customers and responding to their needs, not arm-wrestling Google bots over Quality Score.

I turned Google AdWords off and left it off—FOR AN ENTIRE YEAR.

Sure, Google is still part of my long-term strategy, but it moved from spot Number 1 to spot Number 4. Here is my new world order:

1. Facebook ads
2. Email blasts to paid lists
3. Button and banner ads on homeschool websites
4. Google AdWords

I found an alternative for what I was initially trying to achieve on Facebook. And the alternative turned out to be way better.

I got the leads I needed for my beta test for $4,100 not the $20,000 I had budgeted. And, I built an entire, interconnected community of fans on Facebook for free—after I moved my landing pages to Facebook pages! Because I charged to use the beta HomeSchoolAdvantage service and the advertising was so affordable, my beta campaign broke even. As a bonus, my Facebook community offers suggestions, provides feedback, and continually attracts more customers.

I purchased 15.5 million impressions and 11,000 clicks in my beta program for about 37 cents a click. I spent less than one hour a week managing the campaigns. Do you have any idea how amazing this is?

I used Facebook for this project because it was easier.

I used Facebook for my next project because it was better. Read on—you'll see what I mean. Is Facebook for me? You bet it is, I scored an 8.4!

One last note, and this is very, very important: I did not initially focus on the "social media" aspect of Facebook. Yes, "liking," posting, and interacting with

FACEBOOK WAS FOR ME—TOM'S STORY, continued

people on my fan page has proven to be important over time. But all of this is nearly useless unless and until you have the ability to steadily and reliably get targeted traffic to your website or fan page.

If you want to build a real business that makes money, most of the advice you find in "social media" books demands enormous amounts of manual labor from you at best. And much of that advice is woefully ineffective. If you want to build a real business that makes money, invest $1 in advertising, acquire a customer, and get $2 back. It's faster, it's easier, and it's the most reliable way to grow a company.

Go to www.perrymarshall.com/fbtools for the latest updates and to get valuable resources for more clicks from Facebook for less money.

Chapter 3

A Few Fundamentals

HOW A MEASLY DOLLAR BILL ALMOST GOT ME FIRED

When I was a brand-new, wet-behind-the-ears student of marketing, I had great admiration for legendary copywriters like Gary Halbert, who wrote high-testosterone, hypnotic, grab-you-by-the-throat copy.

But I had a really hard time understanding how to apply their daring approaches and edgy ideas to my customers, who were conservative, risk-averse manufacturing engineers. My company sold B2B, and infomercial-style marketing was not how anybody did things in that business.

> *"First master the fundamentals."*
> —LARRY BIRD

One day the proverbial gun was pointed at my head and I had to make my numbers for the month. I had to sell something. So I called up my friend Phil Alexander, who knew more marketing techniques than anybody else I knew.

At that time, Phil, like me, was pretty green. He had more theory under his belt than practice, for sure. Phil said, "The best way I know of to sell anything is a dollar bill letter."

"What's a dollar bill letter?"

"It's a letter where you tape a one dollar bill to the top of it and you say,

DEAR FIRSTNAME,

As you see, I have attached a crisp new $1 bill to the top of this letter. Why have I done this?

Three reasons:

1. I needed to get your attention, and I knew this would work. You can have this dollar as a gift.
2. Every single day you're losing hundreds of dollar bills just like this one because . . . (blah blah blah).

"Wow, Phil, thanks! What a fantastic idea!"

I quickly sent that letter to 300 engineers, expecting the phone to ring and products to fly off the shelf.

I got . . . nothing.

Ah, the stony austere silence of an offer that makes a thud and generates no interest. How awful I felt.

Plus I'd done it without my boss Mike's permission (literally pulling the dollar bills out of my own pocket), and he was mortified. "You sent THIS goofy letter to 300 engineers?"

His face was red. I could almost see the steam coming out of his ears. "This is crazy! What, are you trying to vandalize our brand?"

I meekly apologized. I didn't even dare ask for the postage money back, let alone my three hundred dollars.

Mike said, "Perry, if you ever do something like this again without permission, don't bother coming to work the next day, cuz you'll be fired on the spot."

"Yessir."

So . . . what really happened and why didn't it work?

First, I did that out of desperation, and that's the worst frame of mind to be in when you're trying to sell something.

Second, I applied a **technique** without understanding the **principle** behind it. The technique was "dollar bill letter." But what's the principle? The principle of all advertising is: *Enter the conversation inside your customer's head.*

I hadn't done that at all. It was probably against company policy for half those engineers to even put the dollar bill in their pocket. So the brilliant idea that I borrowed from Phil that Phil borrowed from the late Gary Halbert was a gimmick, and it almost got me fired.

I resolved to always recognize the difference between a principle and a technique. And make sure the principle *behind* the technique was correct. This chapter is all about the basic principles and vocabulary of Facebook, so you're not just trying stuff willy-nilly.

LEARN THE VOCABULARY TO UNDERSTAND THE TOOL

There are a few fundamentals you, the Facebook advertiser, should understand before you begin spending your hard-earned cash. However, that being said, some of the terms and definitions in this chapter can be a little confusing and overwhelming to the brand new advertiser.

This chapter is meant to be used more as a reference guide that you can come back to again and again as different scenarios come up in your quest for world domination with Facebook. It is okay to quickly skim through some of these terms and get right into chapter 4, so you get started creating your first ad!

Ads

An *ad* in Facebook is content displayed to Facebook users at an advertiser's specific request (see Figure 3.1).

Ready To Make A Trip?

Little Duck offers free guides to ponds and puddles all over the Metro area. Get your FREE GUIDE today.

FIGURE 3.1–A Facebook Ad Displayed Horizontally

These ads are frequently seen in the right-hand column of your Facebook wall, profile, and photo pages. Up to five different ads may show at one time. Of course, where ads are displayed, what they are called, how they work, how they are presented, and how many are shown at a time are subject to change at any time.

Every time an ad is displayed on a Facebook page, a user could potentially read the ad. Facebook calls that an *impression*. An impression is an opportunity for someone to see your ad. If the ad seen in Figure 3.1 had 1.4 million impressions, then the ad had 1.4 million opportunities to be seen.

Impressions does not mean separate people have had the chance to see the ad. Your ad has not in fact been shown to 1.4 million people. The *estimated reach* for this ad is reported by Facebook to be 200,000 people. The estimated reach is the number of Facebook users who meet the criteria the advertiser has selected for people the advertiser wants to see the ad.

If an ad has 1.4 million impressions and an estimated reach of 200,000 people, we know that, on average, each of those 200,000 people has had seven opportunities to see the ad.

Most people do not click on an ad on the first impression. As users browse Facebook, moving from page to page, from their wall to their profile to their friend's wall to their pictures to business pages, the same ads are displayed multiple times.

If the *ad title*—the top line of the ad—is good and the *ad image* is compelling, the ad may eventually capture the attention of a Facebook browser, who then will actually look at it and read the *body text*, where all of an ad can be seen. (See Figure 3.2.)

FIGURE 3.2–Ad Title, Image, and Body Text

If the ad interests the user enough, then the user actually clicks on the ad and is taken to a new destination specified by the advertiser.

Facebook captures and reports the number of times all users have clicked on each ad. They cleverly name this process *clicks*.

How Well Is My Ad Working?

One of the first questions everyone asks is "How well is my ad working?" This question is actually trickier than it first seems because there are many measures of "working."

- Does the ad encourage the users to click?
- Will users do the next step we want them to after clicking?
- Will users ever purchase from us?
- Will users stop buying stuff from the other guy?

All four of these questions may be different ways to define working. Facebook helps us track and answer the first question, "Does the ad encourage the users to click?" You will learn secrets to answering the remaining questions in later chapters.

Facebook reports how well an ad encourages a user to click in a statistic called the *clickthrough rate* (CTR). This rate identifies how many impressions it takes on average before a user clicks on the ad.

CTR is clicks divided by impressions (clicks/impressions).

(10 clicks/1,000 impressions = 1 percent.)

If your ad has had 1,000 total impressions and users have clicked on the ad ten times, then your CTR is 1 percent.

The ad in Figure 3.3 had 376,409 impressions leading to 344 clicks. What is its CTR? Don't peek at the answer. Seriously, calculate this yourself at least once.

Finger Painting Adventure

Free finger painting project ideas. Seven fun-at-home projects for rainy weekends. Click for free video.

FIGURE 3.3–Calculate the CTR for this Ad

Did you get 0.091 percent? If not, do the math again.

The formula: 344 clicks/376,409 impressions = 0.091 percent CTR.

If you are still having trouble getting the math right, don't fret. Facebook reports the impressions and the clicks and calculates the CTR automatically. But it is important that you understand what the CTR means.

Landing Pages

When users click on an ad, where do they go? The page that is displayed after a user clicks on an ad is called a *landing page*. The advertiser specifies the landing page when the ad is created.

You can send a user who clicks on an ad anywhere that does not violate Facebook's landing page policies. You may send users to your own web page or you may send users to other locations within Facebook—such as a Facebook page, event, application, or group.

CPC (Cost Per Click)

Facebook does not display ads out of the goodness of its heart. It wants cold, hard cash. You have to provide a credit card before Facebook will even think of displaying your ad.

Once they have your payment information, they let you create an ad. During this process they ask if you want to *bid* for *clicks* or for *impressions*.

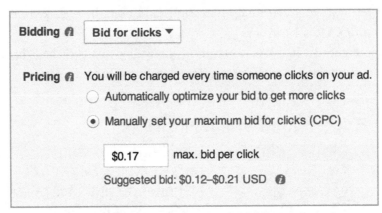

FIGURE 3.4–Pay for Clicks (CPC) Bidding Selected

If you choose to bid for clicks, you will be charged only if a user clicks on the ad. You can specify the amount you are willing to pay for a click, starting at one cent per click. If you say that you are willing to pay 17 cents for a click, then that is the most you will be charged for a click.

Technically, you are *bidding* on the ad space, so what you enter in a field labeled *Max Bid* is the maximum amount you are willing to pay for the click. You are bidding against other advertisers who are unseen and unknown, and you do not really know what they are bidding.

From your perspective, the *bid* word is a bit of a sham. Initially, the higher your bid the more likely your ad will be displayed. After a few thousand impressions, additional factors weigh in to affect the cost of your ad, including the CTR and whether users "like" or complain about your ad.

The good news? Facebook reserves the right to "lower the price" you pay per click. You read that right! They will actually charge you less than you bid, and lucky for you, they do this all the time.

CPM (Cost Per Thousand Impressions)

You may also select to bid on impressions instead of clicks. You actually bid what you are willing to pay for 1,000 impressions of your ad. This is called *cost per impression* (CPM). The advertiser is paying for someone to view the ad whether or not the user clicks on the ad. CPM is frequently associated with brand advertising. If the goal

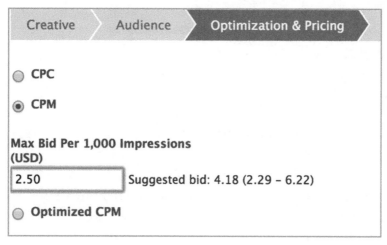

FIGURE 3.5–Pay for Impressions (CPM) Bidding Selected

is only to get the user to see the brand name and not to get a click, then CPM is advertisers' first choice. Of course, we think not trying to get a click is nearly always a mistake in digital advertising.

In the Facebook interface, pay per view is labeled CPM, short for cost per thousand impressions. You are thinking, "M? What is the M for?" Do you remember your Latin?

Mille means 1,000 in Latin.

M is 1,000 in Roman numerals.

Our word *millennium* means a span of 1,000 years.

CPM stands for cost per M impressions (M = 1,000). Get used to that crazy little "M." It is not going away.

You can tell Facebook that you are willing to pay simply to have it display your ad 1,000 times whether or not anyone clicks on the ad.

Did you notice that if you bid CPC you can still calculate CPM, and if you bid CPM you can still calculate CPC? In fact, no matter which way you choose to bid, Facebook will calculate and display both results for you.

Bidding strategy is covered in greater detail in later chapters. If we covered it all now, you might run screaming from the room and that would not help anybody.

Optimized CPM: Optimized CPM is a bid type that shows your ad to people who are more likely take the action you want. With this bid type, you pay for impressions (CPM). For example, if your advertising objective is to get more Facebook page likes, an optimized CPM bid will show your ad to people who are more likely to like your page. Your bid will automatically adjust to help your ads reach the people you care about, but you won't spend more than your budget.

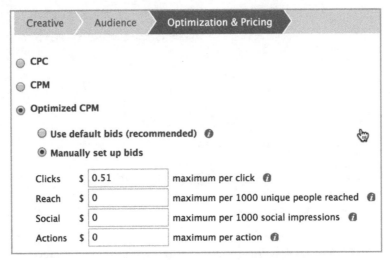

FIGURE 3.6–Optimized CPM Bidding

Reach, Frequency, and Ad Fatigue

Ads display on Facebook multiple times to the same user. The number of individual people who have seen your ad during a specific period of time is reported by Facebook as *reach*. The average number of times each individual user has seen your ad is reported as *frequency*. If you run your ad long enough, your actual *reach* will approach your *estimated reach*. Facebook displays the relationship between *reach* and *estimated reach* in a graphic. *Reach* is displayed as a smaller circle inside of a larger *estimated reach* circle, as shown in Figure 3.7.

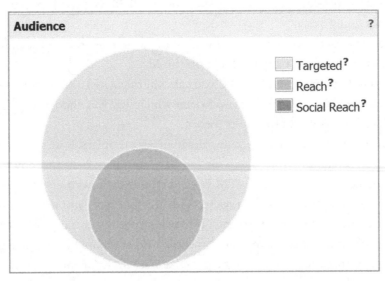

FIGURE 3.7–Relationship between Reach and Estimated Reach

Eventually, an ad may have a *frequency* of 30 or more. An ad with a frequency of 30 has been displayed to each individual reached user 30 times. Even if the ad is excellent, the users still get tired of seeing it, and they stop clicking on it.

This is called *ad fatigue*—your prospects stop clicking on an ad as the frequency gets high simply because they have grown tired of seeing it.

Have you ever watched a television commercial and really enjoyed it? Perhaps you thought it was funny, clever, or emotionally moving. Later, after seeing the same commercial over and over and over and over again—you slowly begin to hate it. If you have had that experience, then you have experienced *ad fatigue* firsthand.

Unique Clicks: The total number of unique people who have clicked on your ad. For example, if three people click on the same ad five times, it will count as three unique people who clicked.

Unique Clickthrough Rate (UCTR): The number of unique clicks as result of your ad divided by the number of unique people you reached. For example, if you received 20 unique clicks and 1,000 unique people saw your ad, your unique clickthrough rate will be 2 percent.

Ad Set: An ad set has one or more ads, a budget, and a schedule. You can create an ad set for each of your audience segments by making the ads within the ad set target the same audience. This will help you control the amount you spend on each audience, decide when each audience will see your ads, and see metrics specific to each audience.

Ads Manager: Ads Manager is where you can manage your Facebook ads. In Ads Manager, you can:

- View all of your campaigns, ad sets, and ads
- Make changes to your bids and budgets
- Stop or restart your ad sets and ads
- Access the billing manager to see your payment history and payment method info
- Access and export your ad performance reports

Social Clicks: Number of clicks your ad receives when it's shown with social information (e.g., Jane Doe likes this).

People Taking Action: The number of unique people who took an action such as liking your Facebook page or installing your app as a result of your ad. For example, if the same person likes and comments on a post, they will be counted as one unique person. People's actions are counted within one day of someone viewing your ad or 28 days after clicking on it.

Social Reach: Number of unique people who saw an ad with social information. For example, if three people see an ad two times each that says a friend likes your page, it counts as three social reaches.

Social Impressions: The number of times your ad was viewed with social information. For example, if three people see an ad two times each and it includes information about a friend liking your page, it counts as six social impressions.

Page Post Ads

This is a news feed ad. You are taking a post from your existing Facebook page and amplifying that post with advertising.

Photo posts and video posts typically get most engagement and organic boost; however, link posts can give you the best ROI on your ad spend in many cases. The reason for this is because the image in your link post will redirect straight to your landing page or offer, unlike a photo post or video post.

If you click on a photo it will open up in a light box so you will pay for that click even if the visitor does not visit your site. If you click to play a video you will pay for that click even if the user does not click the link in your post and visit your landing page. That being said, we have seen video posts outperform all other types of posts in many cases.

FIGURE 3.8–Page Post Image Ad

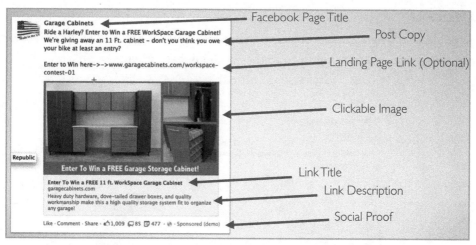

Facebook Page Title

Post Copy

Landing Page Link (Optional)

Clickable Image

Link Title

Link Description

Social Proof

FIGURE 3.9–Page Post Link Ad (Or "Link Post Ad")

FIGURE 3.10–Page Post Video Post

Page Like Ad

A page like ad is where the sole objective is for someone to be able to "like" a page directly from the ad instead of having to go to the Facebook page itself.

FIGURE 3.11–Page Like Ad

Facebook Offers

Facebook offers are used for special promotions, discounts, or any type of offer where you want to bring some scarcity and social proof into it and can be very effective. (Think of the daily deal sites.)

FIGURE 3.12–Gentle Dental Offer

FIGURE 3.13–80/20 Book Offer

> **Go to www.perrymarshall.com/fbtools for the latest updates and to get valuable resources for more clicks from Facebook for less money.**

Chapter 4

Ten Minutes to Your First Ad

HOW I SOLD MY FIRST PRODUCT

When I (Perry) was 14 years old, I sold my first product to my first customer. I built a pair of stereo speakers in shop class at school. I ran an ad in the newspaper, and a guy called and came and looked at them.

He walked out the door with his new speakers under his arm and as he left I clutched his $60.00 check in my hands. My dad was real cool about it until the guy had driven away, but as soon as he was gone, Dad got all excited and gave me a big high five.

> *"Doing business without advertising is like winking at a girl in the dark. You know what you are doing, but nobody else does."*
>
> —STEUART HENDERSON BRITT

That was 15 years before anyone was even thinking about advertising on the internet. To place that ad in the newspaper, I had to mail in a classified ad form to the newspaper with a check, then wait for my ad to appear. From writing my ad to appearing in the newspaper and getting phone calls took about a week.

Now it takes ten minutes.

All that speed has a downside. Do you know how to tell if you are talking to a true Facebook expert? They qualify all of their answers with, "The last time I checked," even if they last checked yesterday.

Facebook changes constantly, so don't get too comfortable just because you did something once before. Instead, learn to be comfortable poking around the interface, clicking on question marks, and reading help text. Questions marks indicate help text is available.

TEN MINUTES TO REACH 250,000 PEOPLE

"250,000 people?" You are thinking, "I thought Facebook was going to help me reach over a billion people!"

It may be true that Facebook could reach a billion people with your advertising message. But be serious, you can't afford to target a billion people. Do you know what is more exciting than advertising to a billion random people across the planet? Advertising to 250,000 people who are hot to buy your product.

By the time you finish this chapter, you will be ready to reach that first 250,000.

FACEBOOK CAN'T AFFORD TO TAKE
SIX BILLION QUESTIONS THIS YEAR

The Facebook Help Center is your one and only real friend supplied by Facebook. And it is not much of a friend. It's like being friends with the sexiest girl in high school who doesn't return your calls and secretly thinks she can do better. Still, she is yours. Type the following URL into your browser to go on your first date: https://www.facebook.com/help/.

Facebook Help Center offers advice on:

- Using Facebook
- Facebook apps and features
- Ads and business solutions

This book is about Facebook ads, so if you want the official latest and greatest scoop on features, rules, and regulations, review the "Ads and Business Solutions" links from the Help Center. They can help clear up a lot of your questions. But they will also generate even more questions that you will probably never get answered.

If you look at other people's accounts you may encounter entirely different features within the ad interface than you see in your account. There is no "one" ad interface Facebook is supporting at any point in time. You need to be comfortable with always learning. The first time you use the advertising interface (or when something changes) click on lots and lots of question marks, the ones that look like this: [?]. They give short descriptions of what you are looking at, as seen in Figure 4.1 on page 33.

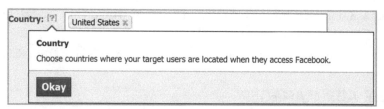

FIGURE 4.1–Clicking on the Question Mark Displays a Description
of the Country Field

Facebook does have several locations where you can submit a question to the Help Center staff. After you submit the question, you are directed to the Help Center. If the question strikes an interest, someone may even get back to you.

When you have a billion free users, you cannot afford to take phone calls to answer most people's mind-numbingly stupid questions. One of the reasons Facebook ads are so affordable is because they are self-service. Facebook, for the most part, doesn't care to talk with you unless you are spending lots and lots of money and need help spending more money. By then, you will probably already know the Facebook ad system better than the rep taking your call.

SET UP YOUR ACCOUNT

To run Facebook ads you need a Facebook profile. If you already have a user account Facebook wants you to use that. If you do not already have a user account, you may create a user or a business account.

Do not create a fictitious user account. That is a great way to get banned from Facebook.

Facebook currently has absolutely insane policies regarding business accounts. In Facebook's mind, there should be one account for every person on the planet, and that is it. No need for an account that is attached to a business.

Yes. Facebook does offer business accounts. But if you already have a Facebook account you are prohibited from creating a business account without permission. Fill out their form and ask for permission; everyone who asks nicely will get the help they need. Do not violate the current terms of service, which requires contacting Facebook, since it may get you banned from the site.

Whether you create a business account to run your ads or you run them from your personal account, you need an account to run ads. Read the following Facebook Help Center sections if you need help creating an account:

- Sign up
- Business accounts

Facebook did implement the help system correctly. You do not have to be logged in to access help!

If you have to manage multiple accounts, you need permission from Facebook.

FIND THE ADS MANAGER

There are a few different ways to find the Ads Manager, once you have already submitted at least one ad, and this changes frequently like so many other features do in Facebook. The easiest way to find it is to just go to: www.Facebook.com/ads/manage/home/.

If you have never created an ad, then you will not have an Ads Manager yet. The way you create your Facebook ads account and get access to your Ads Manager is to create your first ad.

If you already have a Facebook business page, the easiest way to create your first ad is to do a "Boost Post" right from an existing post on your Facebook business page. (Note- "Boost Post" may be called something different by the time you are reading this.)

Keep reading a few more paragraphs to see exactly how to "Boost" a post.

After you boost your first post you can then go to: www.Facebook.com/ads/manage/home/ and you will see your Ads Manager.

The other way to get to the Ads Manager is to go to www.Facebook.com/advertising. Once there, your screen will look something like Figure 4.2, with a large "Create an Ad" button, or something similar.

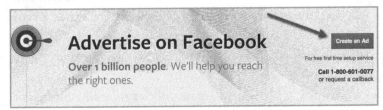

FIGURE 4.2–Create an Ad

If you already have a Facebook ads account you will see the "Manage Your Ads" button, and this will also take you to your Ads Manager.

FIGURE 4.3–"Manage Your Ads"

If you would like to access your Ads Manager but you are not quite ready to run ads yet, then I suggest submitting a "dummy ad." Immediately after creating your first ad you will be taken to your Ads Manager. So, just go ahead and quickly submit an ad with all the default data Facebook already has in there.

Don't worry about targeting, bidding, or anything. You will be pausing the campaign immediately after submission so no ads will actually run and your credit card will not get charged. Remember, you are submitting this ad *just* to get access to your Ads Manager, and you can pause the ad immediately after submission (before it is approved).

Once taken to your Ads Manager, bookmark that page in your browser so it is easy to get to at a later date.

CREATE YOUR FIRST AD

Important: Facebook is an ever-changing beast, and you need to be able to adapt to changes. Things may look different inside Facebook by the time you are reading this, but the core principles will still remain the same. Adapt or get left behind!

You can create ads three different ways:

1. "Boosting" a post from your Facebook business page
2. Using the Ads Manager
3. Using the Power Editor

The Power Editor gives you the most options and is best for advanced Facebook ad management. The Ads Manager is much easier to get started running ads and is the preferred method for beginners. "Boosting" a post is the quickest and easiest way to promote a post on your page; however, it has the least amount of targeting and placement options and is usually not recommended as the best long-term strategy.

Since using the "Boost Post" method is the easiest way to get your content promoted and placed in front of your exact, ideal audience, let's start with this method. Next, we will go through the process to create an ad using the ad manager. We will save the Power Editor option for later, as we have dedicated the entire Chapter 11 to how to use the Power Editor.

The examples in this chapter are showing you how to create a newsfeed ad, which is an ad that doesn't look like an ad. In most cases this is the effective type of ad that you can run in Facebook. It's essentially a Facebook Post that you are promoting and forcing Facebook to display in the newsfeed of your selected audience. The only thing difference between your newsfeed ad and an organic post that a friend of your puts up in Facebook is that your post will display a very small, gray text that reads: "Sponsored." This is very important to understand.

Your newsfeed ad begins as a Facebook post and must be hosted by a Facebook business page. There are several ways to create these posts, (using the Ads Manager or the Power Editor) as we will describe throughout this entire book. But for now, as long as you understand that your newsfeed ads begin as a Facebook post you will be good to go!

BOOST A POST FROM YOUR FACEBOOK PAGE

If you have a Facebook business page you have probably already seen the option to "boost" a post. You can't miss it. Facebook is doing their "darndest" to make it as easy as possible for you to spend money with them. They may not be using the word *boost*; it may be another word: *promote, amplify, ignite,* or some other word that motivates you to put money behind your posts. When Facebook first added this feature it used to be "promote post." Then they started testing "boost" against "promote," and boost won.

The reason we did not go through how to boost a post first in this chapter, even though it is the fastest and easiest way, is because in most cases using the Ad Manager or Power Editor is more effective. Better ROI.

Why? Because you have more options for targeting, ad placement, and so on, in the Ads Manager.

That being said, Facebook is constantly improving the process for boosting a post. They continue to add more targeting options and continue to make the boost post option better and better. The opportunity costs being saved when quickly boosting a post without having to jump into the Ad Manager (which can be overwhelming at first) can be big.

Make sure you test the difference in boosting a post compared to promoting it from the Ad Manager. You may find some posts that get better results from boosting them!

You will see different places where you can easily boost a post (see Figure 4.4). Right below the post itself, in your page insights along the post, or somewhere else. Facebook

FIGURE 4.4–Boost Post from the Post

FIGURE 4.5–Boost Post from Page Insights

typically puts this feature right next to your reach and insights data so you can take a post that may have already received more engagement than an average post and boost it even more.

At the time of this writing Facebook gives you the option to target "people who like your page and their friends" and "people you choose through targeting." We usually do not recommend choosing "people who like your page and their friends," as now you will be promoting your content to people who are not in your target audience. (Targeting friends of your fans is great to do, but only if you combine this targeting with another interest or behavior. And you can only do this in the Ads Manager or Power Editor.)

Maximum Budget

Facebook gives you a maximum budget with this option instead of a daily budget option. After you submit the boosted post Facebook will spread that maximum budget out over a few days, depending on what you choose. Facebook gives you a range to choose from (most likely from one to seven days) in which your budget will be spread out over that period of time. You also have the ability to go in and pause the campaign at any time after you submit it.

The range of budget Facebook gives you depends on the number of fans you currently have. So if you have only 500 fans you may have a range of $10–$100. Of course they now have a "choose your own" option which lets you set whatever amount you choose. Facebook gives you an estimated reach depending on the dollar amount you choose to boost the post with. (See Figure 4.6 on page 38.)

You can choose the number of days your budget is disseminated as shown in Figure 4.7 on page 38.

Choose Your Own Targeting

With the "choose your own targeting" option you have a lot more flexibility with who sees your post. As seen in Figure 4.8 on page 39, you have some basic targeting options, which include interest-based targeting. (By the time you are reading this Facebook will have updated this feature even more, so expect more options here.)

Maximum Budget	**$200.00**	
$10	Est. Reach 12,000 - 30,000	
$20	Est. Reach 27,000 - 71,000	
$30	Est. Reach 35,000 - 92,000	
$40	Est. Reach 41,000 - 110,000	
$60	Est. Reach 55,000 - 140,000	
$100	Est. Reach 83,000 - 220,000	
✓ **$200**	Est. Reach 140,000 - 380,000	
$400	Est. Reach 230,000 - 620,000	
$600	Est. Reach 290,000 - 760,000	
$1,000	Est. Reach 370,000 - 980,000	
$1,500	Est. Reach 450,000 - 1,200,000	
$2,000	Est. Reach 530,000 - 1,400,000	
Choose Your Own		

FIGURE 4.6–Maximum Budget

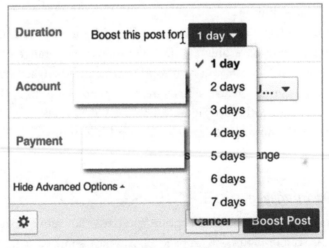

FIGURE 4.7–Number of Days to Boost

FIGURE 4.8–Choose Your Own Targeting

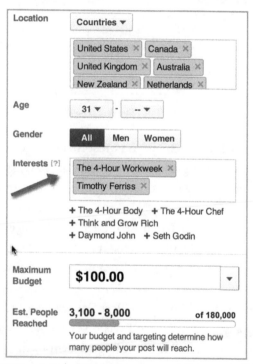

FIGURE 4.9–Selecting Interests and Demographics

As you begin to add interests to the targeting section, Facebook will begin to suggest other similar interests that you may want to add. Facebook will also adjust the estimated reach for the post as you refine your targeting (Figure 4.9).

As you can see, submitting an ad via the boost post method is much quicker than going into the Ads Manager. Yet, in my opinion, the severe lack of any advanced targeting, ad placement, or budget settings heavily outweighs the convenience of use.

CREATE AN AD USING THE ADS MANAGER

As you will see below you have many more options when it comes to creating and customizing your newsfeed ads. You can actually create the Facebook post itself right inside the Ads Manager, even if you haven't yet made a post on your Facebook page.

Step 1: Choose an Objective

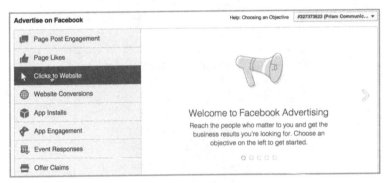

FIGURE 4.10–Choose an Objective

Before you can start editing your ad, you must first choose an objective. The choices for objectives are constantly being adjusted by Facebook, so try to use as much common sense here as possible (also realize that with Facebook, sometimes common sense goes out the window!)

In Figure 4.11 on page 41 we have chosen "Page Post Engagement" for the objective. Facebook's definition for Page Post Engagement is: "Boosts posts to reach more people. Engagement includes likes for your post, comments, shares, video plays, and photo views."

A typical situation you would use Page Post Engagement for your objective is when you are looking to amplify a post on your Facebook page. This may be a photo, a video, or a link to a blog post. Choosing Page Post Engagement in the ad manager is the same objective as when you boost a post right from your Facebook business page. The reason it can be better to do this from the Ads Manager is because you have more options with your targeting, placement, bidding, etc.

The next step is to select your Facebook page and the specific post you want to amplify with your Facebook ads. You must be an administrator of a Facebook page;

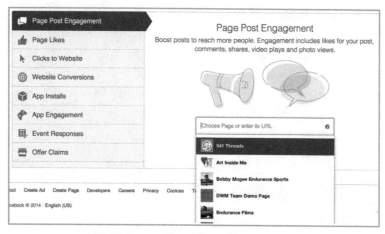

FIGURE 4.11–Page Post Engagement

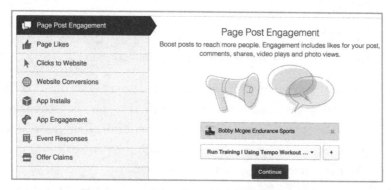

FIGURE 4.12–Page Post Ad Page Selection

otherwise, it will not be available as a choice. After you select your page you will then select the specific post you want to promote. See Figure 4.12.

I recommend being very careful selecting "Page Likes" as your objective. If you do this, please start out using smaller budgets and make sure your audiences are very focused on your exact, ideal target audience. If your goal is to get more fans, then you should create engaging content and creative promotions that motivate people to become fans of your page. DO NOT leave this in Facebook's hands. It is not about how many fans you have; it is about how many highly targeted fans you have. If you have too many fans who are not true fans, this will compromise your organic reach.

If you have a lot of fans who are not true fans, you get penalized in your organic exposure, because Facebook takes a very quick snapshot of the initial engagement of your post.

If a small percentage of your entire fan base engages with this post, then Facebook will assume this is not a very interesting post. So if you have 1,000 true fans and another

1,000 not-so-true fans, those percentages get whacked out pretty quickly, as your 1,000 not-so-true fans will never engage with your content, thus decreasing the percentage of engagement from all of your fans.

In Figure 4.13 we selected "Clicks to Website" for the objective. This choice has recently proven to be a good choice for those looking to drive traffic to a website and generate leads or amplify content.

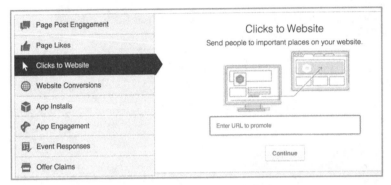

FIGURE 4.13–Clicks to Website

Even if your goal is to get website conversions, using "Clicks to Website" as your objective can get you great results. Sometimes this is better than choosing "Website Conversions" for your objective. It makes sense if you think about it, because your true goal with your Facebook ad is to get the clickthrough to your website. Once they get to your website, your goal may be to get a website conversion.

These objectives are fairly new, and Facebook is constantly working on their algorithms. The goal for Facebook is to use their massive amount of user data and try to make your ad campaigns as smart as possible. So, in theory, if you select "Clicks to Website" they would show these ads to people more likely to click on a link in a post. And if you choose "Website Conversions" then they will show your ads to more people who have a history of making Website Conversions.

The problem is, this is not perfect. If you are looking to generate leads or sales, just because you choose website conversions (see Figure 4.14) doesn't mean you will get better performance than choosing website clicks. In fact, we have seen just the opposite in many cases. You just need to test!

What we have found to be the case is that the "Website Conversions" bidding objective tends to need some "seasoning" time. The longer you are running ads the smarter Facebook will get. The "Website Conversions" options can end up being the best bidding option if you have been running your campaigns for a few weeks or more. (This is also exactly what an agency Facebook rep confirmed can happen on a recent phone call we had with her.)

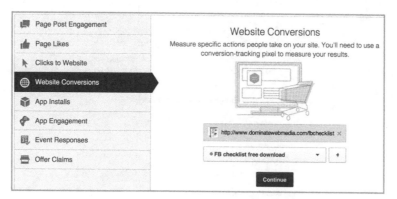

FIGURE 4.14–Website Conversions

If you choose Website Conversions, then you must also select a conversion pixel. If you have not yet created a conversion pixel, then Facebook helps you out here and asks you to create a conversion pixel now. (See Figures 4.15, 4.16, and 4.17 on page 44.)

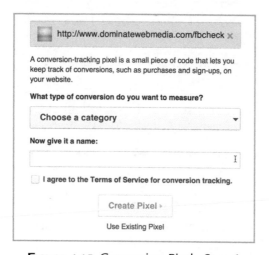

FIGURE 4.15–Conversion Pixel—Step 1

At the time of this writing there are a few other options: App Installs, App Engagement, Event Responses, and Offer Claims. We will discuss these strategies in later chapters.

Once you get inside the ad creator you will have many options on ad placement, ad type, targeting, bidding, budgeting, etc.

FIGURE 4.16–Conversion Goal Category

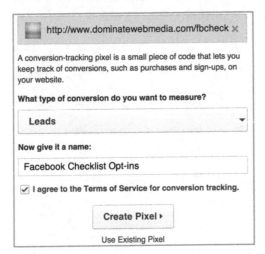

FIGURE 4.17–Conversion Category—Step 2

Step 2: Create Your Ad

After you choose the destination for your ad (a Facebook page post, a website URL, an event, a Facebook Offer, etc.) you will be taken to the ad creator (see Figure 4.24).

If you choose Clicks to Website or Website Conversions, then Facebook will pull an image from your website into the image placeholder. In most cases you will want to replace this image with an image created specifically for this ad. Facebook-recommended image sizes change frequently, so make sure you keep updated on the latest image specifications.

Facebook will usually tell you the recommended image size, as shown in Figure 4.18.

If you upload more than one image, Facebook will create a separate additional ad for each image inside the respective ad set.

FIGURE 4.18–Selecting Your Image

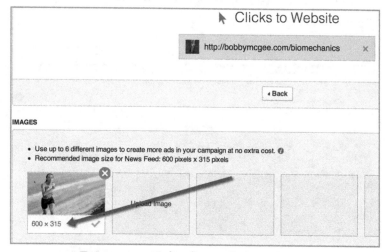

FIGURE 4.19–Uploading a Custom Image

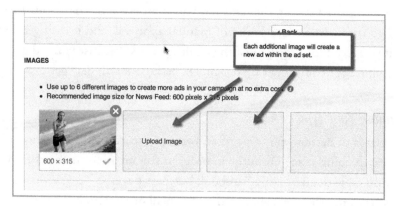

FIGURE 4.20–Uploading Additional Images

The 20 Percent Text Rule

When Facebook first introduced news feed ads, all of us direct-response marketers thought we were in hog heaven: We could literally have a seven-word headline take up half the news feed above the fold. We did this by making our image mostly all text. One big billboard. We could still use a compelling image to grab attention, but having very large text overlaid on top of the image always worked best. (If it was good copy of course!)

After us direct-response marketers had our heyday for almost a year, Facebook finally implemented a 20 percent text rule. The rule states that any image that is sponsored in the news feed cannot have more than 20 percent text overlaying the image.

Facebook has created a free tool you can use to check your image to see if it will pass the test (see Figure 4.21). You can access that here: https://www.facebook.com/ads/tools/text_overlay.

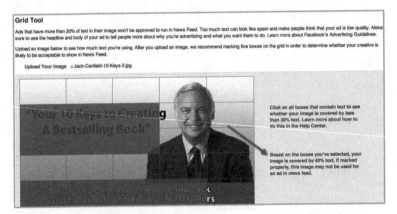

FIGURE 4.21–Facebook's 20-Percent Text Grid Tool

Note: Our experience has shown that many news feed ads will get approved by Facebook's automated system the same day you submit them. Then, sometime the next day it will go through another round of manual approval, and it may get disapproved then. So, if you're submitting against the guidelines, just because your ad gets approved right away, don't get your hopes up too much, because it still may get disapproved!

Step 3: Choose Your Type of Ad

The next step is to decide what type of ad you want to run. Is this going to be a news feed ad? A right-column ad? Or both? In order to run an ad in the news feed you must associate your ad with an existing Facebook business page.

This is very important. The best real estate in all of Facebook is the news feed! This is the oceanfront property you want to stake your claim in.

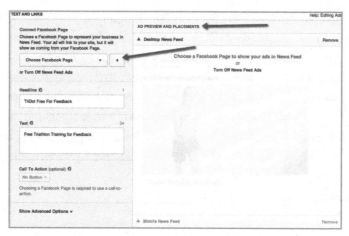

FIGURE 4.22–Connect Your Facebook Page

You have the ability to choose news feed only, news feed and right column, or just right column. We usually don't recommend using the same ad in both the news feed and the right column, because of the differences in image size, ad copy available, etc. However, in some cases you may have a perfect image and ad copy that looks good in both the right column and the news feed. (You may also do this in some cases just in the interest of saving time.)

Notice in Figure 4.22 that you must select a Facebook page to host the ad if you want your ad to show in the news feed. You cannot run a traditional banner ad in the news feed; it must display as a post from your Facebook page. This is also one of the big reasons news feed ads perform so well—because they look similar to an organic post you might see from one of your friends.

Please notice the limited space for ad copy on your news feed ads. This may be improved by the time you are reading this book, but at the time of this writing

FIGURE 4.23–Character Limitations

Facebook has character limitations for the copy that goes in the post, the link title, and the link description. If you create a newsfeed ad like this using the Power Editor you will not have a character limitation in the post area. You do have limitations in the link title and link description sections, but the character limits are larger in the Power Editor than they are using the Ads Manager. It looks like content, not an advertisement.

Note: One other way around these character limitations without using the Power Editor is to create and publish the post on your Facebook page itself, then go into the Ads Manager and run a "Page Post Engagement" ad and select a recent post you have published on your page (see Figures 4.24 and 4.25).

First, create a post on your Facebook page.

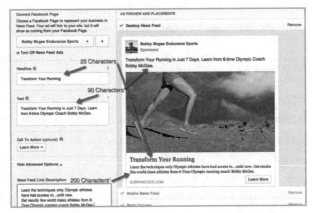

FIGURE 4.24–Existing Post on Your Facebook Page

Next, run a Page Post Engagement Ad, and select a recent post from your page.

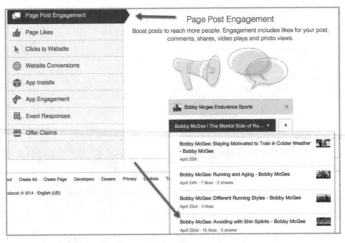

FIGURE 4.25–Selecting a Recent Post

Right-Column Option

If you choose to show your ad in the right column, you will have character limitations for the headline and the body text and will have a much smaller displayed image. Facebook is frequently changing the image specifications, so please make sure you stay updated on the latest image dimensions.

Note: With right-column ads there are no limitations when it comes to text overlaid on an image. So you will want to take advantage of this by testing some images with text on the image calling out the user to take action.

FIGURE 4.26–Right-Column Ad

Step 4: Choose Your Audience

Now we're getting to the fun stuff—choosing your target audience. You can (and should) spend hours inside the Ads Manager just tinkering around searching for different types of interests, topics, behaviors, categories, custom audiences, etc. that you can choose for any specific ad. We discuss more advanced targeting strategies in Chapter 7 and elsewhere, so I will keep it simple for this section.

You will see in Figure 4.27, page 50, that there are a lot of different choices in your targeting. And within each different targeting section (interests, topics, behaviors, etc.) you will see anything from a few dozen options to a few thousand.

In Figure 4.28, you will see the location and demographic targeting sections. You target countries, states, provinces, cities, or zip codes. Notice that you can also exclude locations, like in the example where we are targeting all of the United States excluding Los Angeles.

The "More Demographics" section is expanding all the time, as Facebook gains more and more intelligent data. In Figure 4.28, page 50, you can see some of the subcategories. (This may look different in countries outside the United States.) Much of the data for these dropdowns is derived from offline big data companies, not from the Facebook profile data or actions taken inside Facebook (data from the Partner Categories).

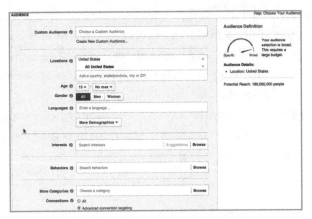

FIGURE 4.27–Choosing Your Targeting

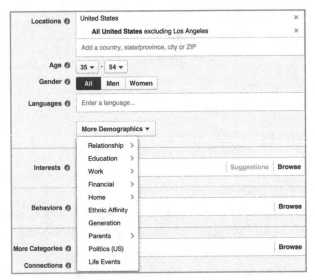

FIGURE 4.28–More Demographics

The demographic targeting includes data like income, net worth, home value *and* composition, job titles, relationship status, and much more. (See Figures 4.29 and 4.30 for a couple of examples.)

The Interests targeting section (see Figure 4.31) is where you can use the dropdown menu to choose different categories, or you can put in anything you can think of that someone might like. The possibilities are endless, with thousands of potential audiences to target.

Facebook used to have a Precise Interest section and a Broad Categories section. Now these two are combined into the one Interests section.

Advanced connection targeting gives you even more options to create hyper-targeted, highly engaging ads. (See Figure 4.34, page 52.) This is where you can target

FIGURE 4.29–Net Worth Targeting

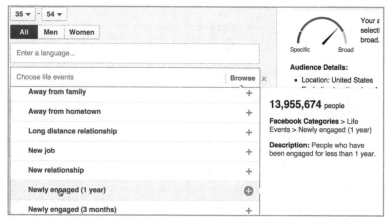

FIGURE 4.30–Life Events

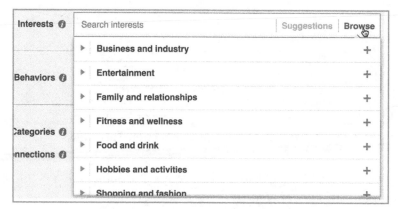

FIGURE 4.31–Interests Categories

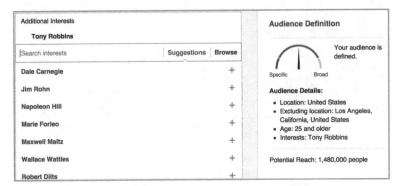

FIGURE 4.32–Tony Robbins Targeting

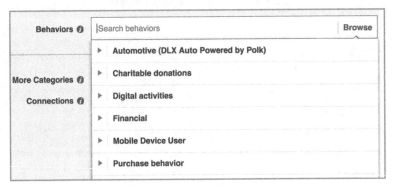

FIGURE 4.33–Behavior Targeting

FIGURE 4.34–Advanced Connection Targeting

only your existing fans (or any Facebook page you have admin access to), or you can exclude your existing fans, or you can target friends of your fans.

The third option, "people whose friends are connected to" (friends of your fans) can be a great option in some cases. For example, you may target someone who likes Tony Robbins and is also a friend of one of your fans. This is an example layering, and in addition to helping keep your ads more targeted, it can give you an extra "social boost."

Many of the users who see your ad will see something like this above the ad "Joe Smith also likes Sam's Crab Shack."

NAMING YOUR CAMPAIGNS AND AD SETS

Campaigns

The next section is where you decide how to organize your campaigns. The best way to organize your campaigns is to name the campaign related to the specific promotion that you are running or objective you are trying to accomplish. For example, you may name it "Free Video Series" or "May 15th Webinar." If you are managing multiple clients or different divisions of your company inside one ad account you will want to add another identifier in front of the title of the campaign, as in Figure 4.35.

FIGURE 4.35–Campaign and Ad Set Name

Ad Sets

You will want to use a different ad set for each different target audience or any other segmenting you are doing. You can have as many ad sets inside one campaign as you want. The more the better.

For better tracking you should place each target audience into a separate ad set. For example, if you would like to target *Rich Dad Poor Dad*, *Think and Grow Rich*, and T. Harv Eker, you should create separate ad sets for each of those audiences. And after those three audiences you may want to add a few more ad sets, such as: Tony Robbins plus income over $125,000, or Tony Robbins plus friends of fans, or Tony Robbins plus a similar audience of your buyers.

There's a ton of different combinations you can test, but the point here is that you need to keep each of these different segments as different ad sets.

Inside your ad sets is where you may want to start testing ad design changes. However, the one major caveat here is that as of this writing Facebook uses their own "optimization" and limits impressions to some of your ads when you have multiple ads inside one ad set. Maybe by the time you're reading this, Facebook has gotten their act together and is not messing with your impressions. But for now don't put too many ads inside one ad set. (Unless you are using third-party software to manage your ads and you have ad rotation rules in place.)

If you have more than one or two ads inside an ad set, you lower CTR, ads will not get impressions, and you will get frustrated. So the best way to test image and ad copy changes is to create separate ad sets for these also. This will give you the best data. Or use third-party software like Qwaya to set up ad rules to run only one to two ads at any one time.

Using software like Qwaya or another ad management tool is only for advanced users who are looking to manage large campaigns and do a lot of testing. I do not recommend using a software program like this until you are very comfortable with the Facebook Ad Manager and the Power Editor. You do not need a tool like this to be successful, and these tools also have some drawbacks and limitations when it comes to creating certain types of ads.

Budget

You can set your budget to a daily budget or a lifetime budget. We always use a daily budget, so we have more control throughout the campaign.

When you are setting your budget you are setting the budget for each ad set, not the entire campaign. So if your planned budget is $100 per day, then you need to figure out how many ad sets you have and schedule accordingly. If you have ten different ad sets then you would need to set each ad set budget to $10 per day to stay at your $100 per day target.

Schedule

You can run your ad set "continuously starting today" or you can set a start and end date. We usually prefer to run continuously and just pause and unpause the campaigns when we want to stop them. In some cases it may be better to schedule your ads, but if you plan on doing a lot of duplicating and pausing and unpausing, then it can be a little easier to sort your campaigns and ad sets when you just pause a campaign.

BIDDING AND PRICING

You have several different options with your bidding, and please realize that this is another ever-evolving feature with Facebook. Facebook's "Optimized CPM" bidding is where they automatically optimize your bid for you. And in many cases you will get the best results using their optimized bidding. (Please see Chapter 9 for more detailed bidding strategies.)

The type of bidding you choose should depend on the type of ad you are running, what your overall objective is, and of course dealing with idiosyncrasies on how Facebook is pricing at the time you are running your ads. We have seen ads perform better using

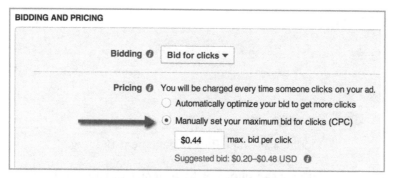

FIGURE 4.36–Bid for Clicks—CPC

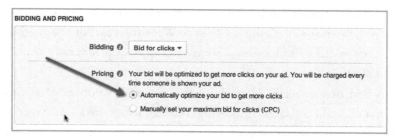

FIGURE 4.37–Bid for Clicks—Automated Bidding (Optimized CPM)

FIGURE 4.38–Bid for Website Conversions—Automated Bidding (Optimized CPM)

straight CPC bidding compared to Facebook's Optimized CPM bidding, and we have seen Facebook's Optimized CPM bidding outperform straight CPC.

If your goal is to generate leads and track the ROI of your campaigns, you may be better off starting with CPC bidding just to be safe and have more control. If you do bid CPC try bidding toward the higher end of the suggested bid range.

After your ads begin to run you can then check the new recommended bid. In many cases it will be lower than the original suggested bid and your cost per click will also be much lower than your original bid. You can then begin to slowly lower your bid by adjusting it down in small increments, until you start to lose impressions.

If some cases you will not have the choice of CPC at all, such as in a Page Post Engagement ad. In this case Facebook will automatically optimize your ad

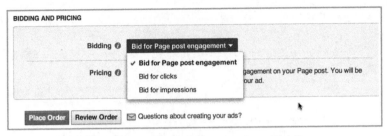

FIGURE 4.39–Page Post Engagement Bidding

(Optimized CPM), but you can choose which objective you would like to optimize for. (See Figure 4.39.)

You will have different bidding options depending on which objective you choose for your ad (i.e., Website Conversions, Clicks to Website, etc.), but the good thing about Facebook's automated CPM bidding is that *you can actually manually optimize your bids when you're using their automated bidding.*

Yes you read that correctly. How about that for an oxymoron? At the time of this writing, if you choose Facebook's automated bidding using the ad manager, you can go into the Power Editor after you submit your ad (or you can just create your ad using the Power Editor) and manually adjust your "Optimized CPM Bidding" by manually setting up your bids. See Figure 4.40 for an illustration; this is what we call OCPM—Bid for Clicks.

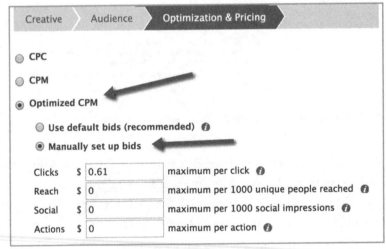

FIGURE 4.40–Optimized CPM—Manually Bidding For Clicks (In the Power Editor)

Breaking It Down

The main point to take away here is, if you are a beginner, use CPC bidding to be safe. Then start testing Facebook's automated bidding. Then go into the Power Editor and manually adjust Facebook's automated bidding.

Chapter 5

Selling on the Front Porch, at a Party, and at the Coffee Shop

WHERE SELLING MEETS SOCIAL

Have you ever been to a party or any social gathering and met "that guy?" You know . . . the one who 30 seconds after he shakes your hand is already pitching you his financial planning services, or insurance plans, or his "business opportunity" that will help you enjoy a residual income for the rest of your life.

The conversation goes something like this:

"Hi, I'm Joe. How are you?" He says.

"Hi, I'm Keith. I'm doing great, how about you?" You reply.

> "*Let us make a special effort to stop communicating with each other, so we can have some conversation.*"
>
> —MARK TWAIN

"Oh, that's great!" He says half yelling, with his face about ten inches from yours. "You know, I've had a great week too. Busy! I've been helping people get one step closer to becoming financially free all week long. Are you financially free yet? I'd love to help you put the right pieces in place to create a residual income for the rest of your life. My schedule has a couple openings next week. I'd love to get together with you and see if I can help you out. Would Tuesday at 1:00 P.M. work, or Wednesday at 10:00 work better?"

After quietly listening and nodding your head, what do you want to do?

If you're anything like me, you want to seize him by his shoulders, twist him around, and kick him his rear end out the front door!

Nobody likes "that guy" or "that girl" who is always selling something at a party or social gathering.

However, some of the biggest deals and some of the biggest sales ever made have been born from two people meeting at a party or a coffee shop.

Of course, any savvy business owner or entrepreneur understands that it might take three, four, possibly five or six connections with the same person before you have actually built a *real* relationship that may lead to an appointment or a meeting.

Keep reading for another example of the right way to sell at a party.

Just imagine if you could clone yourself (or your best salesperson) and start attending parties, social gatherings, and coffee shops all over the world, building relationships along the way. You're planting seeds along the way with all these new friends and peers, in order to eventually move a percentage of them into your organization as clients or customers.

And just imagine an army of these clones attending several networking events each month connecting with your existing customers and potential new customers.

CLONE YOURSELF AND CRASH ANY PARTY IN THE WORLD

Would you like to mingle with high rollers with a net worth over $1 million at the Metropolitan Museum of Art in New York City?

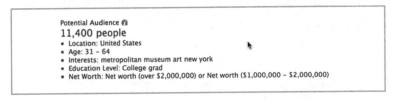

FIGURE 5.1–Boost New York Metropolitan Art Museum

Would you like to simultaneously attend all the best BNI chapter meetings around the world? Or your chamber of commerce? Or Rotary International?

FIGURE 5.2–Chamber of Commerce, BNI, Rotary Targeting

These are just two examples of some basic targeting inside the Facebook Ads Power Editor. The possibilities are endless.

HOW DO YOU REALLY MAKE MONEY WITH FACEBOOK AND SOCIAL MEDIA?

If you were to count up every article ever written about how you can make money with social media and compare that total to the number of articles written about how you cannot make money in social media, you may end up with the same total for each list. Everyone seems to have an opinion.

So how do you know which side is correct?

You don't, without doing at least a little research first.

One way to do this is to go to www.IsFBforMe.com and fill out a free quiz that asks you ten questions you can easily answer in 60 seconds and gives you a score of 1 to 10.

You shouldn't be asking the question: "*Can* I make money with social media?" You should be asking yourself: "*How* can I make money with social media?"

It is not a matter of *if*. It is a matter of *how*.

How can you tap into the vast array of targeting possibilities with Facebook, Twitter, LinkedIn, or any other major social ad platform? How can you craft a "Facebook appropriate offer" to move a Facebook user to taking action with you or your company?

After overseeing millions of dollars in ad spend (mostly on Facebook), several billion impressions, several million clicks, several million dollars generated, and several hundred thousand subscribers generated, it has become fairly easy for me to spot a winner or a loser, without having to even look at the ad campaigns or analytics.

How does this come so easy for me now?

Because I fully understand the frame of mind users are in when they are logged into a social media network. The number-one reason social media is a lousy place to sell stuff is that people don't go to Facebook to make decisions. They go to Facebook to *avoid* making decisions!

This is a social environment. They are not searching in Google for a solution to a problem. They are not browsing an online store looking for a product. This is no different than "that guy" you meet at the party who pitches you 30 seconds in, who you want to toss out the front door. Most people attend parties to get away from work or making decisions.

BACK TO THE PARTY

Let's go back to the party and start over. Imagine meeting that same person at a party and the conversation goes a little different this time. Maybe something like this:

"Hi I'm Joe, how are you?" he says.

"Hi I'm Keith. I'm doing great—how 'bout you?"

"I'm doing great, too, now that the week is over," he says with a sigh of relief.

"Long week, huh? What do you do?" you reply.

"Yep, it was a pretty long week, but a good one though. I'm a financial advisor," he says. "I specialize mostly in helping 30- to 50-year-old folks raise the money they will need for their kids' university or college tuition and still have enough left over to *actually* retire when they want to. It's pretty engaging. What about you? What do you do?" he asks.

"I'm a business consultant. I help entrepreneurs and small businesses put in the right systems to be able to scale their business while simultaneously reducing the number of hours of work per week they work *in* the business. Yeah, I have a five-year-old and a seven-year-old, and I keep thinking that college is going to sneak up on me a little too fast."

Joe sincerely replies, "There's a great tax loophole that 90 percent of parents don't know exists. And it's ideal when children are under ten. Google '529 plan' sometime; if you're just a little strategic you can sock away an extra 20K or so while your kids are growing up. Anyway . . . so are your kids playing sports or into any activities keeping you busy?"

The conversation moves on. Maybe you ask more about his financial advising services, maybe you don't. But when you leave the party you don't feel like you have to wash your hands after meeting Joe. Maybe you even tell your wife or husband about the college fund loophole Joe told you about, while driving home.

The next day, as you are driving to work, you drive past a billboard on the right side of the road and you see a photo of Joe and the name of his company on the billboard! That billboard has probably been there for a month, but you never really noticed it until now. The message on the billboard says:

"Give Your Child a Head Start For College. Start Small and Save Big. Visit www.SaveForCollege.com to fill out the quiz to find out how much money you will need put away when your child turns 18."

You think to yourself, "Oh wow, that's Joe, the guy I met last night who gave me that funding tip."

Do you think you would go visit his website and fill out a survey, or even possibly schedule a call or appointment with him?

Maybe. Maybe not.

But my guess is that you'll have a much higher likelihood of visiting his site and taking action after he provided some value and tipped off his authority by giving you that insightful nugget of information, *without* trying to sell you something. He gave you an "aha" moment at the party. He whetted your appetite just enough to leave you wanting more—and luckily he had some good systems in place to make it easy for you to follow up (a billboard on your way to work).

Facebook advertising is no different. However, the great thing about Facebook is you can be automatically building relationships and providing value with potential customers or clients simultaneously all over the world, with strategic systems in place to transition some of those new acquaintances into customers.

SELLING ON THE FRONT PORCH

Imagine you live in a small town in a big, old house on Main Street. The house has a large front porch that extends its entire length and even wraps around the side. People in town walk up and down the street to see what's going on, to meet and chat with friends and neighbors, and perhaps stroll to the library or the theater.

You are sitting on your front porch as people walk by on a warm, summer evening. You sit quietly, sipping lemonade, commenting on the heat, and playing checkers with your neighbor. Many who walk by wave or say hello. Some even stop, lean on the rail, and visit for a while, talking about nothing in particular but sharing news: births, weddings, deaths, gossip—who is in a new relationship or who is arguing with whom.

A few of those who pass by even join you, finding a seat on the front porch to watch others walk by. You welcome them with a fresh glass of lemonade and a snickerdoodle cookie.

Those who join you on the porch also see friends passing by. Sometimes they invite their friends to join them on the porch. They may sit together on a swinging bench and talk for a while, sharing pictures just picked up at the five-and-dime and telling tall tales. Some folks walking by shout a quick hello and a short bit of news without even slowing their pace.

This casual, dynamic, social environment is Facebook.

Facebook is where people connect with friends, family, and acquaintances. *Facebook is the new town square.* People do not go to the town square to search for the answers to a problem or to buy life insurance. They go to meet people, to see and to be seen, to interact.

Facebook is not about *what* people are doing right now, it is about *who* people are: what they like, what they believe in, and with whom they like to associate. Facebook is where people share announcements, opinions, and insights not for any particular objective, but just to share. To connect. To be alive.

Can you sell on the front porch? Absolutely.

What you are about to learn is nothing new. People have been selling from their version of a front porch for centuries. What is important to recognize is that the front porch is not the market; it is not the boardroom; it is not the mall. You do not conduct business on the front porch in the same way you do in these other locations.

Learn this lesson and you crack the code to effective Facebook advertising.

THIS IS NOT YOUR FATHER'S ADWORDS

Selling on the front porch is not the same as selling with Google AdWords. (It took us a while to figure that out.) AdWords is an absolutely amazing tool produced by Google to display ads in Google search and across the internet. However, those who have extensive experience with AdWords may find Facebook advertising a little frustrating.

You may have had a thrilling and positive experience selling on Google. Then you take those exact same ads to Facebook and flop. What happened? Facebook looks almost the same, but looks are deceiving in this case. Facebook is not AdWords.

Try a real-world example. Bring up one window for Google and another window for Facebook. We are going to pretend that we are users interested in buying a guitar. In Google type in the word "guitar" and press Enter.

Instantly, Google shows natural search results related to guitar. We describe Google search as the "Yellow Pages" when we are talking to older people. It is where you go to look things up. When we say "Yellow Pages" to younger people, they look at us funny and say, "Oh, you mean like Google."

As Google delivers links to textual information about guitars, it also simultaneously displays ads related to guitars.

When looking at a screen full of information related to their Google inquiry, most users probably don't recognize what is a search result and what is an ad. If Google does its job well, users shouldn't care because the search results and the ads are of equal interest to them.

These ads are purchased by advertisers who specifically request that their ads be displayed when the word "guitar" is entered into the search bar. A simple concept, right? If someone types in a specific word or phrase you want to advertise to, then Google displays your ad associated with that key word or phrase. Simple.

Now go to Facebook.

Facebook also has a search feature, but it is primarily focused on searching Facebook, Facebook pages, your friends, likes, and interests. Facebook is not focused on searching the entire internet for you. It is NOT the Yellow Pages or Google.

In Facebook type in the word "guitar" and press Enter.

Notice anything interesting about the ads shown in Figure 5.3 on page 63? Not a single ad about guitars!

Not a lot of choices either!

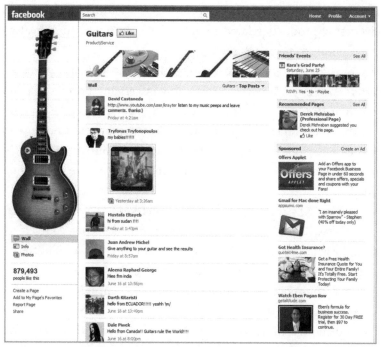

FIGURE 5.3–Not a Single Ad about Guitars

The ads you see at the right-hand side of the page in Facebook are not ads based on what you are doing right now, which is searching the word "guitar." Rather they are ads focused on who you are as a person: your age, your sex, your marital status, and the pages, TV shows, and other things you're into.

In Google you get to sell to the specific need that the user is digitally shouting at you. The user is saying "Hey, I am thinking about a 'guitar' right now," and you, as the advertiser, get to shout back, "Hey, I've got great deals on guitars."

No so on Facebook.

If you were to stand on your front porch and yell at everyone walking down the street that "I have a great deal on car insurance," some people might stop by and talk with you, but most would move to the other side of the street.

So is there an effective way to sell on the front porch?

You bet there is. It all begins with adding value, and with a snickerdoodle, a glass of lemonade, and a game of checkers.

ADD VALUE BEFORE YOU RECEIVE A DIME

Selling on the front porch is about engaging people where they are, based on their personal likes and interests. People stop by the front porch because they see something they find interesting and want to learn more. This is what makes Facebook such a great tool for advertising products related to art, beliefs, music, culture, health, fitness, or anything that appeals to personal interests.

If you were selling pottery on the front porch, how would you approach it?

For starters, you begin by having incredibly interesting pottery in plain view. You choose pieces that stop people in their tracks and make them come up onto the porch and see what they are. You engage people there. You make them smarter about pottery. You answer their questions about pottery; you converse about art, artists, clay, and kilns.

You may even have a pottery wheel on the front porch where you demonstrate how a pot is made.

When people stop by for lemonade and snickerdoodles, you invite them to try the wheel for themselves. There's nothing like trying to make a pot yourself to appreciate why you might be willing to pay $150 or more for amazing pieces of pottery art made by hand, a piece of pottery you can cherish for years to come.

Selling on the front porch is about adding value and engaging the customers so that they want to spend time on the front porch.

If they spend enough time, see the products, learn about them, and do so in a way that engages and entertains . . . guess what? They stop by the front porch the next time they are in town. The more people stop at the front porch, the more people hang around,

---

A MASTERFUL UNIQUE SELLING PROPOSITION OVER 100 YEARS AGO

Can you name a magician who lived more than 100 years ago? Did you say Harry Houdini? Houdini was the master of the unique selling proposition (USP). In his case, a USP was a new illusion that nobody had ever seen before. Houdini was a marketing genius. You can probably name one of his USPs more than 100 years after it was introduced. Can you name one of his illusions?

Did you think of the Chinese water torture cell?

His USPs worked, and he attracted large audiences. Of course, other magicians were always copying him and ripping off his ideas. Can you name any of his contemporaries? Not unless you're a magician yourself.

Being first with a string of USPs is a powerful advantage. Don't worry about being copied, worry about being great.

---

the more people learn about pottery, and the more they want to own a nice piece of pottery themselves.

Done correctly, the entire process doesn't even feel like selling. Why? Because it isn't selling; it is being social. It is a natural extension of your customers' old (or even newfound) interest in pottery. They ultimately ask you, "How much does this one cost? I really love it."

This scenario is real, and it has real and very practical applications in Facebook.

It you are trying to sell pottery on Facebook, do not drive your users to a page that says, "Buy this pot right now for only $150." If they are not interested in buying a pot right then (and Facebook users are not shopping), then you will miss the real opportunity and will probably not sell enough pots to pay for the ads.

So what might you do instead? It depends on your unique selling proposition (USP). Your USP is the front porch story you tell about why your product or service is so special. *Unique* is the critical word in USP. You have to display something that nobody else offers, does, or promises. Tell your front porch visitors stories about your USP.

It may be a story about quality, service, a satisfaction guarantee, or even artistry. Is there:

- Something you can guarantee uniquely?
- An experience your customer will have with you that he or she will have nowhere else?
- Something memorable to tell them that nobody else is saying?

You may be continually refining your USP as your business develops.

Once you have your USP, you must craft interesting and engaging content that reflects your USP. Are you selling pottery as an investment? Art form? Dinner plates? Are you selling to 20-something hipsters? Forty-something professionals? For each one of these, you may craft a different front porch experience.

If you are selling beautifully hand-crafted pottery for forty-something professionals to give as gifts, you may offer visitors to your porch a free guide to the 15 most stunning pieces of pottery you have ever seen. You may talk about how the pieces are made, why they are special, and why discriminating individuals might enjoy such a magnificent piece of pottery.

Pictures, videos, cartoons, testimonials—all about pottery—support your front porch conversation and validate your USP. We always encourage capturing your visitors' email addresses through at least one special offer that only comes via email.

Do you have a piece of pottery that is so exceptional that visitors to your front porch would urge their friends walking by to stop and see that piece? Is it beautiful, provocative, or funny? If so, then feature it and encourage your visitors to invite their friends to engage.

PLAYING WITH CUSTOMERS: A NEW WAY TO ENGAGE

Do you have 1,000 fans on your Facebook page but almost no interaction from them? It is probably because you are not playing with them. Playing leads to interaction, interaction leads to information, information leads to interest, and interest leads to sales. This is the way of the front porch.

BEING FRIENDLY, TRULY FRIENDLY

Selling on the front porch is not new. For years I (Perry) have been encouraging my clients to engage their customers with a website with a strong landing-page offering, relevant conversation, and value-added information.

I encourage my students not to focus initially on their products or service offerings but to first provide free information around their products and services. If the potential customers request more information around the product or service and we collect their contact information, then we have a lot more space to work with them until they are ready for a sale.

The goal, once you pay for a click, is to begin to build a relationship with a customer. One where they like you, appreciate your expertise, and actively desire to purchase from you.

Ten years ago, I said if you are selling ink for a commercial printer, first offer your potential clients a free paper (now perhaps a free video) on how to save money on ink. Include every good suggestion you can find on how to save money on ink without mentioning your product or service. Only in the last point might you note that you sell high-quality commercial ink for 35 percent less than your nearest competitor.

This strategy works precisely because it is not just a tactic, it is a way to demonstrate that you are actually there to help. You are not out to make a quick buck but to build a relationship. You are selling on the front porch.

BEING FRIENDLY, TRULY FRIENDLY, continued

The conversation built around helping your prospect find ways to save on ink could be followed with a series of messages in an email autoresponder that describe other ways to get more value in the printing process, saving paper, saving electricity, etc. Adding value for your customers, making them want to visit your Facebook page or open your email, is key.

Eventually, when they want ink, guess who they will think of first. Does this work?

"Is This THE Richard Sheridan?"

Just ask Richard Sheridan, founder of Menlo Innovations, who runs a now world-renowned custom software development firm based on lean and agile techniques. Sheridan wasn't always world-renowned. When he was first setting up shop in his basement in 2001, he and his partners turned on the TV and witnessed the attack on the World Trade Center. New business, no office, no customers, undercapitalized—and an economy that had turned itself off.

In early 2002, Richard and his team started implementing front-porch techniques for their very specialized B2B products: high-end training, consulting, and software development using agile software development techniques.

They put together an information campaign with the specific purpose of telling every secret they know about agile software development. They wrote papers, made public speeches, sent emails, and provided literally thousands of free hours of training. And they attracted readers from more than 100 countries within their first year.

Of course, they also had an AdWords campaign, a dedicated website landing page, and an autoresponder. They didn't sell—they chatted on the front porch about software, process, and what they had learned. Anyone who ordered their papers received dozens of emails, often highly technical, containing every bit of good advice Menlo could provide. FREE.

One day Richard Sheridan answered the phone. "Hello, Menlo Innovations, Rich Sheridan speaking."

BEING FRIENDLY, TRULY FRIENDLY, continued

"Rich Sheridan. THE Rich Sheridan? We've been reading your papers. Can you come on down here and talk to us?"

Care to guess who called?

Care to guess who knew his name?

Care to guess who already considered Rich Sheridan a *somebody* who was interesting to talk to?

It was Coca-Cola. "The Coca-Cola Company" on the other end of the phone was excited to reach "The Rich Sheridan."

Would you like Coca-Cola to be your customer? Or your version of Coca-Cola? Would you like *them* to call *you*?

Then master selling on the front porch. Harness the fundamental principles that have been working for millennia, because they have never been truer than they are on Facebook. The fundamentals don't change. The tools and tactics change; the strategy remains.

Engage your customers with value-added experience so they enjoy hanging out on your front porch. Get as many leads as possible on your front porch, playing checkers, eating snickerdoodles, and occasionally even learning something interesting or important. When the time comes to purchase a product or service, who do you think they will be most inclined to buy from?

Coca-Cola may soon be calling you, too.

THE THREE-LAYER FACEBOOK FUNNEL

Throughout this book you will see a lot of different tactics, tips, and advice for your Facebook ad campaigns. We share many different *specific* strategies that have been proven to work on Facebook—proven to move users into taking action. All these strategies may feel overwhelming, and some of it may even feel a little contradictory. But what I want you to do right now is try and think very holistically about the long-term goals and objectives for your upcoming campaigns and for your entire business.

If you want to really stand out from your competition and make Facebook a never-ending gold mine that you can be digging into for years to come, then put some time into thinking very strategically about everything you do on Facebook. I want you to start thinking about everything you do as part of a three-layer Facebook funnel.

I was first introduced to this three-layer funnel by Dennis Yu, a brilliant Facebook advertising marketer whose company manages some of the most successful brands on Facebook.

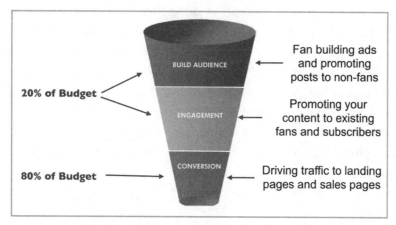

FIGURE 5.4–Three-Layer Facebook Funnel

In Figure 5.4, you see a graphic of the funnel and that it consists of three separate layers: build audience, engagement, and conversion. With your Facebook ads you should always be thinking of how you can be focusing on all three of these layers. Now, don't try to create one ad that does all three.

Create multiple ads or posts that will each achieve one of these goals. (However, in Chapter 14, I take you through my ninja tactic called the "Promoted Post Retargeting Loop" that achieves all three of these goals simultaneously!)

First Layer: Build Audience

Think of the first layer of the funnel as meeting your husband, wife, or partner for the first time. Your goal is to get them to like you first. Not to take them home to bed ten minutes after you meet. (Well, hopefully that's not your goal. Unless your goal is to rack up as many one-night stands as possible and never truly have a deep relationship with anyone.)

There are several ways to run audience-building campaigns, some of which include:

- Page like ads: using Facebook's "page like" objective when running campaigns
- Running "click like if you love baseball" types of ads
- Using a like-gated landing page, where the user must first click like in order to view the rest of your message

- Running a contest or giveaway encouraging or requiring people to like a page
- Running news feed page post ads, as a certain percentage of people will "like" your page during these campaigns

Second Layer: Engagement

If you are using an email autoresponder at any level then you will understand the engagement level. This is where you deepen the relationship with your prospects, where you nurture them with your high-value content. (If you are *not* already using an email autoresponder, please start ASAP. You cannot be successful on Facebook without having some type of lead generating and nurturing campaign in place. Period.)

Engaging on Facebook is obviously different than sending emails to your subscribers; however, the reason I use this as a comparison is to get you into the frame of mind of creating compelling content to keep your audience engaged and moving toward eventually becoming a customer or client. And great marketers understand that for every one promotional email they send out, they will send four, five, or more content-rich, nonselling emails.

This is how you engage on Facebook. Yet the best part about Facebook is that your audience isn't required to subscribe to your email list. They don't even need to become a fan.

Is it better if they become a fan first? Yes, of course it is; once they're fans you know they have raised their hand telling you they want more content from you. However, even if they are not fans but you know they are inside your exact, ideal target audience, then you can still create high-value content and amplify that content into the news feed of those folks!

Creating high-value, nonselling content and amplifying that with Facebook ads in the news feed is how you engage with people and move them from strangers to friends, and eventually to customers.

Third Layer: Conversion

The final layer of your Facebook advertising efforts is conversion. This is where your sole purpose is to convert visitors into leads, prospects, and customers. The one very important thing to understand about this layer is that you may have some campaigns running that are taking new, cold traffic right into the conversion phase.

Example: ads driving traffic to a free lead magnet offer. And you may have some campaigns running that are taking users that you have *already* engaged with in the past.

80/20 YOUR THREE-LAYER FACEBOOK FUNNEL BUDGET

Assuming you have designed an offer that can convert cold traffic on Facebook into leads or customers, you will want to start thinking about getting more strategic with your ad budget and content that you promote with Facebook.

Even if you have an offer that is converting, you still want to look for ways to scale out into broader targeting groups, have longer lasting power, and build a community of raving fans and followers along the way. The way you do this is by implementing this three-layer funnel strategy.

Here is an example of how you might use your Facebook ad budget:

- Dedicate around 10 percent of the budget on building your audience and getting new fans. (The blind date.)
- Dedicate between 10 and 20 percent on amplifying high-quality content with Facebook ads and increasing engagement.
- Dedicate 70 to 80 percent of the budget driving traffic to high-converting landing pages to your lead magnets or other offers.

Please understand that these numbers can sway in a big way, depending on the company or brand or according to the promotional schedule. For example, we will go through some periods where almost 100 percent of the budget is dedicated to promoting blog content only, and no opt-ins-required or selling is happening. This may be leading up to a big product launch where the budget may shift to 90 percent conversion focused and only 10 percent content and engagement focused.

Use your best judgment here for your specific situation!

Go to www.perrymarshall.com/fbtools for the latest updates and to get valuable resources for more clicks from Facebook for less money.

Chapter 6

How to Create Offers that Make Customers Salivate and Pine for More

FROM 15% TO 50%

When we wrote the first edition of this book, we had a vexing problem:

Facebook was appropriate for maybe 15 percent of businesses out there and a waste of time for everybody else.

That was great for the 15 percent, but if the 85 percent bought our Facebook guide thinking it was going to give them the big breakthrough they were seeking, they were in for a rude surprise. The last thing we wanted was a bunch of one-star Amazon reviews from angry, frustrated readers.

> *"We make a living by what we get. We make a life by what we give."*
>
> —WINSTON CHURCHILL

We needed to *dis*qualify people who shouldn't be using Facebook. So we built the www. IsFBforMe.com quiz. We intentionally designed it so that 85 percent of people would score a 6 or below. The results page would tell them to go away and do something else, and only people we could help would be left.

You know what? That actually worked! The first edition has 4.8 stars out of 5 on Amazon, as I write this, nearly two years after it was first printed. There is no way that many people would be happy if we were "trying to get everybody."

Not only that, the Facebook scoring tool itself went viral. All kinds of experts and websites have been recommending it ever since.

After Facebook got its act together, we redesigned the tool. Now the tool tells only 50 percent of people to go away. Which is about right. Facebook is pretty good for about half the businesses out there. For the other half, not so much.

This is a *very* effective approach. I (Perry) call it "Empowering the customer to sort himself out."

Most of your competitors will never do this, because they falsely believe they need everybody. The fact that I'm ready and willing to tell a "4" that they should find some other way to advertise automatically gives me that much more power when I'm talking to the "9" and I tell him he should put every possible bit of effort into making Facebook fly.

In my book *80/20 Sales and Marketing*, I explain that sales and marketing is not a "convincing people" process as most people suppose; it is first and foremost a *disqualification* process.

Before you sell anything, you need to get rid of the people who don't belong in the room in the first place. This is the marketing strategy of disqualification.

I always try to design landing pages not only to attract the person I want but to repel the person I don't want. Great marketing polarizes people.

Please notice the trend:

> 1998—"Sign up for our free ezine"—and yes, people actually built nice fat email lists with nothing more sophisticated than that
>
> 2003—"Enter your name and email address to get our free report on . . ."
>
> 2010—"Enter your name and email address to get this software utility for free. Normally valued at $49"
>
> 2015—"Your score is 6.8 on a scale from 1 to 10. To get a customized report explaining exactly what it means and how to improve it, fill in this form . . ." or "You can get *80/20 Sales and Marketing* for 1 penny plus shipping, instead of paying $17 on Amazon . . ." (that's my offer by the way, it's at www.Sell8020. com).

Do you see the pattern? The increasing level of value you must deliver in order to collect an email address or sales lead? That's lead-generation inflation. You gotta deliver value, baby.

Here is a list of lead magnets that work great with Facebook.

- Self-diagnostic
- Cheat sheet or checklist
- Free report, guide, or industry bulletin

- Coupon
- Tool kit or resource list
- Free tool, plugin, etc.
- Free video series
- Survey or quiz
- Webinar, teleseminar, or Hangout
- Contest or sweepstakes
- Live event
- Tip or hack
- Free book plus shipping
- Bargain-priced physical product (impulse buy)

Your offer is more important than your Facebook ad or your landing page copy. You MUST deliver something sexy and desirable. Failure to deliver serious value in exchange for a sales lead is one of the biggest causes of failure. You can't give people boring stuff and expect them to respond.

STOP MAKING YOUR ADS LOOK LIKE ADS!

Try focusing on making your ads look as much like content as possible. Everyone is always talking about creating images that stand out, adding borders, contrasting back-grounds, funny pictures, etc. to get higher clickthrough rates. Try making your ad *not* look like an ad! (This only works with news feed ads and is not relevant for right-column ads.)

If you can make your page post ads look and feel more like high-quality, organic content, you will get much higher quality visitors clicking through on your ads. You will also get a lot of social boost from likes, comments, and shares. (Of course, if you're going to do this you must be promoting high quality stuff, not crap.)

When you are running native advertising or content advertising like news feed ads, make it look like content and send the traffic to content! And I'm not talking about content you can only consume after you opt-in with your contact info, I'm talking about content you can freely consume without giving anything in return. (For more on promoting content see Chapter 14.)

Please remember that it is almost impossible to generalize the topic of your Facebook offer to fit every business out there. Every situation is different. You may have two different businesses selling the exact same product or service, and a free video series works great for one business and bombs for the other.

Or two companies both have essentially the same free tool they're giving away as a lead magnet, and they both have similar lead conversion rates. But one company is getting a positive ROI and the other company is burning through cash on a daily basis.

Small hinges swing big doors.

Here are just a few things that may seem small but can make a major impact and swing a campaign from a winner to a loser:

- Exactly what the person gets in exchange for "playing ball" with you.
- The headline and subhead on the landing page.
- The congruency of the landing page compared to the Facebook ad.
- Using a video compared to not using video.
- Video quality. One person may resonate with the user; another person may not.
- Retargeting segmentation. One company may not retarget at all. One company may only retarget leads that didn't buy. And one company may have different retargeting campaigns running for every step in the sales or nurturing process.
- Email follow-up sequence. One company may have a super basic seven-email sequence, and another may have a complex, deeply automated 35-email sequence with several automation triggers and actions set up to send highly relevant emails to move leads along smoothly.
- Price point. A $2 change could be the difference-maker. Or maybe it's a $150 increase.
- Upsells, cross-sells, and down-sells.
- Targeting.

THREE PILLARS OF FACEBOOK ADVERTISING SUCCESS

Success with Facebook advertising has three pillars:

1. The offer
2. Audience targeting
3. Ad copy or creative

All of those pillars provide vital support to your campaign. They're all essential and together they'll determine your success on Facebook. You're going to create an offer that people will want; decide who you want to show it to, and write the words that persuade them to take it.

One pillar, again, is much more crucial to your success than the other two. Your *offer*.

Before you can do anything else, you must get the offer right. You have to give your audience a hook that will cause them to click through or opt-in or want to learn more.

Whenever we take on a new client, we will NOT start running ads until we know that we've got an offer—and not just any offer, but one that's appropriate for Facebook.

After much experimentation and close tracking of results, we now have a list of different kinds of offers that we know work well on Facebook. In this chapter, we introduce you to a number of different offers that we've found to be the most effective.

They're pretty straightforward. You've probably seen these offers plenty of times before. You might even have used them plenty of times before. You shouldn't have any problem promoting them to an audience with Facebook ads.

1. Checklists, Cheat Sheets, Guides, and Reports

You'll certainly have seen these before: simple information products that offer readers quick nuggets of valuable information. The copy itself might take the form of a picture of the product on the left and some hard-hitting copy on the right, often incorporating a number so that leads know that they'll be able to absorb that knowledge very quickly.

We *know* these work.

The example on the left in Figure 6.1 is one that I use. The one on the right comes from Ryan Deiss.

FIGURE 6.1–Checklist, Cheat Sheet, or Simple Report

The lifetime opt-in rate that I typically see on an offer like this is around 40 to 50 percent. That's a high rate, and it's coming partly *because the people seeing these offers will already have seen something from me at least once.* They might have seen a Facebook video ad or I'll have used retargeting to show the offer to people who have already clicked through to my website. The offer is coming from someone with whom they already have some sort of relationship so I know they're interested in clicking.

But it's still the offer that's key.

Persuading someone to play a video in a Facebook news feed is very different from persuading someone to give you their email address.

Offer people quick bits of valuable information in the form of checklists, cheat sheets, guides, or reports and they'll be persuaded to click.

2. Tool Kits and Resource Lists

Tool kits and resource lists are another form of information product but one that offers the *means* to achieve a goal rather than the knowledge to achieve a goal. The difference isn't huge. It lies mostly in the content—a list of essential data sources or software products, for example—and in the wording of the copy. The product itself might still be a report, but the copy might mention "tools" or "resources." ("Tools" is better.)

FIGURE 6.2–Tool Kit or Resource List

Clay Collins of LeadPages™ once published a post about his highest-converting offer. It offered his audience "Five Free Tools" and converted like gangbusters. I copied it for one of my offers. You can copy mine for one of yours.

But the offer doesn't have to contain a number of different items. The Motley Fool, which is said to have invented the basic squeeze layout, did very well with an offer to tell audiences about "the one stock they need to own." (See Figure 6.3 on page 79.) The simplicity of that offer can be just as persuasive.

To get that one resource, all audiences needed to do was enter an email address to watch a video. Very simple and very effective. You can find plenty of templates online that will let you churn out offers like these very quickly.

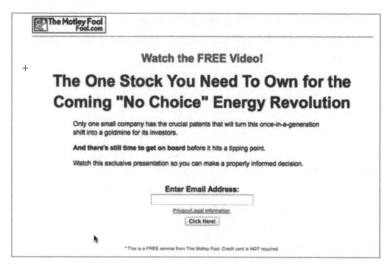

FIGURE 6.3–One Specific Tip, Resource, or Hack

3. Video Series

Videos make for good offers because not everyone wants to read. People often just want to sit back and watch, and they'll pay for that ease with their email address. We've seen great results with a couple of different kinds of offers for video series.

FIGURE 6.4–Free Video Series

The offer shown in Figure 6.4 for an athletic audience is very specific. Audiences can see that they're going to be running like an Olympic athlete. And the offer is for the first video. There's no great commitment from the audience there. They can see the first video, and if they like it, they can watch more. It's short and to the point and guides audiences very effectively to the action button.

For a product with Jack Canfield and Steve Harrison where they help authors create bestsellers, we used a long-form landing page where there were several screens of sales points, features, and testimonials.

The result was a lower opt-in rate but much higher sales conversions from those opt-ins.

4. Webinars

Facebook ads are awesome for promoting webinars. We saw great results when we promoted John Lee Dumas's podcasting secrets. The landing page was very straightforward: headline; quick video from John; reasons to attend the free webinar; and a simple reservation form below the date and time.

Again these work even better when someone has already seen you. Once someone has already received value from you, they'll be more likely to pencil in a date in their calendar to get more value. That value could take the form of a checklist or even just a video on your news feed or blog.

Anything that helps to ensure that your offer doesn't come on their very first contact with you will help to improve your results.

5. One Tip

We've seen how offering a single resource, such as The Motley Fool's essential stock, can make for powerful offers on Facebook. A single tip can have the same effect, and it can even be used to bring leads into a funnel that ends eventually in high-ticket items.

For example, we had a previous client who had a service offering that was over $5,000 that centered around helping couples deepen their relationship. But you can't just sell a $5,000 service with Facebook ads—that's way too expensive for a first impression. We needed a process that created trust and familiarity before hitting them with the full product offering.

The Facebook ad and landing page offered just a single tip that drew a lot of curiosity: "The real secret of making your partner fall head over heels in love with you all over again!" This landing page was getting a 40percent-plus conversion rate and the word "heels" was even spelled wrong!

That's a big result that comes from the offer of a single piece of information.

In fact, they got a lot more. As shown in Figure 6.5 on page 81, the landing page offered an entire book about relationships that usually costs $30. The lead could get it for free plus $5 postage and packing. At that point, they were already in a funnel. They would then be taken through the next step in the funnel, which would include direct mail, a phone call, etc., to move the buyer prospect closer to that $5,000 service.

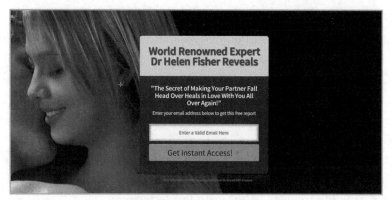

FIGURE 6.5–One Tip

6. Free Book Offer

We could have chosen a different route for the photography session. The most efficient customer acquisition that we've ever experienced—cheaper even than in the glory days of Google—came when we used Facebook to offer our *80/20 Sales and Marketing* for a penny (see Figure 6.6).

If you've got the content to give away, it's a hugely valuable strategy. You can try both methods to see which works best: Either make the offer for the book, or offer the most outstanding and valuable piece of information within the book.

You'll find that the most effective strategy is the one that offers the most value to leads, but both will work.

FIGURE 6.6–Free Book Plus Shipping

7. Physical Products

So far, I've only discussed offers of digital products. They're instant, easy to order, and simple to deliver, but you can also play on people's impulses and offer physical products. Ryan Deiss had a success offering a "Survival Business Card" and is still having success with a free "Credit Card Knife." They are both free—just a few bucks for shipping— limited, and looked really useful. You can think of it as a kind of physical version of those tool kits I described earlier.

The choice of product is critical. It has to be something that people would pick up without thinking too much. If you can imagine it in the rack next to the cash desk at Home Depot or Staples, you're on the right line of inquiry.

Again, the idea is just to get people to click, leave their details, and start moving through the funnel.

FIGURE 6.7–Free Credit Card Knife

Another great example of going right into the sale for a physical product is Dollar Shave Club (see Figures 6.8 and 6.9 on page 83). Because they have a low enough price point, which makes it an impulse buy, they can drive traffic right into their offer. They have an under-$10 offer and make money on the monthly subscription and the upsells.

MAKE THE OFFER SPECIFIC AND GET A COMMITMENT

That's a long list of different kinds of offers that we've found to be very effective on Facebook. Clearly, when we're putting together campaigns for clients, we make sure that

FIGURE 6.8–Dollar Shave Club, Step 1

FIGURE 6.9–Dollar Shave Club Step 2

we match the offer to the audience and to the final product. But this is the toolbox we're always choosing from.

Whenever you make an offer, the lead should know exactly what's on the table. Even when you're offering a tool kit, the benefits of that tool kit are always clear and specific. Those ads you've seen on the sides of nearly every website offering "1 tip for a flat belly" work in exactly the same way.

They're everywhere because they work, and they work because they're specific.

Whenever you make an offer through Facebook, you should always be looking for something that you can put *before* your main core product or service to build rapport or get a small commitment. It doesn't have to be anything as complex as a complete funnel filled with upsells and down-sells. Even something as simple as a testimonial video inserted into the news feed can prime the lead and prepare them for the offer.

For example, we once had a client who was trying to promote a $3,000 training program via automated webinar. The landing page wasn't very exciting, and I didn't think it would convert well on Facebook. They didn't have much in the way of content that we could use to build value before making the offer, but they did have a testimonial video.

We put that in the news feed, promoted it, and filled the lower third of the screen with an ad urging them to register for the webinar. The result was an ROI as high as two to one.

Every successful Facebook campaign starts with a good offer or lead magnet. Get it right, make it specific, then test it, and you'll have your first pillar in place.

Go to www.perrymarshall.com/fbtools for the latest updates and to get valuable resources for more clicks from Facebook for less money.

Chapter 7

Targeting

YOUR OWN CUSTOM DEMOGRAPHICS COMPANY AT YOUR FINGERTIPS

Have you ever wished you had a crystal ball so you would spend your precious money on reaching only the people who are going to *buy*?

Have you ever looked at a bunch of customer information—let's say, an email or snail mail list on a spreadsheet—and wondered which one of those people is going to buy next?

That's exactly how I felt. So enlisted the services of a high-end demographics

> "*People don't notice ads, they notice what interests them and sometimes it's an ad.*"
>
> —Howard Gossage

consulting company, Kristalytics. They showed us that 60 percent of our sales were coming from 3 percent of our customers. Eighty percent of our sales leads were never going to buy, ever. Suddenly, for the first time we could predict which ones they were going to be.

We discovered that only a certain slice of the world ever became quality customers. There was a very consistent pattern of what neighborhoods and cities they lived in, what their buying patterns were, their postal codes, and financial situations. One city or county might be 20 times more likely to bring us a customer than the one right next to it.

We built a profile of our customers. As we began supplementing our electronic marketing efforts with direct mail sent to a laser-targeted section of our list, the ROI of our direct-mail efforts doubled. Before that, direct-mail drops were a crapshoot. Since then, it's become a reliable money machine.

When you can predict, with accuracy, which names are going to buy and which ones won't, you possess a secret advantage over your competitors.

Guess what: You no longer have to commission a custom demographics company in order to get powerful targeting. Today, demographic and psychographic ad targeting is built right into Facebook. This is a *major* key to making your Facebook ads profitable!

BLOW AWAY ALL OTHER MEDIA CHANNELS WITH STRATEGIC FACEBOOK TARGETING

There is no other advertising platform with the targeting capabilities that Facebook has. This is a bold but true statement. The data Facebook gathers on a daily basis is mind-boggling. It's data from user profiles, user actions such as liking or sharing a post, liking a page, joining a group, downloading an app, or any other Facebook activity a user can do.

Facebook also has data from mortgage loans, student loans, auto and motorcycle loans, and purchase data, lease agreements, grocery shopping rewards programs, frequent-flyer programs, charitable donation activity, and much more offline spending data.

Facebook also has data from every mobile platform Facebook controls, partners with, or acquires. Do not take this one lightly. We are just in the early stages of the capabilities and possibilities with Facebook and mobile and how this will affect us advertisers, and Facebook is holding their cards very close to the vest regarding how much data and how much targeting will be possible over the next few years.

When it comes to your targeting, the more hypertargeted you get, the more successful you will be. It is that simple. You can start broad, but you will want to begin narrowing down your targeting and creating new ad sets for every different segment combination you can think of.

The average person (and journalist) is paranoid about how much data Facebook has. Most of these fears are unfounded. The reason it's important to me and you as marketers is: *We don't want to show our ads to the wrong people!* This rich data is a major reason why Facebook went from dog to hottest thing on the web after the company went public.

TARGET AUDIENCE RESEARCH

Before you begin running ads, you need to spend some time researching your target audience. Even though the Ads Manager itself is a great tool for researching and brainstorming for potential audiences to target, you should spend some time doing your due diligence with some other great resources.

I will list some suggestions on the next few pages for gathering data to prep for your campaigns, but feel free to use any resource you have found to be helpful in learning about your target audience.

Target Audience Spreadsheet

Before you begin your target audience research, open up an Excel spreadsheet, preferably a Google Doc spreadsheet, where you can start an ongoing list of potential target audiences. Brain dump everything you find onto this spreadsheet. All potential audiences. You can organize it later.

Facebook Graph Search

The best place to start your research is right inside Facebook, on the search bar. My favorite search is "pages liked by people who like (insert Facebook page here)." You can search for pages liked by fans of your Facebook page, your competition's pages, thought leaders in your space, or any other type of page.

You can do topic-related searches (pages liked by people who like "public speaking"), you can search for people who like certain pages or interests, and tons of other kinds of searches. Get creative here!

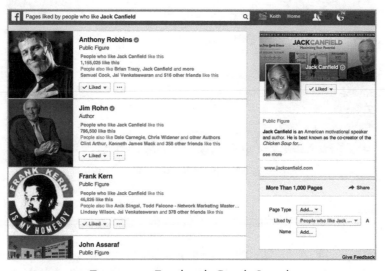

FIGURE 7.1–Facebook Graph Search

Facebook Ads Manager

There's no better place for your target audience research than inside the Ad Manager or the Power Editor! Get inside the Ad Manager and start putting in some of the interests you found in your Facebook search into the "Interests" section in the Ad Manager. If the interest you put in the Ad Manager is an available interest to target, then Facebook will give you a list of "suggested interests" in a dropdown menu. Add all of those interests into your spreadsheet. Then select one of them and check and see what new interests are suggested.

Note: Not all Facebook pages are available as interests to target in Facebook. There is no exact guideline for how many fans a page needs to have to show up as a target audience; however, it does need to have a significant number of fans (normally at least 10,000 or 20,000 or more, but sometimes less).

Facebook Audience Insights

How about combining the power of Facebook search; targeting in the ad platform, offline affinity, and demographic data; and putting everything into one amazing tool?

Welcome to Audience Insights.

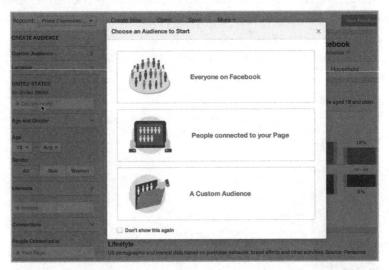

FIGURE 7.2–Facebook Audience Insights

Facebook Interests and Activity Affinities

With Audience Insights you can analyze a custom audience of your subscriber or customer database, you can analyze your Facebook fans and friends of fans, and you can analyze any Facebook interest, topic, or behavior that Facebook has accumulated data on.

Offline Behavior Affinities

With Audience Insights you can find offline commonalities and trends within any interest, list, or audience. You can run affinity reports (on any interest, list, or audience)

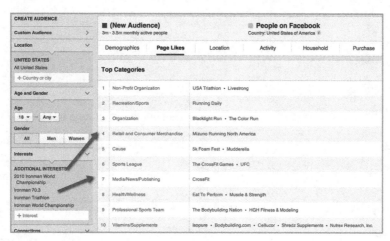

FIGURE 7.3–Top Categories for People with Ironman Triathlon Interests

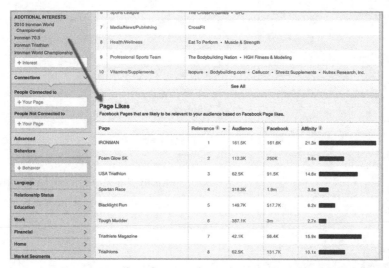

FIGURE 7.4–Top Page Likes for People with Ironman Triathlon Interests

on behaviors such as language, relationship status, job title, income, home value, family size, life events, and much more. You can also overlay this information with a custom audience, your fans, or a Facebook interest to find more affinities. And the best part: You can turn any Insights data result into a new target audience that will be saved inside your Ads Manager or Power Editor.

In Figure 7.5 on page 90 you will see a list of advanced targeting options. Each advanced targeting option has either a dropdown of additional subcategories or a window you can enter in a more advanced targeting search. (See Figures 7.6. and 7.7.)

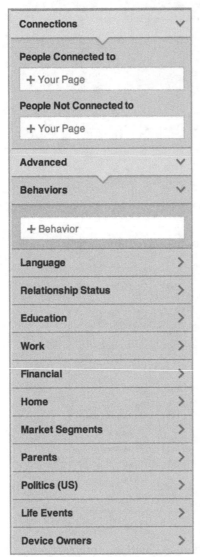

FIGURE 7.5–Advanced
Connections—Behaviors

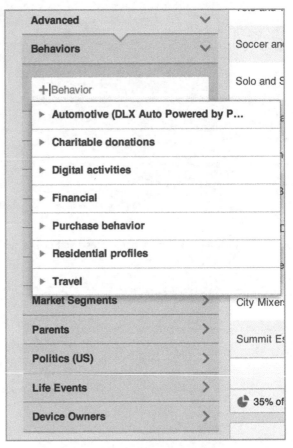

FIGURE 7.6–Advanced Targeting
Insights—Behaviors

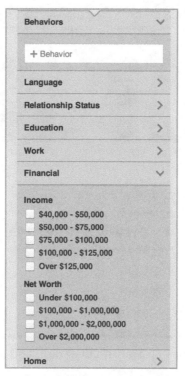

FIGURE 7.7–Advanced Targeting Insights—Financial

You will also find many other useful insight reports, such as lifestyle, location, activity, relationship status, job title, household data, purchase data, and more.

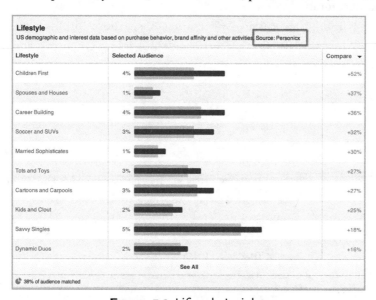

FIGURE 7.8–Lifestyle Insights

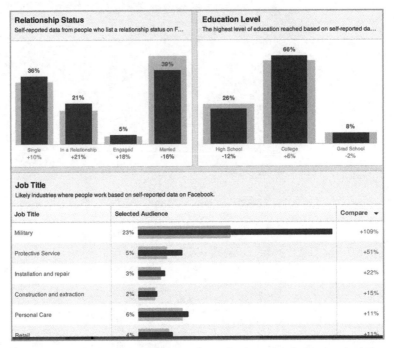

FIGURE 7.9–Relationship Status, Education, and Job Status Insights

Google

Go to Google and search for thought leaders in your market, books in your market, etc., and see what you can find. For some searches Google will show other related searches in the right-hand column.

Search for leading forums in your market. Visit those forums and look for hot topics, and also take the URL for that forum and plug it into Quantcast and SimilarWeb.

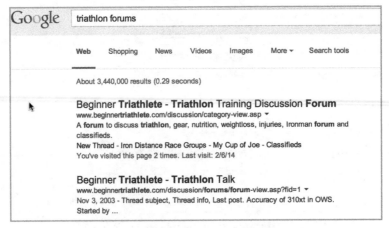

FIGURE 7.10–Search for Forums in Your Market

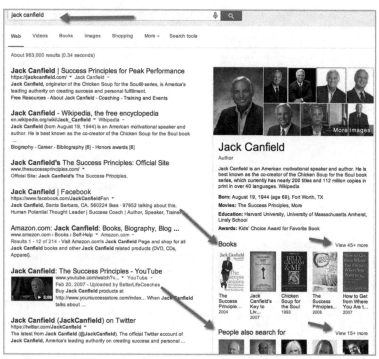

FIGURE 7.11–Google Search

SimilarWeb and Quantcast

You can find demographic data, affinity data, and general competitor analysis data at www.Similarweb.com and www.Quantcast.com that can be super helpful in your research phase. These are both free resources. But be aware that a lot of sites you enter into these sites might not have enough traffic to have any results so you may need to try other similar sites.

FIGURE 7.12–SimilarWeb Data on the www.BeginnerTriathlete.com Forum

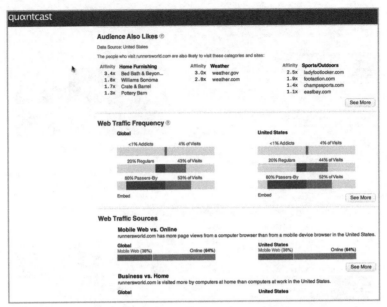

FIGURE 7.13–Gathering Affinity Data with Quantcast

Amazon

Amazon is an excellent place to find more potential audiences along with other game-changing insight, like discovering the true needs, desires, and frustrations of your target audience. With Amazon you can do a search, click on one of the top results, then scroll down and look for "customers who bought this item also bought this" and "what other items do customers buy after viewing this item," and look for what sponsored listings are showing up near that search.

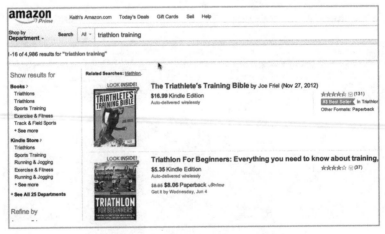

FIGURE 7.14–Amazon Book Search

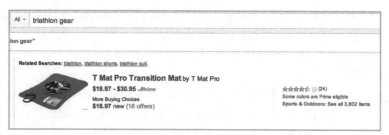

FIGURE 7.15–Amazon Product Search

But don't stop there. Read through the customer reviews and look for pain points and favorite aspects of that product that people talk about. This is gold for your ad copy and landing page copy!

TARGETING OPTIONS

Facebook organizes their targeting by different sections inside the Ads Manager or Power Editor, and this structure is another ever-evolving piece of the Facebook ads game. I'm going to take you through some of the different targeting segments inside Facebook through the next few pages, but please be aware that there may be some options not available to you at the time you're reading this, due to recent changes by Facebook or because of your geographic location.

Some of the data Facebook gathers through their various partners is slowly rolling out to countries outside the United States; some of that "offline spending data" is not made available by other countries, due to different regulations.

As mentioned before you will have a few more options with the Power Editor with things such as your targeting, ad placement, and conversion tracking; however, as of late Facebook has been really improving the regular Ad Manager. The targeting options are almost the same as the Power Editor.

If you haven't already, please make sure you go pick up the latest Facebook ads program we have over at www.PerryMarshall.com/fbtools, and join our inner circle of Facebook ads experts. You will also want to visit Keith's site at www.Dominatewebmedia. com where you'll find a ton of free trainings, checklists, and programs to keep you on the cutting edge and adept with all the Facebook changes.

Facebook is continually breaking up the different targeting options into different subcategories inside the Ad Manager, giving you more and more options to focus your targeting better. For example, not too long ago we had only four options: demographics and location, precise interests, broad categories, and connection targeting.

As of this writing we now have: demographics and location, custom audiences, more demographics, interests, behaviors, more categories, and connection targeting. The more subcategories we have the better, as this gives you more layering opportunities, which we will discuss in more detail in this section.

Interests Targeting

The Interests category of targeting has replaced the original Precise Interests category and combined it with the Broad Categories. Within the Interests section you can search for almost any type of interest you can imagine. You can select specific Facebook pages, like "Tony Robbins" or "Nike," or you can select topics, books, movies, etc. (See Figures 7.16 and 7.17.)

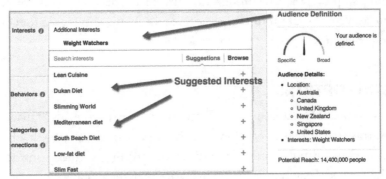

FIGURE 7.16–Weight Watchers Interest Targeting

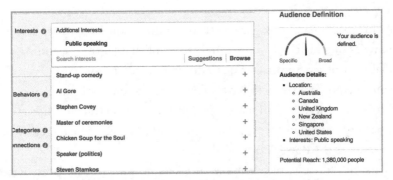

FIGURE 7.17–Public Speaking Topic Targeting

GET IN AND PLAY AROUND

The best thing for you to do is to get inside the Ad Manager or the Power Editor and just start playing around and searching for potential interests. Facebook will give you tons of suggestions to help you find more even potential interests, *and* it will really help you brainstorm more ideas.

FIGURE 7.18–More Interests

Advanced Demographic Targeting

Facebook is constantly adding more demographic targeting options, and in Figures 7.19 through 7.22 you can see some of the types of options you have available in the More Demographics section.

FIGURE 7.19–More Demographics

FIGURE 7.20–Work Demographics

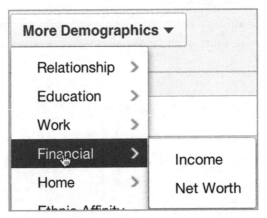

FIGURE 7.21–Net Worth Demographics

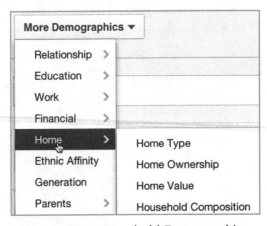

FIGURE 7.22–Household Demographics

Behavior Targeting

How would you like to know more about your potential customers than they know about themselves? Have you ever read the stories about companies like Target, Macy's, and Babies "R" Us sending out offers to expecting mothers still living with their parents, letting the "cat out of the bag" before they had a chance to spill the beans to their mom or dad? The parents would wonder why they were getting all these promotions on prenatal vitamins, diapers, baby food, and other products only an expecting mother would be interested in.

Up until Facebook changed the game only large companies with deep pockets had the ability to utilize and profit from this offline spending behavior data.

Not anymore.

With a credit card or a PayPal account and a Facebook account, you can now tap into this abundant amount of data and take your business to the next level.

Here are just a few of the behaviors you can target inside Facebook:

- Annual salary
- Net income
- Type and style of vehicle or motorcycle
- Vehicle price or vehicle age
- Type of charitable donations (political, religious, animal, children's, etc.)
- Digital activities
- Insurance renewal month (no, that is not a misprint)
- Business purchase behavior
- Grocery shopping behavior
- Retail shopping behavior
- Buyer profiles ("gamers, gadget enthusiasts, green living, healthy and fit, luxury brand purchasers, outdoor enthusiasts, skiing, spa enthusiasts, sportsman, trendy homemakers, etc.)
- Residential profiles (likely to move, recent home buyer, recently moved, etc.)
- Travel habits
- And much more

You can see a few examples of these behavior targets inside Facebook in Figures 7.23 to 7.26 on pages 100 and 101.

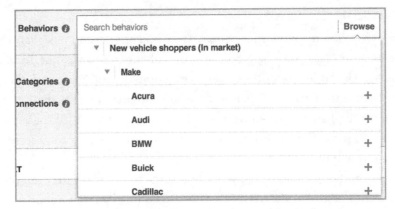

FIGURE 7.23–Vehicle Purchase Behavior

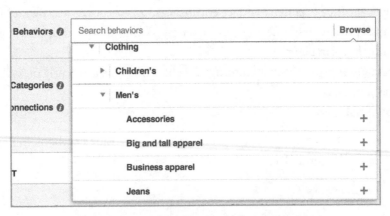

FIGURE 7.24–Online Behavior

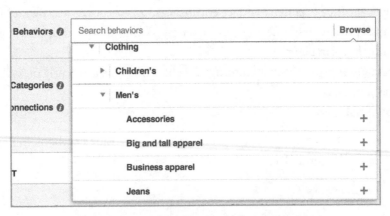

FIGURE 7.25–Clothing Shopping Behavior

FIGURE 7.26–More Behaviors

Custom Audience Targeting

Want to supercharge your email marketing? You can now export any email or phone list as small as 20 people and upload that list into Facebook as a new target audience. Facebook will then go through a mining process of matching up all the emails to their database. After about an hour, you will now have a new target audience in your arsenal called "a custom audience."

For example, if you upload a list of 10,000 emails (CSV file), you may have 6,500 of those emails match up with the Facebook profile emails. That would be a 65 percent match rate. You can expect around a 30 to 70 percent match rate, depending on the quality of your list.

FIGURE 7.27–Create a Custom Audience

FIGURE 7.28–Choosing a Custom Audience

How many different ways can you ring the register from custom audiences? Here are just a few examples to get your mind spinning:

- Not getting 100 percent open rate on your emails? Then run a custom audience news feed page post ad that will be sure get in front of all your subscribers on Facebook.
- Looking for more sales conversions on your leads? Run a Facebook video ad showing a testimonial video from one of your happy customers, with a link in the post taking the user to your sales page, product page, or shopping cart.
- Looking to wake up a dead list? Or run a promotion to unsubscribers ethically inside Facebook? Then run a campaign with a compelling new offer to these Facebook users.
- Looking to nurture existing customers and subscribers with high-value content, warming them up to eventually make a first purchase or buy another product or service? Then run custom audience engagement ads that drive people to your content and build up more goodwill.
- Looking to get more reviews for your product or book on Amazon and improve your ranking? Then run a custom audience Facebook ad asking people: "If you liked my book please leave a review on Amazon. We'd love your feedback!" Then link directly to your Amazon product review page.
- Looking to retarget visitors on mobile who originally visited your site on a desktop device? Or viceversa? Then run a Facebook website custom audience campaign and reach people on any device (aka "Facebook Website Retargeting").

As you can see, the possibilities are endless.

Right-Angle Targeting with Lookalike Audiences

Another new feature that is constantly being improved is Facebook's "Lookalike Audiences" or "Similar Audiences." This is where Facebook will take any existing custom audience you select and create a new, completely unique group of users with similar likes, interests, and behaviors.

FIGURE 7.29–New Lookalike Audience

Each time you create a new lookalike audience you are able to optimize for "similarity" or "greater reach." I usually recommend optimizing for "similarity," as the audience Facebook creates will still be fairly large. The more targeted, the better.

In fact, because a lookalike audience by itself is usually a broad audience, we recommend being careful targeting *only* a lookalike audience. In some cases you will be OK targeting *only* a lookalike audience without any other interests selected, but be careful here. The more hyper targeted you can get, the better off you will be.

You can even create a lookalike audience from fans of a Facebook page you have admin access to or from a conversion tracking pixel! So you can be creating dynamic, constantly updating lookalike audiences from only the visitors who are converting into leads, prospects, or customers. This has been an absolute game changer for our client campaigns.

The Holy Grail of Targeting: Layering

Do you have a product or service that would benefit more people, if they *just* knew it existed. If they *knew* the story behind your brand, they would love you.

Keep reading carefully if this is you or a client of yours. If you are selling crap then go ahead and stop reading now, because this type of marketing doesn't work very well on crappy products and services that are just ripping people off.

The one thing we know about Facebook ads is that the more precise your targeting is, the better your ads will perform. However, the razor-sharp marketers with good sales funnels in place are always looking for ways to be able to scale out into wider and broader audiences and still keep a positive ROI.

One of the best ways to do this is to use a technique we call "audience layering." The basic strategy here is to find a target audience inside Facebook that may be normally too broad to get good results and overlay that audience with one of your similar audiences.

In the example below you will see that the interest target of "triathlons" is pretty broad: the "Potential Audience" is 4,800,000 people. This is too big. The advertiser in this case offers training curriculums to triathletes who want to improve their performance. Hardcore athletes.

With the general "triathlons" interest you may be getting a lot of regular folks who are not really hardcore athletes. They may just have a friend who runs in triathlons. Or they may have expressed interest in an event like the Boston Marathon, which is a big U.S. annual event.

They typically do much better when targeting small, more precise audiences, like individual races, such as "Ironman Triathlon," "Ironman World Championship," "Ironman 70.3," etc.

So how do you scale out into that 4,800,000-person audience but leave out the riffraff?

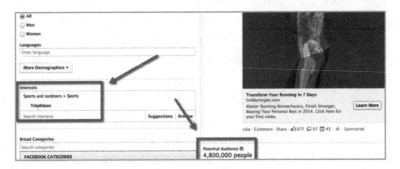

FIGURE 7.30–"Triathlons" Audience (inside the Power Editor)

You layer that audience over one or several of your lookalike audiences.

You will see in Figure 7.31 on page 105 that when you target only the lookalike audience, you are *still* targeting a large potential audience of 740,000 people.

Yet when you target someone who "likes" triathlons *and* is also part of the lookalike audience Facebook created from the "BM Contacts," you will see the potential audience decrease to 58,000, a much more hypertargeted audience! See Figue 7.32.

As you can hopefully imagine, there are countless variations of layering that you can cook up and test with your ads.

Layering with Connection Targeting

Another version of layering that works well is using the connection targeting feature combined with an interest or behavior. For example, in Figure 7.33 on page 106 we are

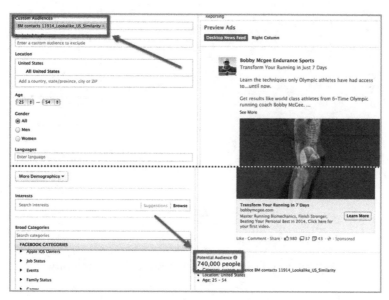

FIGURE 7.31–Similar Audience of Email List Targeting

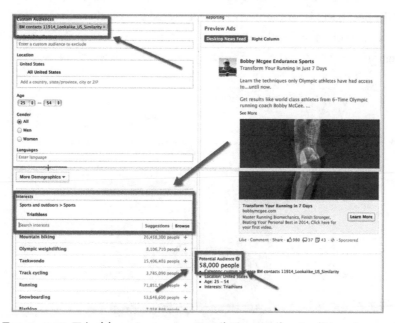

FIGURE 7.32–Triathlons Interest + Email List Similar Audience Layered

targeting people who like "Triathlons" and whose friends are connected to the Bobby McGee Endurance Sports Facebook page (friends of fans targeting).

By choosing the friends of fans option it will significantly reduce your target audience, so if your page has a very low number of fans, then the audience may be a little

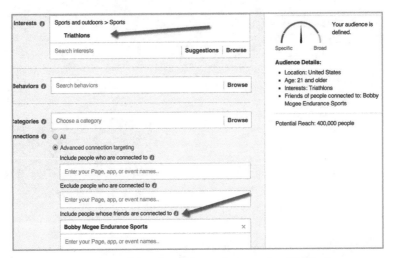

FIGURE 7.33–Friends of Fans Connection Targeting

too small for you to gain any traction doing this. You are reducing your target audience, but you are also increasing the likelihood that you will resonate with that audience.

And the best part about connection targeting is the social credibility you are getting when people see your ads. Facebook will add one or two names of the friend who is a fan of the page that is running the ad. See Figure 4.34 for an illustration.

FIGURE 7.34–Friends of Fans Connection Targeting

Chapter 8

That Quirky Little Image Is Everything

MY BANNER AD EPIPHANY

For a long time I believed banner ads were a waste of money. An ad agency style, "dotcom" scam for branding-oriented companies who knew nothing about direct response. That was because of some banners I bought from a trade magazine website in the late 1990s.

Then one day I decided to take my best pay-per-click text ads and crank out some banners. I hired Laura at BannerAdQueen.com to do the graphics ,and we fed the ads into the machine.

> "*The secret of all effective originality in advertising is not the creation of new and tricky words and pictures, but one of putting familiar words and pictures into new relationships.*"
>
> —LEO BURNETT

She tried all kinds of different visual approaches with 20 different ads. Her best ad got ten times the response of the worst ad; and even the worst one got a better CTR than my text ads. Plus the top two banners slaughtered my old text ads. Traffic doubled almost overnight, the cost of the clicks was about a third of the text ads, and I had a rude but happy awakening:

Dude, good banners are WAY more powerful than simple text! I've been a raving fan of banners ever since.

DRAMATICALLY IMPROVE YOUR CLICKTHROUGH RATES WITH BETTER IMAGES!

Image is everything in Facebook ads. The picture is 70 percent of the game. It is flat out more important than the text.

The ads are formatted by Facebook to project an image of the site as a friendly and social place. Facebook's goal is to have the ads "seamlessly integrate into the Facebook experience." Of course, your goal is a little different. You want to interrupt the users, force them to look at your ad, capture their interest, and compel them to click.

To stand out, you have to interrupt whatever the users were going to do and have them focus on you—your ad, your landing page. There are really only a few tools to help your ad stand out, the biggest being your ad image. Perhaps 80 percent of the click-effectiveness of your ad will be determined by the image you choose and the headline you provide for that image, with 70 percent coming from the image alone.

Images are so important to your ad that you should never fully convince yourself you really know what you are doing when you choose them. Instead, select and test lots of images, and never stop trying new ones.

THE SECRET IS TO BUY CUSTOMERS, NOT JUST GET CHEAP CLICKS

As much as you want to be focused on finding or creating images that stand out and grab the user's attention, you need to be mindful of who you *really* want clicking on your ads. Do you want a ton of cheap clicks and bragging rights about your clickthrough rate? Or do you want only potential buyers clicking on your ads?

I'll take the buyers.

Facebook rewards you for having higher clickthrough rates on your ads. We know this. In general, the higher the CTR of your ads, the lower the cost per click. However, there's a fine line that can be easily crossed, which is going from having a high CTR and low CPC to getting too many unwanted clicks.

NEWS FEED IMAGES VS. RIGHT COLUMN

When you're thinking about images and messaging to put on your ads, you really need to understand the subtle differences and impact points that affect your message, your clickthrough rates, and your conversion rates when you are running a right-column ad compared to a news feed ad.

In the right column, your ad will be very small. In the right column your ad will be just one of several ads on the sidebar. In the right column your ad will *be in the sidebar* and not in the main news feed where the user's attention is focused.

With a news feed ad, your ad will be large. In fact, with a news feed page post link ad, just the image alone (at the time of this writing) is 1,100 percent bigger than a right-column image.

With a news feed ad you will have more area in the post and the image title and description areas for ad copy.

In some cases your news feed ad can take up the entire news feed above the fold for the user. In Figure 8.1, you see the difference between a news feed ad and a right-column ad. The news feed ad is impossible to not see. A right-column ad can easily be lost in the sea of other ads and distractions on Facebook. In this example I took the screenshot from the very top of the browser to the bottom of the browser.

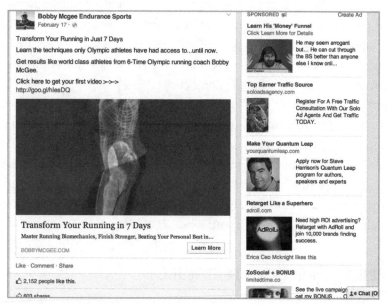

FIGURE 8.1–News Feed Ad Taking Up the Entire News Feed

If you are scrolling the news feed, do you think you would notice the Bobby McGee Endurance Sports ad? Of course you would.

So, the real question you need to ask yourself is: "How can I get the user to not merely *notice* my post and click for pure curiosity's sake, but be compelled to click on it and take the next action I have planned for them after they click?"

How does this ad or post reflect on your brand? Does it exude professionalism? Does it represent your product or service well? When someone clicks on your sponsored news feed posts, they are subconsciously already starting to make judgments and decisions about your product or service. Or you, if you are branding yourself.

Now don't get me wrong, people are judging you by the ad you place on the right column also but in a much different way. The average user spends much less time looking at a right-column ad before clicking on it. It is almost a subconscious action.

So with a right-column ad, mission number one is to grab the user's attention. Mission two is to get them to click. And mission three is to get them to take the action, whatever that may be.

With a news feed ad, Facebook has done 90 percent of the work for you by putting your ad in the news feed. Your number-one mission is to get the user to click on your image, link, video, offer, or whatever you are promoting with your post. And number 2 is to get them to take action on the next step or on the next page.

Please don't misunderstand me. I am not saying that it's not important to stand out with a news feed ad. I'm saying that you need to try and think holistically and intelligently about every campaign you are creating. Your news feed ads are content ads, not just display ads. You are generating a lot of brand awareness and reputation with your news feed ads, even when people don't click.

The average clickthrough rate for a right-column ad is around .04 percent. If you are getting into the .10 percent range with a right-column ad, you're probably doing a great job with your ad copy and image, depending on the situation, of course. The average CTR of a news feed ad is about 2 percent. This means that your news feed ads have about a 50 times higher likelihood of getting clicked on than your right-column ads!

Now that you understand the big picture, it's time to focus on creating images that give you high clickthrough rates without a bunch of wasted clicks.

NEWS FEED 20 PERCENT TEXT RULE

Whenever you have any type of Facebook ad in the news feed you are not able to have more than 20 percent text overlaying the image. When news feed ads first came out, they didn't have this rule, and we direct-response folks were in "hog heaven," making huge text-only images that made it impossible for the user to miss the main headline or call to action.

Facebook has created an online tool where you can upload your image to find out if it will pass their 20 percent text rule. You can access that here: https://www.facebook.com/ads/tools/text_overlay.

NEWS FEED IMAGE TIPS

In most situations the best type of news feed ad to run is a page post link ad, where the image is a clickable redirect. When you click the image it takes you directly to your landing page instead of popping open as light box window like an image post does. The image dimensions are changing all the time and change for every device they are displayed on, so please visit www.PerryMarshall.com/fbtools to get the updated dimensions. However, the main thing to understand is that a link ad image is going to be a landscape style image. (Currently the image ration is 1.91:1 image width to image length.)

In-Action Photos

Photos (or a still frame of a video) where you or your product is in action are great images for news feed ads. They're authentic, they stand out, and they are typically very congruent with your landing page. In-action photos can be of you, of your product, your typical customer, or any type of in-action you can think of. See Figures 8.2 below and 8.3 on page 112.

FIGURE 8.2–In-Action Teaching Image

FIGURE 8.3–In-Action Swimming Photo

Calls to Action in Your Images and Posts

You can get creative with text and/or imaging by adding calls-to-action on your image.

FIGURE 8.4–Call-to-Action Button in the Image

Facebook also gives you a few options of call-to-action buttons you can add to page post link ads. See Figures 8.5 and 8.6 on page 113.

The main idea to take home here is to figure out ways to make your images stand out, look professional, and have strong calls-to-action. A great way to help your images

FIGURE 8.5–Learn More Button

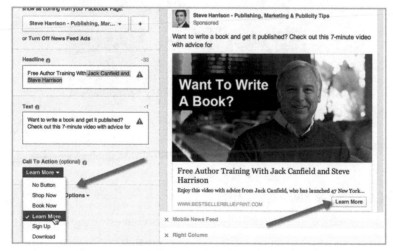

FIGURE 8.6–Call-to-Action Button Feature

stand out is to try to use colors that clash with Facebook's colors. Images with bright backgrounds and dark backgrounds work great, as they really pop out from Facebook's light blue and white.

In Figure 8.7 the brand Como does a great job of creating a professional-looking image, with clashing colors, an image of the actual product, and a great use of text on the image. "Create Your Own App" is clear, compelling, and congruent to their landing page.

FIGURE 8.7–Como Page Post Image Ad

RIGHT-COLUMN IMAGE TIPS

As I explained earlier, with the right-column ads, you have one more hurdle to overcome: You have to stand out from the crowd! Some great ways to stand out are by using borders, clashing backgrounds, strange images, emotional connecting images, and faces.

In Figure 8.8 you will see two ads that really stand out. Since the images are black and white it is difficult to illustrate the contrast, but the ZoSocial ad has a bright green border around it, making it pop. And the Como ad, just below that, has the entire backround of the image as a solid bright green color, with black text overlaid on top. These two ads stand out way more than the other two ads in the screenshot. The other thing Como did a good job with was how they changed the shape of their image. It is not a normal rectangle like every other image. They rounded the corners, which makes it stand out.

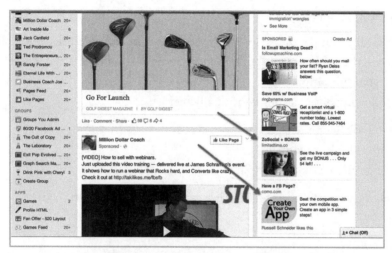

FIGURE 8.8–Right-Column Ads Standing Out

FIGURE 8.9–Orange Right-Column Ad

Orange is another good color for standing out in the sidebar. Take a look at Figure 8.9, and think about which image stands out most. The orange one, of course.

MORE FACTORS THAT CAN HELP YOUR CTRS AND CLICK COSTS

Below you will find more factors that can make a difference in your performance that you can think about when looking for images and photos for your ads.

Use Pictures of People

Facebook is all about people, so look for images that include pictures of people. Pictures of people are the backbone and lifeblood of Facebook, and they make great images to include in your ad campaigns.

The following observations continually test true:

- Men look at women.
- Women look at women.
- Women also look at children.

No matter who you are targeting, it is hard to go wrong with pictures of women.

Selling to Moms?

Test pictures of kids. Cute kids, dirty kids, happy kids, and what else? We hope you said "crying or screaming kids." Pictures of crying and screaming kids evoke a strong emotional reaction that interrupts. The crying child in Figure 8.10 was a very successful image for me (Tom) that I still use today.

If you are looking at lots of pictures of kids, the crying kids are just like green eggs and ham—you spot them a mile away. Every mom immediately relates to a crying kid: "Yes, please, help me get this kid to stop crying!"

Boy Crying

An image does not have to be pleasant to interrupt. This image triggers an internal response that captures attention.

FIGURE 8.10–Images You Do Not Like May Be Great Triggers

Where Are They Looking?

If you walk into a crowded room and look around at all the people, who do you think you are more likely to notice?

- A person looking at her friend
- A person looking directly at you

Of course, you'll notice the person looking directly at you. It is a primal response. Deep inside of your head your brain sees a person looking directly at you as a possible threat or love interest—both get your attention.

All things being equal, images of people are more effective at interrupting when they are looking directly at you, as in the image in Figure 8.11.

I'm Looking Right At You

You know you want to click on me, don't you? I'm looking right at you and smiling. Click now.

FIGURE 8.11–People Looking at You Catch Your Attention

Figure 8.12 illustrates another automatic response we have, which is to look where other people are looking. On a landing page, have the image of a person looking directly at the action you desire. If you want them to press a button or fill out a form, post a picture of a person looking at the button or the form.

Looking Down Left

It is hard not to look where she is looking. Make sure you want people to actually look there.

FIGURE 8.12–Have People Look at Action Items on Your
Landing Page or in Your Ad

Pictures of Things

If about half of the ads in Facebook use pictures of people, the other half include pictures of things. If you have a picture of a thing, make it a good picture. If you are selling a digital camera and you include a poor quality picture of a digital camera, well, you get what you deserve.

Selling mortgages? Test a picture of a house. Selling cameras? Test a picture of the camera.

Selling car insurance? Test a picture of a wrecked car. For male targets, use a picture of hot sports cars. For female targets, try pictures of a child safely buckled into a child car seat.

Selling pizza? Test a picture of a mouth-watering piece of pizza. For male customers, test a picture that combines pizza and football. For females, test pictures of children eating pizza. Does this sound too sexist? Then test the same picture for males and females and let the demographic reports sort them out for you. We bet, however, they sort the same way. But don't guess—test and see for yourself. Don't be afraid to harness stereotypes to your advantage. Many times, "stereotype" is just a not-so-sexy term for psychographics.

Selling jewelry? Sell romance. Text that complements a close-up picture of a heart-shaped pendant draped over two lovely breasts.

Selling cat products? Test a picture of a cat. Or, better yet, test a picture of a kitten, too.

We can think of 1,000,000 more ideas for images. TEST. Test lots and lots of different images. The main thing to test: **A picture of what you are selling!**

This seems perhaps a bit too easy, but the reason it works is simple. If you are advertising tires for a local tire store, post a picture of a tire. In your community, somebody needs to buy tires for his or her car, right?

When this person sees the tire ad, he or she is actually interrupted by the image of a tire. Why? Because he or she is already spending some mental energy thinking about the need to buy tires soon. The tire image triggers these individuals. Now, do you have something interesting to say to this potential customer?

Pictures with Words

Facebook lets you include text in the image, and it adds a new dimension to your ad. If you include a word or two in your picture, it is essential to include text that is readable in the very tiny image size available. Many images we have seen with text are truly awful, with text that is unreadable.

Done properly, text in the image box will be much more visually powerful than the headline—meaning it will be read first.

These images are really, really small, so pay attention to the text in the image and to the contrast between text color and background color. Contrast needs to be high, like that in Figure 8.13, for the text to be readable.

FIGURE 8.13–The Words Embedded in This Image Will Be More Powerful Than the Headline

Pictures of Words

A powerful technique you should test is simply making the entire image a word that is a trigger word for your target audience. What are some examples of making your entire image a word?

A language tool has as its image the words, "LEARN FRENCH," as shown in Figure 8.14. A movie theater has as its image the word, "CINEMA."

A local cupcake shop has as its image the words, "HEY Cupcake!"

Of course, these words can be really simple or very fancy. They can be all one color or every letter can be a different color from the rainbow. Images that include text may be endlessly creative with different fonts, styles, shapes, and colors. And they may be framed in different colors, too, if you simply change the background color around the text in an image.

FIGURE 8.14–Everyone Will Read These Words

How many times have you driven by a highway billboard that interested you—but it was so crammed with text you couldn't read it? Facebook images are micro-billboards. So please, if you use text in your images, take a long, hard look at the image text and ask yourself, "Is this easily readable?"

If it not easily readable, then go back to the drawing board and start again. If a word image works well for your business, continually changing its color, background, and framing helps prevent ad fatigue.

FIGURE 8.15–Using Text as Your Image

Strange or Silly Images

The goal is attention. So don't be afraid to try strange or silly images like the one in Figure 8.16. Be the shiny new object—the most interesting thing on the page. Ads that fall into this category tend to fatigue more slowly.

FIGURE 8.16–Silly Image That Somehow Interrupts

The boy's eyes looking up and the slight smirk on his face tell an interesting story all on their own.

Groupon ran an ad with an image of a little piglet in red rain boots standing in the mud. You cannot help but want to click on the little pig. It is adorable. Unfortunately the landing page after you clicked on the little pig was the same boring, old Groupon sign-up offer—what a waste.

If the landing page had been a Facebook page full of more adorable baby pig pictures or videos, Groupon might have been able to get that page to go viral and still include their discount offer on the page. Groupon, are you reading this? We want more baby pigs!

Connecting Images to Text

Finding new images can be fun. Thinking up new copy for your ad can be difficult. Use new images you discover to inspire new text—new headlines and body text. Use new images to start a new story. Make the story good enough, and you get the click.

A mother told me (Tom) a story about her daughter so enjoying using HomeSchool Advantage that she asked for an alarm clock to wake her up in the morning. When I saw the image in Figure 8.17, it reminded me of the testimonial, and I decided to share the story in an ad. The ad performed very well.

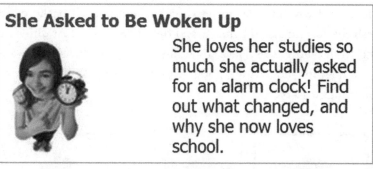

She Asked to Be Woken Up

She loves her studies so much she actually asked for an alarm clock! Find out what changed, and why she now loves school.

FIGURE 8.17–Use a New Image to Inspire a New Story

ONCE YOU FIND SOME GOOD IMAGES, FIND SOME MORE

No matter how good your images are, your ads will fatigue with time. And your ad will fatigue even though there are still many new customers on Facebook who will want to purchase from you; they just don't want to click on your tired, old ad with that tired, old image.

Even before you first turn on a new ad, you should be planning for how to keep your ad going with new images after ad fatigue sets in. The first time you create an ad, go looking for at least three different images that can support the ad. Then plan from the very beginning to rotate multiple images through each and every ad—without necessarily even changing the text.

Some of your customers will be interrupted by people crying, some by people covered in finger paint, and some by people smiling; plan to use all three. Other people will not be interrupted by a person at all but will pause for the picture of a delicious cupcake. We want them all, for with the same ad we can rotate in the picture of crying, painting, and smiling people, and cupcakes too.

The good news is that images are so powerful in Facebook that you do not need to struggle to create the perfect headline and body text for the ad anymore. Seriously, in search advertising you are frequently sweating every last hyphen to make an ad work. In Facebook, mediocre ad copy with a funny image may get a ton of reasonably priced clicks—it is great!

It is easy to change the image and get dramatically better CTR in Facebook. It is harder to see a dramatic improvement just by changing the text. This is great news for beginners, because it is a lot easier to find compelling images than to write compelling copy. Simply learn to take careful note of images that catch your attention and use those images.

IMAGE EXTREME MAKEOVERS

You can add a border to an older image or change an image's background color as a way to refresh the ad, enhance the image, and fight ad fatigue. Test different colors and styles, as shown in Figure 8.18. Have something that is boldly colored—a bright color such as yellow, hot pink, hot orange, hot green—something like that. That's a shiny new object. Liven things up a bit.

FIGURE 8.18–Try Different Colors and Textures around Your Images

QUICK-DRAW ADS

Two gunslingers slowly enter into the dusty street of a frontier town, faces grim. It is a faceoff. They are about to shoot it out and settle their scores like men.

The shopkeepers, seeing men with cool determination in their eyes and guns on their hips, dive for cover. Mothers hustle children to safety.

A challenge of nerves, speed, and skills is about to occur. If you can draw fast and shoot true, victory is yours. Speed is essential, but so is accuracy.

Men already practiced in the fine art of quick draw show no fear. Their lives depend on the quality of their practice.

Your life does, too.

Not as dramatically, of course. But your life as a Facebook ad-slinger is totally dependent on your ability to produce and test new ads quickly.

How quickly can you go to your favorite image site, find a new image, duplicate a working existing ad, upload a new image, and launch the new ad?

How quickly can you do the same adjusting to the title and copy, too?

See if you can do this in seven minutes or less. Practice the art of ad-slinging. It will still take some time for Facebook to approve your ad—but that is not the challenge. The challenge is: Can you get in the habit of creating new and exciting ads without making it a long and laborious process?

Your mission, should you choose to accept it, is to survive in the world of advertising by developing the skills to move fast and move true.

Draw!

HELP! MY BEST-PERFORMING IMAGE JUST GOT REJECTED

Facebook requires that your images be relevant to your product or service. Images of beach-bathing beauties in swimsuits are fine if you are selling swimsuits but will likely be rejected by Facebook if you are selling tablet computers. If your ad was rejected but you think your image was relevant, create another ad and submit it again. Different reviewers will have different perspectives on images in ads.

Facebook is trying to be a family-friendly place. Although you are supposed to be at least 13 years old to create an account, it is almost certain that even younger children are present.

Facebook immediately deletes those younger users when it finds them. Facebook seeks to balance freedom of expression with prudent censorship in a single site that crosses all traditional boundaries of cultures and state. It is almost a guarantee that Facebook will hack off everybody everywhere eventually.

Facebook reviewers will make mistakes.

If you think they have made a mistake with your ad, you do not have much recourse. Submit it again and fill out a contact form. If you spend enough money, send an email directly to your Facebook contact. Otherwise, crank out another ad.

Once I (Tom) had my best-performing ad rejected when I changed a target. The reviewer claimed the ad was violating some sort of policy but was unspecific about how. This was an ad that had already been displayed millions of times to other targets.

So I waited a few days, created a new ad from the ground up that was exactly the same, and submitted it again. Accepted. Remember, there are humans in the chain, and different humans will have different opinions about what is acceptable.

By the way, my rejected ad was totally relevant and contained absolutely nothing remotely objectionable. Not even close. You could display the ad in church on Easter Sunday and nobody would take offense. Go figure.

FINDING IMAGES

You can find free images online in places like Wikimedia Commons (http://commons. wikimedia.org). Never use an image you find on the internet unless you know its license allows you to use it in an ad. The license terms for images in Wikimedia Commons are included with the images.

Flickr.com is also a great place to find free royalty-free images. However, you need to make sure you read the copyright rules closely, as many of the images are copyrighted. You want to use the images with "Creative Commons" licensing.

Such excellent, low-cost commercial images are available that it is easy to use an image with a clear knowledge of its license. Unless you purchased images 20 years ago for commercial use, you have no idea how amazingly reasonable and simple this is. It is the best money you will ever invest in your ad. Some places to look for images:

- *Big Stock Photo* (http://www.bigstockphoto.com) offers high-quality, commercial images for decent pricing. They also have a membership where you can download a certain number of images every day for one monthly price.
- *Fotolia* (http://us.fotolia.com/) offers high-quality, commercial images for low prices, often for $1 to $4. The site's smallest images are frequently sized 400 x 300, scaled at 72 dpi, and can sometimes be loaded directly into Facebook without additional cropping.
- *iStockPhoto* (http://www.istockphoto.com/) carries excellent photos, although they can be a bit pricey.

In all cases, when using images you did not create, remember to confirm that the copyright holder will allow for the commercial use of the image on a site like Facebook.

SOFTWARE TO EDIT IMAGES

If you are going to advertise on Facebook, you need to get some software that will let you do basic editing of images. Here are some great options:

- Pixlr (www.pixlr.com): A free online "Photoshop for dummies." Pixlr is great because it's way easier to use than Photoshop and there are great tutorial videos. It also integrates with Google Drive.

- Canva (www.canva.com): An amazing online tool that makes it easy to add text layers, edit images, find royalty-free images, etc. Go check out Canva and start using it.
- PicMonkey (www.picmonkey.com): A free online tool for adding text to images, editing images, etc.

SORRY, ANIMATORS!

Facebook does not allow for animated or flash images in its standard ads. Seriously, think how obnoxious the site would become if they gave us a tool that powerful to visually interrupt its users. Even I might stop using it if they did that.

> **Go to www.perrymarshall.com/fbtools for the latest updates & to get valuable resources for more clicks from Facebook for less money.**

Chapter 9

Superior Bidding Strategies in Facebook

USING CHECKERS TO WIN AT CHESS

When my friend and colleague John Paul Mendocha was 17, he dropped out of high school, hitchhiked to Las Vegas, and spent four years as a professional gambler.

One afternoon, John faced off with the third-best chess champion in the state of California in an informal match. John's chess skills were *not* special by any means. In poker he was a ninja, but in chess he was an ordinary guy.

But John's poker experience had taught him a thing or two about how to play games.

John won the match.

His pal was stunned. "How did you do that? How did you beat me? I'm the number-three chess player in the freaking state, for crying out loud! What was your strategy?"

John refused to say.

For weeks his friend hounded him. Finally, he cornered him. "John, you HAVE to tell me what you did. Please. We're friends. I want to know."

"OK, dude. For a bottle of Jack and a carton of Marlboros, you're on."

> "*V*ictory is a fleeting thing in the gambling business. Today's winners are tomorrow's blinking toads, dumb beasts with no hope."
>
> —HUNTER S. THOMPSON

"Deal."

John replied, "You played chess. I played checkers."

"Huh?"

"You've got all these deep strategies for how to protect your queen, how to maneuver your rooks, when to move your pawns. You've been honing your craft for years. I don't know all that, so I treated every piece the same and I lurched my guys forward. Just the way you do in checkers.

"You had no grid for what was going on, so I did stuff you would never anticipate. The fact that you're a seasoned pro was actually a *dis*advantage, because I was playing by a different set of rules. Even though I was obeying the official rules of chess. I used a checkers strategy. It wasn't guaranteed to work, but on that day it did."

"Wanna play again?"

"No."

John continues: "Time to pay up. I sure could use a smoke right now. Your turn to run down to the 7–11 and pick up my Jack and cigarettes."

Bidding strategies on Facebook are a lot like that. Sometimes you win by superior strategy. And sometimes it works simply because you're running on a different set of rules than everybody you're competing with. That's why it pays to understand all the different bidding strategies.

HOW MUCH SHOULD YOU PAY PER CLICK? WRONG QUESTION.

The right question is: What should you pay *for* in the first place? And what should you be optimizing for?

You have all your ad creatives uploaded. You have all your precise interests and custom audiences loaded up and ready to go. You even have your demographics for your ideal audience nailed down. All the preparation and all the planning and all the strategizing are finally coming together, and you're ready to pull the trigger on your first Facebook ad.

The last step is to simply figure out how much you want to pay in order to get your awesome new ad showing in your ideal customer's news feed.

So you click over to the Optimization & Pricing tab in the Power Editor, and suddenly everything comes to a screeching halt. Unbeknownst to you, you're suddenly faced with a myriad of bidding and pricing options that you've never even heard of before. (See Figure 9.1 on page 129.)

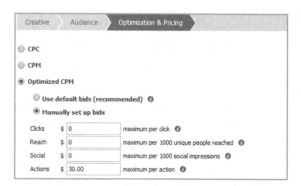

FIGURE 9.1–Bidding in the Power Editor

CPC VS. CPM BIDDING

Bidding on Facebook used to be easy.

It was simple—all you needed to do was to figure out whether you wanted to bid per click or per impression.

The "Pay for Click" (CPC) bidding option is very straightforward. You simply pay if and only if someone clicks on your ad. This is also referred to as pay per click (PPC), which was first popularized by Google AdWords.

The other type of bidding is "Pay for Impressions" (CPM). If you did CPM, you pay a preset or variable amount of money for every 1,000 times your ad is displayed. With CPM, you pay regardless of whether or not anyone clicks on your ad.

Most direct-response marketers and internet marketers feel that CPC is somewhat safe, whereas CPM is more risky. After all, why would you pay and have no idea whether or not someone will click on your ad?

CPC seems like the safe choice, right?

If you are doing media buys or banner ads through any of the online advertising networks, CPM is typically the only bidding type these networks offer. So in those cases, you don't have much of a choice. You set up your ads and your targeting, and hope that your creatives garner enough clicks so that you get a return on your advertising investment.

CPC certainly does cut your risk, but if done correctly, CPM can actually lower your risk even further and get cheaper clicks than CPC. In most cases, we use CPC bidding, especially when we are first testing ads. The beauty is that in Facebook, every type of ad can bid either way. Some types of ads are better suited for certain types of bidding.

BIDDING STRATEGIES FOR FACEBOOK

With over seven different types of bidding options in the Power Editor and a dozen or so in the Ad Manager (depending on your ad objective), what kind of bidding should you do for your ad?

The answer is, as always with Facebook, *it depends on your objective*.

Facebook's objective is to move your money to their bank account. There's nothing wrong with that; they have every right to make money from advertisers. They've created an amazing platform to allow advertisers to place their message in front of their ideal audience, and it's their right to maximize profits.

It's also your right to maximize your return on advertising spend, and minimize *their* profits while maximizing *your* profits. But with all the confusing options on bidding, it makes it very challenging for any advertiser to reach that objective.

When Facebook first rolled out its advertising platform, there were two choices for bidding: CPC or CPM.

CPM and CPC bidding are still distinct within Facebook as separate bidding options, but in many types of bidding, they are now intertwined, which poses a vexing problem for many advertisers.

This gets most people very confused when they see the "Optimization & Pricing" tab in the Power Editor. And it's even *more* confusing—and vague—when using the Ad Manager.

MATCH YOUR FACEBOOK BIDDING TO YOUR AD OBJECTIVE

As when using the Power Editor or the Ad Manager, one of the biggest decisions you'll need to make—and oftentimes before you even start choosing your audience or your creative—is you need to determine what *ad objective* you want to use.

As mentioned previously, in the Ad Manager there are many choices (see Figure 9.2):

FIGURE 9.2–Ad Objective Options

As shown in Figure 9.3, there are plenty to choose from in Power Editor:

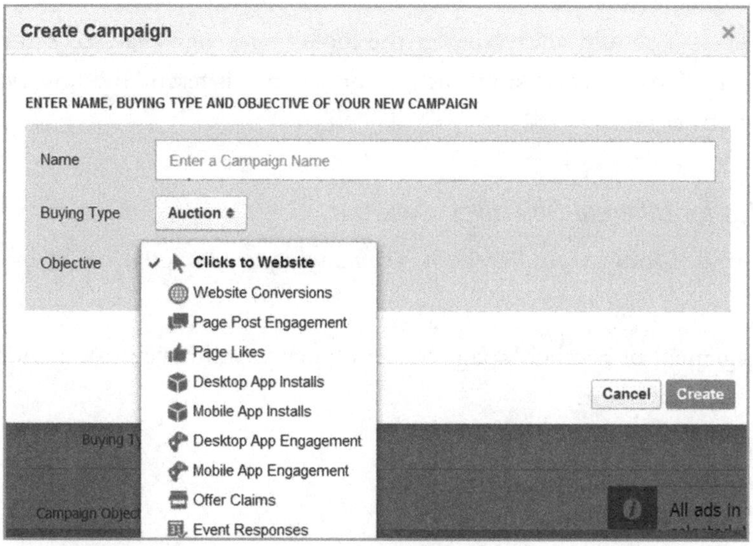

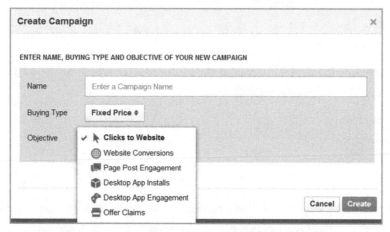

FIGURE 9.3–Power Editor Bidding Options—Auction

FIGURE 9.4–Power Editor Bidding Options—Fixed

Each ad type has its own best type of bidding. Having said that, however, there are no hard-and-fast rules when it comes to bidding in Facebook, but in our experience there are certain types of bidding that work best for the certain types of ads you are creating (Facebook refers to this as "Objective" instead of "ad type" like we do here).

The ad type selection is completely dependent on the particular goal you are looking to achieve. So before we get into bidding types, we need to review objectives and then match the best type of bidding based upon your objective. When it comes to bidding and

Facebook, when you have a bidding strategy that matches your ad objective, you have a winning formula for success.

However, you should always be on the lookout for new ways to bid and should allocate some of your advertising budget for testing different bidding types for the different ad objectives.

Different Ads for Different Objectives

When you're designing your Facebook ad campaign, your goal could be any of the following:

- Engagement of Facebook page content (page post, image post, or video post)
- Off-site conversion
- Off-site website traffic increases
- Page likes
- Mobile app installs
- Desktop app installs
- Desktop app engagement
- Mobile app engagement
- Facebook offer claims
- Promotion of events

With so many objectives, it's easy to get confused as to which one you should use for your business. For simplicity, we will focus on:

- Engagement
- Conversions
- Traffic increases
- Likes

These things are what most direct-response marketers are most interested in.

If you are a pure-play direct-response marketer, you'll be tempted to set up all of your ads with the goal of website conversions. Although you can do quite well with this single objective, conversions tend to increase when you mix in other types of non-promotional content to warm up your potential audience and potential customers.

One thing is certain though: In nearly 99 percent of cases, you should choose "Auction" instead of "Fixed Price." There are always exceptions, but with the auction bidding type, you maintain far more control.

When you're setting up your Facebook ad campaign for direct response, the typical ratio of ad segmentation should be as follows:

- 10 to 30 percent post engagement and like ads

FIGURE 9.5–Fixed vs. Auction

- 70 to 90 percent promotional ads with the goal of an off-site conversion

With that in mind, each type of Facebook ad has its place within a campaign and each has its own bidding strategy.

Page Post Engagement Bidding

Page post engagement ads are ideal for boosting or "igniting" current posts on a Facebook page to gain greater exposure and build credibility for nonpromotional content. They are used primarily for engaging and interacting with fans, friends of fans (FOFs), and ideal customer audiences with the content posted on a particular Facebook business page.

In choosing this goal, Facebook automatically optimizes the post for engagement (likes, comments, shares, video plays, image clicks, etc.) so when you are bidding on these types of ads, use Facebook to gain maximum exposure for your advertising.

Page post engagement ads are not typically used for conversions or to take action on an outside URL but are primarily used to promote content to:

- Custom audiences (CAs)—email lists and/or contacts
- Fans
- Friends of fans
- Similar audiences
- Precise interest

These types of ad are very effective at increasing likes, and in most cases are better ad objectives than "Page Likes" for general promotion of content to an audience. With page post engagement ads, the likes come naturally based on the quality of the content.

When it comes to page post engagement ads, news feed desktop and/or mobile are ideal locations.

Recommended bidding: Fully Optimized CPM. Facebook is extremely adept at optimizing these types of ads, which are used to gain "engagement" with your followers, fans, or other audiences.

Remember, the objective in these types of ads is not necessarily a conversion or a click to your website (although it can be as a side benefit). The primary objective here in a page post engagement ad is to *engage*.

In Facebook terms, "engagement" can include clicking the image, playing the video, igniting the post, sharing the post, clicking the link in the post to your website—any number of actions that increase engagement with your audience.

So let Facebook optimize this for you. This type of bidding looks like this in the Ad Manager:

FIGURE 9.6–Page Post Engagement Bidding

And like this in the Power Editor:

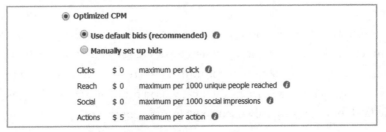

FIGURE 9.7–Page Post Engagement Bidding—Power Editor

Clicks to Website Bidding

Clicks to Website bidding is typically used for the most powerful of all direct response ads on Facebook: the Page Post or Link Post ad. When the post is clicked, it immediately takes a visitor to an off-site website or landing page to take some sort of action.

When choosing this type of ad, Facebook automatically optimizes the ad for the highest number of clicks from the ad to the target URL, and they are typically used for content that has some kind of off-site conversion goal.

With Clicks to Website ads, desktop and/or mobile are ideal locations for these types of ads, although these can be used in the sidebar as well.

With Clicks to Website ads, it's vital that you have a fairly solid sales funnel, as you will be sending lots of visitors to your off-site URL. This type of ad is typically used when there is a positive history of conversions on a particular page or website.

Clicks to Website ads may not be recommended for advertisers who are just starting out and have never tested their landing pages or website conversions. Having said that, Clicks to Website ads give you the opportunity to get some of the lowest CPCs available in Facebook.

Recommended bidding: Either Optimized CPM (OCPMC) bid for clicks or straight CPC.

This type of bidding looks like this in the Ad Manager:

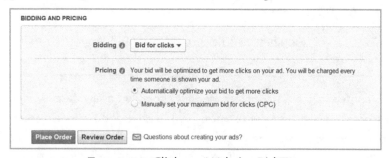

FIGURE 9.8–Clicks to Website Bid Type

However, in most cases with this type of bidding, Facebook will automatically optimize your ad the way *they* want your ads optimized. The only way you can find this out is to log in to your Power Editor to see.

When you choose this type of bidding in the Ad Manager, you may be shocked see this in the Power Editor:

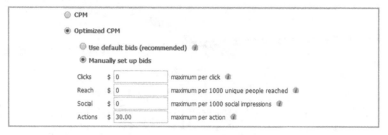

FIGURE 9.9–Clicks to Website Bidding—Power Editor

Unless you have an extremely high-end product or service, you probably don't want to optimize your bidding at $30 for a website action!

This is the default setting in Facebook for this type of bidding. This is why we highly recommend primarily using the Power Editor for all your ad creation. However, if you choose to continue using just the Ad Manager, you can set your bidding this way to set your bids correctly:

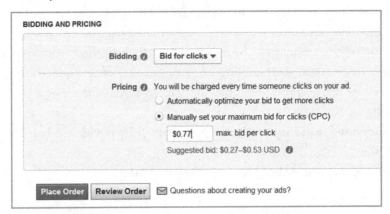

FIGURE 9.10–Clicks to Website Bidding

If you're married to the Ad Manager, consider going on a few dates with the Power Editor, especially when it comes to setting your bidding. You can also create all your ads in the Ad Manager and then optimize them in the Power Editor. Regardless, it's highly recommended that you set all your ad bidding inside the Power Editor.

When you choose to use Clicks to Website ads in Power Editor, OCPMC will look like this:

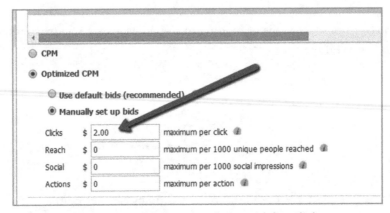

FIGURE 9.11–Clicks to Website Bid for Clicks

When you're using this type of bidding, there is no confusion in Power Editor, whereas in the Ad Manager, you never really know what Facebook will do. And as an advertiser, you want to control your own destiny—do not let Facebook control it for you.

Website Conversion Bidding

Website Conversion ads are some of the most popular ads on Facebook, especially for direct-response marketers. The goal for these ads is clear: conversions. That conversion could be a purchase, a registration, or a simple email opt-in. No wonder they are the most popular type of ads in Facebook for generating leads and sales.

These ads are used for promoting off-site actions and work best when you are promoting Link Post ads—either ones directly on your Facebook page or unpublished Link Post ads done through the Power Editor.

One of the greatest features of the Power Editor is that you can set up multiple conversions by setting up multiple conversion pixels. Website Conversion ads are very effective at measuring a series of conversion steps as a prospect travels down your sales funnel.

Website Conversion ads are used interchangeably with the Clicks to Website ads to create an off-Facebook conversion. We use them greater than 50 percent of the time when using promoted posts for lead generation.

These types of ad should be tested against Clicks to Website ads to see which converts at the lowest possible cost per lead and are best used in the news feed desktop and/or mobile and occasionally in the sidebar. As always, if sidebar ads are used, these ads should be separated out in a separate ad set or a separate campaign to keep your conversion data clean.

Recommended bidding: Either straight CPC or Optimized CPM—bid for clicks (OCPMC)—and if you're adventurous in Power Editor, Optimized CPM, or bid for conversions (OCPMCVR).

The vast majority of the time you use Website Conversion ads, you should bid straight CPC. In some cases where you're not getting as many conversions as you need, split test OCPMC in a separate ad set as outlined in Chapter 16.

When setting up this kind of bidding in the Ad Manager, it will look like Figure 9.12 on page 138.

As with Clicks to Website above, Facebook will automatically optimize your ad the way *they* want your ads optimized. You'll have to log in to your Power Editor to fix this.

When you choose this type of bidding in the Ad Manager, as mentioned above, you'll see the same shocking revelation as you did in your Clicks to Website ads:

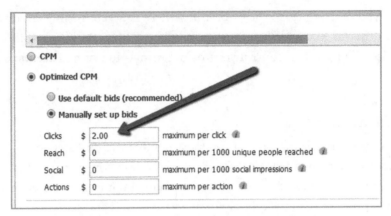

FIGURE 9.12–Bid for Website Conversions

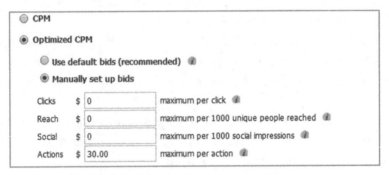

FIGURE 9.13–Facebook Automatic Bidding

Once again, this is why we recommend primarily using the Power Editor for all your ad creation.

The correct way to set this up in the Ad Manager is like this:

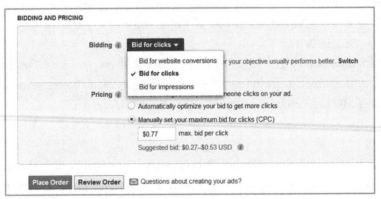

FIGURE 9.14–Bid for Website Clicks

And in the Power Editor like this for CPC:

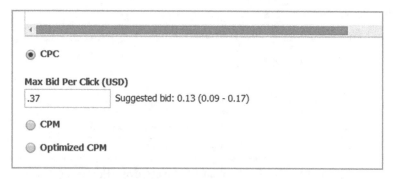

FIGURE 9.15–Cost per Click Bidding—Power Editor

And like this for OCPMC:

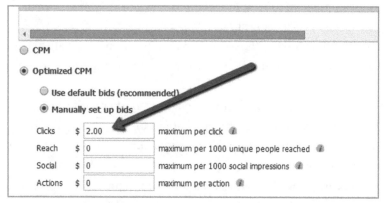

FIGURE 9.16–Optimized CPM Bid for Clicks (OCPMC)—Power Editor

Although optimized CPM for conversions is relatively experimental as of this writing, it's worth a test. If you have a singular conversion pixel firing at a very specific dollar amount for your conversion goal, it's worth a try. We've tried it on many occasions for conversions that have a high relative value, and it has yielded inconsistent but promising results.

However, as Facebook becomes more and more sophisticated, it's a worthwhile bidding strategy to employ when you're using Website Conversion ads. This bidding will look like Figure 9.17 on page 140 in Power Editor:

Page Like Bidding

Page likes, although we may see less of these ads in the future, continue to be a very popular form of advertising on Facebook. As their sole purpose is used to increase page or page post likes, many businesses want to implement these ads to gain more fans for their page.

⊙ Use default bids (recommended) ⓘ
⦿ Manually set up bids

Clicks	$	0	maximum per click ⓘ
Reach	$	0	maximum per 1000 unique people reached ⓘ
Social	$	0	maximum per 1000 social impressions ⓘ
Actions	$	5.00	maximum per action ⓘ

FIGURE 9.17–Bid for Website Conversions—Power Editor

But in most cases, they don't know *why* they want more fans for their page.

Truth be told, most businesses want more likes just to *get* more likes, as if Facebook is some kind of popularity contest and the most fans win a prize of some sort. They're playing checkers when they really should be playing chess.

If your goal is to gain more fans, you should always ask yourself this question: Why do I actually want more fans, and how is this going to help me sell more of my product or service?

If the answer is that you don't know, then don't bother with these types of ads.

However, if you have a strategy to gain more fans from your ideal target customer audience so that you can then ultimately market your product or service to them, then Page Like ads are worthwhile doing.

Page Like ads are typically used as an adjunct to main content promotion through the ad types mentioned above. They should not be used for conversion or for content engagement but only for building a base of fans that can be marketed to at a later date.

This type of ad is typically used as a sidebar-only ad and because of this is not recommended for marketing to mobile devices. Audience size for Page Like ads as a general rule should be very large—one million or more.

Recommended bidding: Optimized CPM.

This type of bidding looks like this in the Ad Manager:

BIDDING AND PRICING

Bidding ⓘ   Bid for Page likes ▾

Pricing ⓘ   Your bid will be optimized to get more Page likes. You will be charged every time someone is shown your ad.

Place Order   Review Order   ✉ Questions about creating your ads?

FIGURE 9.18–Page Like Bidding—Ad Manager

This type of ad is probably the only one that is best set up through the Ad Manager, but it can be set up through Power Editor as well. It should look like this:

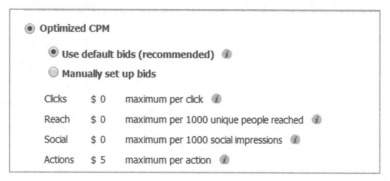

FIGURE 9.19–Page Like Bidding—Power Editor

COUNTERINTUITIVE FACEBOOK CPC BIDDING STRATEGIES

In nearly every type of ad, you will be faced with the question of *how much you should bid*. If you think about it this way, you are bidding on the ad space when you bid on Facebook ads. As an auction market advertising platform, you're bidding against anywhere between a handful to hundreds of other advertisers for that very same space.

In every type of CPC bidding, you enter the maximum you're willing to pay for the click in the field labeled "Max Bid." As for the unseen advertising competition you are competing against, you have no idea what they are bidding. Don't be deceived here—the "bid" word does not necessarily mean that's what you will pay *nor will it always be the maximum amount that you bid!*

In many cases, we've set our maximum bid at a certain level, and our costs per click exceed that maximum bid, although this is rare.

Initially though, the higher your bid, the more likely your ad will be displayed. After several thousand impressions, Facebook will start to weigh other factors that affect the cost of your ad—whether you are bidding straight CPC or OCPMC.

Although Facebook has never revealed their behind-the-scenes formula for how they determine CPC, we do know that the largest single factor that affects your CPC is clickthrough rate (CTR). In essence, the higher your CTR, the lower your CPC.

It's a simple formula that if your audience likes your ad (*and this kind of "like" is not to be confused with "like" in Facebook nomenclature*), the lower your CPC. This is why it's so important to have targeting that perfectly matches your ad creative. The more your audience clicks on your ad, the lower your overall cost will be.

The good news is that once you have some impressions and a track record with Facebook, they begin to lower the price you need to pay per click automatically. In this case, you almost never pay for what you bid; in fact, *you pay less!*

Yes, they will actually charge you *less* than you bid, and they do this quite frequently the longer your ad runs.

You can see this CTR data in your Ad Manager, Power Editor, or in Reports.

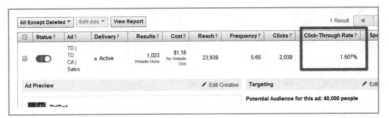

FIGURE 9.20–Ad Reports

CPC Strategies for Maximum Impressions

There are dozens of ways to optimize your CPC bidding in Facebook, but one strategy we use more than any other is:

■ Bid high
■ Fail fast
■ Optimize faster

When you are using CPC or OCPMC bidding, you'll often times be confronted with a situation like this:

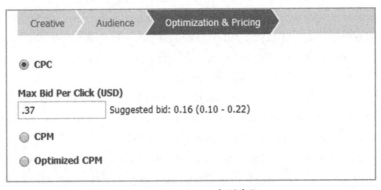

FIGURE 9.21–Suggested Bid Ranges

What should you do? Should you bid lower, bid right in the middle, or bid above? Here are the three likely scenarios:

1. *Bid lower.* You will not get any impressions and will never find out how effective your ad is.
2. *Bid middle.* You'll get some impressions, and you will find out over time how effective your ad is.

3. *Bid higher.* You'll find out immediately if your ad is amazing or if it needs serious work. You may pay more—but as long as you keep an eye on it as soon as it's launched, you can minimize your losses.

If you want to get fast results, we recommend strategy number three. If you can't possibly take a look at your ads at least once per day, you may consider strategy number two. Our typical bid strategy is to bid 50 percent or more over the highest end of the range. So, in this case with this CPC bid, we bid $.37 which is roughly 50 percent above the top end of the range.

If your CTR is on the high end of what Facebook considers a "good CTR" (in the range of 2 percent plus, with 3 to 10 percent being extremely good CTR), your CPC won't be anywhere near your max bid. In fact, it will be much lower.

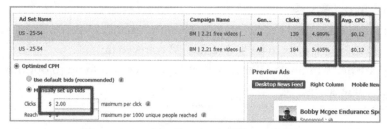

FIGURE 9.22–Monitoring CTRs and CPCs

But in the case of Figure 9.22, you can see that there is a very high CTR at 4 to 5 percent, which led to extremely low CPCs even though our bids were not optimized whatsoever. In cases like this, which are somewhat rare, cost per click gets down to a ridiculously low level because the ad and targeting is so focused. The goal of every ad is to get to this CPC level—although many of them never will—*but it's something to shoot for!*

How to Optimize Your CPC Bids for Winning Ads

Your ads are live and you're getting lots of impressions and you're getting some conversions—so far so good. Now it's time to start optimizing.

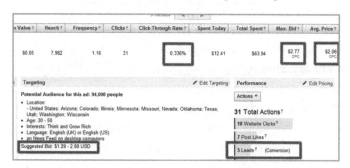

FIGURE 9.23–Reviewing Progress

In Figure 9.24, we have an ad that falls into this scenario:

- It's getting conversions (22 leads).
- It has a high CTR (2.332 percent).
- The current bid is relatively high at $1.27.
- The average CPC is $.40.
- The suggested bid range is $.28 to $.60.

So in this case, what do you do to optimize?

You're obviously getting a good number of leads, your ad is producing with a high CTR, and your average CPC based on your initial test is far lower than your max bid.

The next step is to slowly creep down your bidding from the higher level to just above your average CPC. This way, you don't lose impressions but you slowly lower your average CPC in the process.

This audience is 84,000 people, and has roughly reached 25 percent of that audience (19,869), so you have a ways to go before this ad starts to fatigue.

In the case of a winning ad like this, here is what we would do to optimize the bids: The rationale is this:

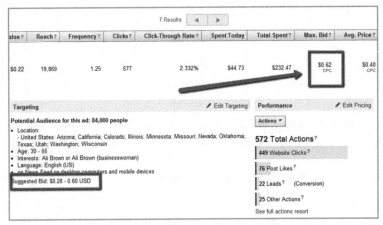

FIGURE 9.24–Optimizing Your Bidding

- Since this is a winning ad, I don't want to lose impressions, so I bid just above the top end of the suggested bid range of $.60. My bid is $.62.
- Because I'm not bidding below my current CPC, I will not lose impressions but instead my average CPC will likely go down because my max bid is the *ceiling* I will pay. Therefore, it squeezes Facebook to lower my overall bid.
- I will continuously keep an eye on this ad and lower my max bid as my average CPC decreases in step with my new max bid.

In the case of a winning ad, this is a winning bidding strategy.

How to Optimize Your CPC Bids for Borderline Ads

Not all of your ads will be home runs like the ones above, and most will be what we call "borderline ads." These are the ads that are converting but at a higher cost per conversion than you want but are not so terrible that you don't want to pause them entirely.

This type of ad requires a completely different strategy of optimization. One such ad is the one shown in Figure 9.25:

Here we have an ad that falls into this scenario:

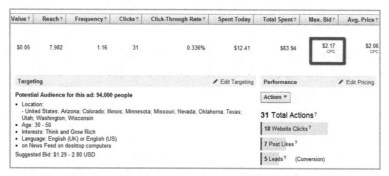

FIGURE 9.25–Optimizing Your Bidding for Borderline Ads

- It's getting a fair number of conversions (5 leads).
- It has a mediocre to poor CTR (0.336 percent).
- The current bid is relatively high at $2.77.
- The average CPC is $2.06.
- The suggested bid range is $1.29–2.80.

So with this ad, how should you optimize?

You're getting a medium number of leads, but because of the extremely low CTR, your average CPC is far higher than our winning ad in the previous section.

This ad is clear evidence that *CTR determines CPC*. This ad is in the same campaign and has the same basic targeting as the winning ad in the previous section, but it's producing very different results.

In this case, you want to *squeeze down* your max bid in order to force Facebook to either show the ad less or you to pay less per click. The best way to optimize is to change your ad, targeting or any other number of factors to increase that CTR is much as possible.

In the case of a mediocre ad like this, Figure 9.26 shows what we would do to optimize the bids:

The truth of the matter is, this ad may not make it. But we want to optimize it because *it is actually producing at a cost per lead that's in line with our goal.*

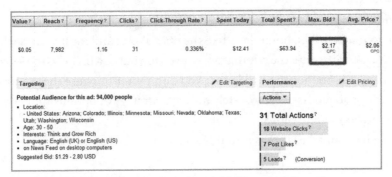

Value?	Reach?	Frequency?	Clicks?	Click-Through Rate?	Spent Today	Total Spent?	Max. Bid?	Avg. Price?
$0.05	7,982	1.16	31	0.336%	$12.41	$63.94	$2.17 CPC	$2.06 CPC

Targeting   ✎ Edit Targeting   **Performance**   ✎ Edit Pricing

Potential Audience for this ad: 94,000 people

- Location:
  - United States: Arizona; Colorado; Illinois; Minnesota; Missouri; Nevada; Oklahoma; Texas; Utah; Washington; Wisconsin
- Age: 30 - 50
- Interests: Think and Grow Rich
- Language: English (UK) or English (US)
- on News Feed on desktop computers

Suggested Bid: $1.29 - 2.80 USD

Actions ▾

31 Total Actions?

18 Website Clicks?

7 Post Likes?

5 Leads?   (Conversion)

FIGURE 9.26–Optimizing Your Bidding—Bidding Down

Having said that, we want to do better. By bidding lower, *but not undercutting our current CPC*, we will squeeze down our cost per click in the short term. The better long-term solution, however, is to improve the targeting and ad creatives to get to a higher CTR and a lower CPC. But for the time being, this will lower our CPC and make our ad more effective.

The many bidding options in Facebook mean you can play checkers, chess, Battleship, or backgammon, depending on what makes the most sense. As you get success with the methods we've recommended, feel free to experiment with variations. Many times you'll reach customers no one else is reaching.

Chapter 10

Who Cares If the Ad Is Cheap? Are You Making Money?

ADS IN CONTEXT

When I (Perry) was brand-new to search marketing, one of my fellow marketing maniacs, Yanik Silver, told about a fascinating case study. The keyword "typing lessons" was getting more than 100,000 searches per month, and the cost per click was under 10 cents. It looked like a golden opportunity: You could get lots of traffic for cheap.

> *"Being good in business is the most fascinating kind of art. Making money is art and working is art and good business is the best art."*
>
> —ANDY WARHOL

But there was a problem: There were so many free, online typing courses, hardly anyone was willing to pay for products. So even though the clicks were cheap, getting a good return on investment for that traffic was tricky.

The principle applies to any kind of advertising, online or off. Just because it's economical doesn't mean it pays.

Your success in Facebook advertising is not measured by your clickthrough rate or cost per click. You must understand how the ad campaigns impact your business's bottom line.

You have to be able to describe clearly each step in your sales process. What you can't describe, you will not measure. What you do not measure, you cannot manage.

A potential customer clicking on an ad is the first step in a chain of events that hopefully ends with money in your pocket. Are your current ads making you money?

To answer this question, start by putting labels on the people in your sales funnel based on where they are in the sales process. This allows you to describe the funnel more effectively and to measure and report on each stage of the sales process. Any labels will do, provided you have a clear definition for them. In this chapter, we use the following labels:

- **A lead:** someone who clicks on a URL you have provided them. The click may be from an ad, organic search, affiliates, purchased email list, silly videos, or any other source. The key to being a lead is a person has specifically clicked on your link. She is now in your hands, and you are guiding her on a journey.
- **A prospect:** a person who opts into at least one offer you make and provides you with additional contact information. A prospect is followed up with additional marketing and sales materials. If the prospect has not yet paid us, then he is counted as a prospect and not as a customer.
- **A customer:** a prospect who has purchased a product from you or otherwise generated revenue.

For your ad campaign to succeed:

- Leads must become prospects.
- Prospects must become customers.

This is hard to learn, but traffic is not necessarily your friend. Having millions of leads that never produce customers is not a win. It is a wasted expense. It can destroy your business.

The goal of your campaign is not to increase traffic; it is to increase sales. And everything prospects do after they click on the ad is part of a choreographed dance from first click to closed deal. All of this must occur at a cost that is reasonable enough so that profit is generated.

There are many parts of the dance, and each part should be tracked. You are seeking to drive the prospect to measurable actions you can use to judge the effectiveness of your marketing decisions, from initial ad to final call to action. Measurable actions include the following:

- Clicks
- Likes
- Visits

- Opt-ins
- Purchases
- Refunds
- Complaints
- Referrals
- Repeat business

If you track and measure only CTR, you are getting only a tiny part of the story!

FACEBOOK CONVERSION TRACKING

The great thing about Facebook's conversion tracking (which is much improved since the first edition of this book) is that you can now track many of these key performance indicators (KPIs) within the Facebook reporting tool.

This gives you the ability to dive deep into which ads, images, landing pages, audiences, placement (news feed or right column), desktop users, mobile users, etc., are giving you the best cost per action.

It is easy to set up Facebook conversion tracking. It's a simple two-step process.

1. Create a new conversion pixel

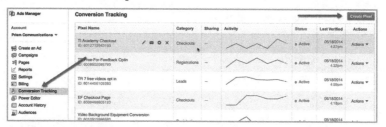

FIGURE 10.1–Creating a Conversion Goal (Pixel)

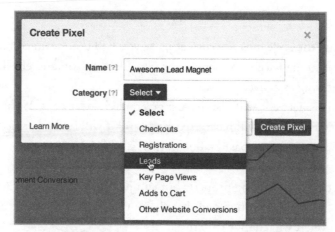

FIGURE 10.2–Naming Your Conversion Pixel

2. Copy the conversion code and paste it onto the "thank-you page" of whichever goal you are trying to accomplish, as shown in Figure 10.3. If you have a landing page where people enter their contact info to get a free report, then the conversion pixel does not go on the landing page. It goes on the very next page the visitor lands on after submitting their information. Or if you are tracking checkouts, then the code goes on the payment confirmation page, not in the shopping cart.

FIGURE 10.3–Copy Conversion Code

After pasting the code into the correct page, you will then want to reload that page once and return to the Facebook Conversion Tracking section and check to see if your pixel is now showing as active.

If the status is active it will also have a green circle next to it. If the pixel was not installed correctly then you will have a red circle and it will be "unverified." And if your pixel has not fired within the past 24 hours, then it will show "inactive" and have a gray circle.

If it is inactive, it is working properly but you just haven't had a visitor to that page within the past 24 hours. If you reload that thank-you page and return to the Facebook conversion section, it will change to active.

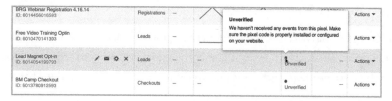

FIGURE 10.4A–Conversion Pixel—Active

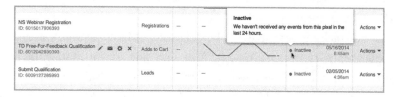

FIGURE 10.4B–Conversion Pixel—Unverified

FIGURE 10.4C–Conversion Pixel—Inactive

TRACKING THE DESTINATION URL

Facebook allows you to select the destination URL for your ad. You can use a special tracking URL as the destination URL. A tracking URL tracks a click to a conversion and helps you later calculate the cost per conversion. The special tracking URL is created by a third party, which records clicks and helps calculate conversion costs. This is very powerful and easy to do and makes calculating conversion rates and costs relatively simple.

All of your ads from all of your various traffic sources should use tracking URLs, in addition to using Facebook conversion tracking. This gives you two sources of tracking, and this is important, as there are always hiccups and some cases where the tracking is off for no apparent reason.

If you use a customer relationship management (CRM) software like Infusionsoft, Ontraport, or Salesforce you may want to create tracking links using your CRM.

Google Analytics provides powerful and free URL-tracking tools you can use to track and tag destination URLs. You can track where a lead comes from and what percentage of those leads reaches a conversion event (opt-in list or sale).

The URL builder in Google Analytics allows you to specify your original destination URL, and it creates a new destination URL to insert into the ad. You can provide tags for:

- Campaign source (referrer: Facebook);
- Campaign medium (marketing medium: banner ad);
- Campaign term (targeting used: U.S. males 18–24);
- Campaign content (describe the ad itself: post, sponsored story); and
- Campaign name (name used in Facebook).

Later, Google Analytics provides reports to track clicks all the way from an original ad to a final conversion event, even if the conversion event occurred days later. You can even enter the cost per lead into Google Analytics, and it will calculate for you the cost per conversion.

There are also some great solutions that make creating tracking links simple, whether you use a CRM or you use Google analytics. One that we use and recommend is Improvely (www.Improvely.com).

Another ad-tracking resource is HyperTracker. Many people are nervous about using Google Analytics because Google also sells ads to you and your competitors. If you are spending a lot of money and don't want the ad salesman to also run your analytics, you may use an independent party tool like HyperTracker to track URLs and conversions. You can watch a video at http://www.video.hypertracker.net, or go to http://www.hypertracker.com.

FACEBOOK REPORTING: METRICS TO MEASURE YOUR SUCCESS

There are several good ways to monitor your most important metrics within the Facebook Advertising interface. Each one has its place in monitoring performance.

1. The Facebook Ad Manager ("Campaigns" on the left–hand column in Ad Manager).
2. The Power Editor (on the left-hand column in Ad Manager; this tool only works in the Google Chrome Browser). Yes, you really can use the Power Editor for reporting purposes, too.
3. Facebook Reports ("Reports" on the left-hand column in Ad Manager).

Also, to measure the engagement on your page, you have Facebook Insights. You can find it when you are on your Facebook page (it's a link at the top-left of the page called "Insights"). This reporting tool has also improved a lot over the past year and is very useful to determine how much engagement each post gets (likes, shares, and comments) and a whole lot more.

A few of reasons you don't want to skip this chapter:

1. Because it will help you waste less and use your advertising budget more effectively.
2. Specifically this will help you choose the right columns in the Facebook Ad Reports.
3. Less is more. Information overload is no fun! I'll show you what to focus on. And I'll give you ideas once you export your data into Excel.

Even if you have been running Facebook ads for a while, you might think you need to create a lot of different ad sets split up by age groups, demographics, and test these different groups against each other. Or you could just cheat and use Facebook Reports to tell you where to dive deep!

With Facebook Reports you can just run fewer ads and initially create more generic targeting segments. Your reports will then show you what is working and what is not.

Based on that info, you can then create more specific ads and targeting for those segments that are promising. These reports can save you a lot of time and money.

If you have seen or used Facebook advertising a couple of years ago you might remember the "old" reports format in Facebook. Well, those old reports were often not so useful. But the new reports are really good, as you will understand after reading this chapter.

Each use depends on what you need to know and how much time you have available. I am using all three options regularly.

For quick daily "overview" metrics I would recommend the Facebook Ad Manager ("Campaigns").

For deeper insights into your stats on a daily basis, you can also use the reporting side of the Power Editor. If you aren't using the Power Editor now, I recommend you just forget about this one for now and go straight to the "Reports" in Facebook's Ad Manager.

If you invest money in advertising on Facebook you have to look at your ad metrics. Who doesn't want to know their ROI? How much did you spend on ads, and how much profit did you get from it?

You will find a lot of useful data; your most important information is hidden in plain sight in the Facebook Reports!

Ad 1: Facebook Ad Manager–"Campaigns" (Quick Daily Monitoring)

For quick daily monitoring, without the Facebook Reports, in the Facebook Ad Manager you just click "Campaigns" in the left column of Figure 10.5 on page 154.

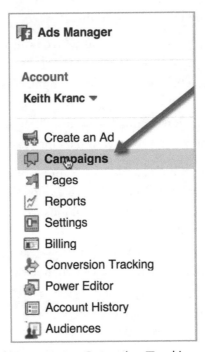

FIGURE 10.5–Campaign Tracking

This lets you focus fast on the big picture. In the Facebook Reports section you can choose more than 40 options to monitor actions. It's important to not get overwhelmed; otherwise, you will not take action based upon the data you are looking at.

I will guide you, so keep reading—it will become very clear which metrics you want to look at.

FIGURE 10.6–Campaign Overview—Cost

FIGURE 10.7–Campaign Overview—Results

You first look at the columns "Results" and "Cost" (see Figure 10.6). If you click on either, it will sort ascending/descending.

"Results" gives you the total number of "actions" during the selected time frame. Each "Action" is based on the "Objective" you chose when you created the campaign. The column next to the "Results" is "Cost"; this will tell you how much each "Action" has cost you. You want this number to be as low as possible, of course.

A 0.00 CPA (Cost per Action) is possible—it does happen in our campaigns. This is seen mostly when used with the campaign objective called "Post Engagement." That means you could have a cost per action of maybe 0.003 which is rounded to 0.00 by Facebook.

On a daily basis you can sort your ads on Spend or Cost Per Action to get an idea of where you stand.

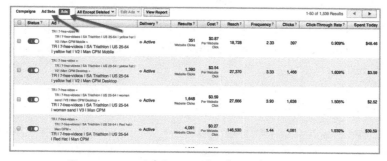

FIGURE 10.8–Ad Sets and Ad Level Reporting

Without leaving the screen you can click on "Ad Sets" or "Ads" and see the picture shown in Figure 10.8.

Here, still without going into the "big" Facebook Reports section, you can check on several other metrics, including one called "Frequency."

Depending on the placement of your ad (desktop news feed, mobile news feed), a too high frequency can lead to ad fatigue. A general rule of thumb is to not let the "big" news feed ads have a frequency of more than 2 or 3, and for the right-hand-side column ads, not let it be more than 30.

However, this depends a lot on your market, and some people have reported frequencies of up to 900 without getting any spam complaints!

You want to avoid annoying people at all costs by showing your ad too often; they could hide the content and give negative feedback to Facebook about your ads. This is something you want to prevent. That´s why you will check your metrics like Frequency regularly.

The preferred "fast action" metrics I like to focus on in this "simple" *screen* report are:

■ "Results"—e.g., post engagements or Page Likes, etc.
■ "Cost"—per action*
■ "Reach"—number of unique visits

- "Spent Today"—total spent today
- "Total Spent"—total spent in the period selected
- "Start Date"—Start date campaign
- "End Date"—End data campaign

*Actions are counted each time someone shares, likes, or comments on your page or post; responds to your event; installs/uses or spends credits in your app; or claims or shares your offer.

An action is attributed to your ad performance when it happens:

- Within 24 hours of someone viewing your ad
- Within 28 days of someone clicking on your ad

Recap: You can use this tool on a daily basis to get a quick indication how your ads are performing.

The Power Editor Reporting

The second way you can look at your metrics is from inside the Power Editor. If you don´t know what this is or don't use the Power Editor, then don't use this solely for reporting purposes.

However, reporting within the Power Editor gives you even more data than the "Campaigns" option we just discussed within the Facebook Ad Manager.

Here you can also customize the columns you want to see for ads, ad sets, or audiences. For each of these three views you can select the fields you want to see as illustrated in Figure 10.9.

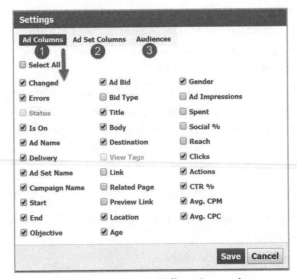

FIGURE 10.9–Power Editor Reporting

The settings for reporting within the Power Editor are pretty good! If you use the Power Editor, then this is something you definitely want to try.

If you already work with the Power Editor you are probably an intermediate or advanced user. Maybe you haven't realized yet you can customize the view (columns) here too. This will enable you to look at some metrics without leaving the Power Editor.

Recap: If you already use the Power Editor, this is a quick way to assess more detailed metrics from your campaigns.

Reports in the Ad Manager

Recommended use: Once a week or more, often depending on your spend. The higher the spend, the more frequently you want to look at this.

This is one of the secret weapons of many successful Facebook ad managers. This is the reporting tool that you will be using regularly to analyze your campaigns in more detail.

FIGURE 10.10–Reports

You can access the Facebook Reports in two ways:

1. In the Ads Manager (https://www.facebook.com/ads/manage), you click on Reports in the left-side navigation bar; or

2. You go straight to: http://facebook.com/ads/manage/reporting.php

Now you click on the button "Edit Columns," and a window will pop up:

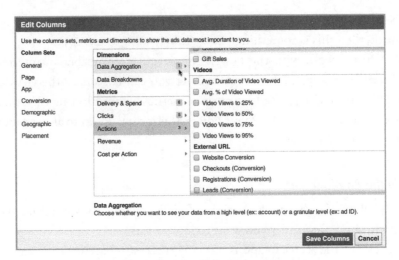

FIGURE 10.11–Edit Columns

At the time I counted there were more than 150 different columns to choose from. Facebook has several predefined sets of columns: General, Page, App, Conversion, Demographic, Geographic, and Placement.

The 150+ columns you can select to be shown in the report are divided over two main categories:

1. Dimensions (Data Aggregation and Data Breakdowns)
2. Metrics (Delivery & Spend, Clicks, Actions, Revenue, Cost per Action)

The "Data Breakdowns" category under "Dimensions" in particular gives a very nice set of "columns," such as: Age, Gender, Age and Gender, Country, Placement, and Destination.

Facebook will break down the performance based on each of the metrics you choose. This is powerful. No doubt. You will find out which age groups, genders, and the like are responding best to your advertising efforts. This allows you to determine very quickly how a single ad performed by country, placement (mobile, desktop, etc.), or age group without having to split test with several ads. And it gives you the performance of your ads based on total action metrics (conversions, for example) and cost per action metrics.

Facebook has a good help section on their own site about "Ads Reporting." You can visit that page here: https://www.facebook.com/help/510910008975690.

Now, before you visit that Facebook help page, I recommend you finish reading this chapter, because I provide you with data you can put into action that you will not find there.

Just having access to over 150 columns of info doesn't automatically help you. We live in the Golden Age of Information Overload. You need to know what to focus on. 80/20. I will give several solutions for this.

The general consensus on measuring advertising success (on Facebook) is to focus on things like number of clicks, the CTR, reach (number of unique users who saw your ad), CPM, etc. Well, we tend to look at other metrics first.

No doubt those are useful numbers to give you the big picture. But it´s unlikely that they link back directly to the most important goal you had in mind for your ads—an action—which also happens to be a separate column in the Facebook Reports. This column gives you the total number of actions that happened as a result of your ads.

You should know your number-one goal of your ad. Facebook even helps you with this, because before you create a new campaign it asks you what *your primary objective* is. This could be Clicks to Website, Website Conversions, Page Likes, Video Plays, Shares, App Installs, or Event RSVP.

Depending on how fast you are spending on Facebook you could look to the more detailed Facebook Reports once or twice a week. It all depends on the type of company you work for, too. Do they like to see very detailed reports regularly, or are you or your company more "hands on"?

The following are some possible settings on how to use the Facebook Reports. You can choose your own or adjust them to your own specific situation, but here are some of my favorite settings.

- *Results*—e.g., Post Engagements or Page Likes, etc.
- *Cost per Action*—Like Post Engagement, Page Like, etc.
- *Reach*—Number of unique visits.
- *Spent Today*—Total spent today.
- *Total spent*—Total spent in the period selected.
- *Revenue*—Somehow you need to determine the total revenue related to your Facebook campaigns.

For more information you can also visit the help sections within the Ad Manager as shown in Figure 10.12.

If you click on "Reports Help" under the "Ads Manager Reports Guide," you have a short and concise overview of the options available in the Facebook Reports.

FIGURE 10.12–General Reporting Help

With Facebook Reports you can:

- Select only the Facebook metrics you want to see (customize your report).
- Save customized reports (!), and schedule these reports to run at specific intervals and have them sent to you by email at predefined times.
- View all the other metrics by "Dimensions": Age, Gender, Age and Gender, Country, Placement (mobile news feed, right-hand side, etc.), Destination (external URL, etc.). As you can see, you have to select a dimension by selecting a radio button, which means you can select only one at a time. The rest of the "Metrics" columns, which you can then customize below, will be shown through that dimension.

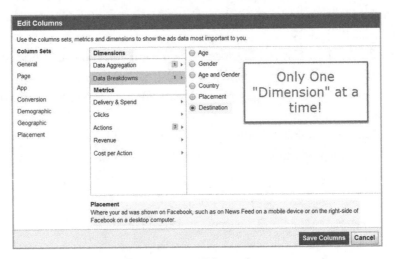

FIGURE 10.13–Dimensions

Try this for yourself:

1. Click "Edit Columns" and choose the columns you are interested in. Choose columns like Dates, Campaign, Frequency, Spend, or Actions. Select the action you want to see (e.g., "Leads" or "Page Video Plays", etc.). When you´re done, you click "Save Columns".
2. In some cases you may like to see a report for one specific campaign only. Then apply "Filters." For example, if your campaign name has a specific word describing its use in it (e.g., "Mother's Day") you could use this as a filter. You then get the report with only those words in the campaign names. You can further filter by Ad Set Name and Ad Name, too. It looks as shown in Figure 10.14 on page 161:
3. Now you select the date range (today, yesterday, past 30 days, etc.). Together with this filter you can also indicate how much time is grouped on each row.

FIGURE 10.14–Adding Filters

4. Save a report for the settings you just selected, like Figure 10.15:

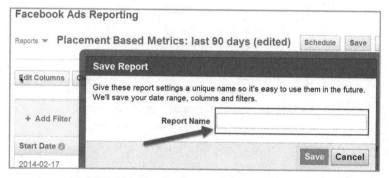

FIGURE 10.15–Saving Your Filtered Reports

Give it a name that is meaningful to you and somebody else who could get a copy of the scheduled report. Then schedule it to run regularly and have it sent to the emails you specify.

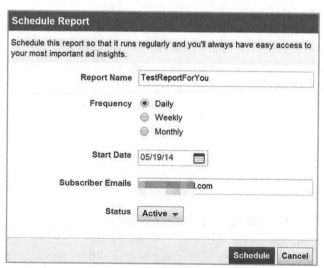

FIGURE 10.16–Scheduling Custom Reports

As mentioned before, if you want to generate a report quickly, you can select the predefined column sets, as shown in Figure 10.17 on page 162.

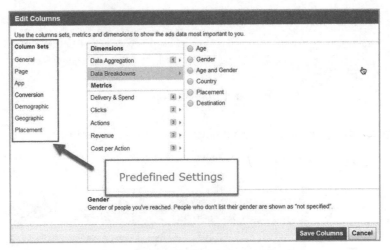

FIGURE 10.17–Pre-Defined Report Settings

The list of pre-defined columns sets is:

- *General*: Includes campaign, reach, frequency, impressions, amount spent, cost per 1,000 impressions (CPM), cost per click (CPC), clicks, clickthrough rate (CTR), and actions.
- *Page*: Includes campaign, page likes, page engagement, and cost per page like.
- *App*: Includes campaign, app installs, app engagement, mobile app installs, and cost per mobile app installs.
- *Conversion*: Includes campaign, conversions, checkouts, registrations, cost per website conversions, cost per checkout, and cost per registration.
- *Demographic*: Includes account, age, gender, reach, and frequency.
- *Geographic*: Includes account, country, reach, and frequency.
- *Placement*: Includes account, placement, reach, and frequency.

By default, actions are counted when they're taken within 24 hours of someone seeing your ad or 28 days after clicking on it.

If there are action metrics (e.g., page likes, conversions, etc.) in your report and you want to see metrics for a different action attribution window than the default, click on "See Advanced Settings" and select "Use a custom action attribution window" to choose from other available options.

Once you hit "Save Columns," the report will be shown on the screen.

You can really dig into the most important metrics, or KPIs, for your business or client.

Now you can look at the data on the screen or do what most Facebook ad managers do: export data. (See Figure 10.18.)

FIGURE 10.18–Exporting Reports

The deepest insights can come from *exporting* the data to Microsoft Excel or .csv files. You can now sort and play with the data without limitations.

You can unleash formulas on your data to provide you with insights that are not in the standard report.

You will have to connect the final revenue outside Facebook back to the Facebook ad spend. This is where you can determine your ROI. With the available data you can now do useful things like adding calculations (formulas) in separate columns. For example, if you have the revenue generated by the Facebook campaigns, you can calculate in a separate column spend-to-revenue ratio: the lower the number, the more money you get for every dollar you spend.

> **Go to www.perrymarshall.com/fbtools for the latest updates & to get valuable resources for more clicks from Facebook for less money.**

Chapter 11

The Facebook Power Editor

WITH GREAT POWER COMES GREAT CLUNKINESS

When it comes to online advertising software, Google AdWords has its AdWords editor, an incredibly useful tool for bulk uploading ads and optimizing PPC campaigns. It's the Cadillac of online advertising software.

Facebook has it very own online advertising software called the Power Editor. And although the Power Editor is extremely useful for larger advertisers, it's a far cry from Google's. To be fair though, the AdWords editor has been perfected over many years of usage, hundreds (if not thousands) of iterations, and input from thousands of very smart PPC advertisers since the mid-2000s.

> "*The best way of difficulty is through it.*"
>
> —WILL ROGERS

The Power Editor, although a very useful tool, hasn't yet benefited from this kind of widespread usage and perfection, so trying to compare the two is like comparing a brand-new MacBook Pro to an old IBM punch card system.

But setting aside its clumsiness, the Facebook Power Editor is a very effective tool for large-scale advertisers. When you start to get really serious about your advertising in Facebook, you'll reach a point where you'll start to outgrow the Ad Manager. This is where you need to start learning how to harness the power inside Facebook's Power Editor.

THE "POWER" INSIDE THE POWER EDITOR

There's a reason why the Power Editor in Facebook has the word *Power* in it. It's because it's a powerful platform to not only create ads but to also optimize and weed out the ads that are no longer working to achieve your advertising goals.

The Power Editor is especially useful for agencies that deal with massive amounts of ads from multiple clients. It's a far easier way to manage all these accounts than the Ad Manager is, and although it has its faults and quirks, it's become the centerpiece ad management tool for Facebook.

The Power Editor gives you so much more flexibility and usability when creating your ads. For example, while using the Power Editor, you can have multiple conversion pixels for each one of your ads, which is especially useful for campaigns with longer or multistep sales funnels.

Also through the Power Editor, you can create unpublished, or what's referred to as "dark," posts for your Link Post news feed ads. You can also add conversion tracking links in your Page Post ad and have the flexibility to use different URLs you show to your visitor.

There's also many other handy functions that make large campaign creation far less time-consuming, including duplication of previous campaigns, ad sets, and ads well as mass deletions of added mistakes and/or ones that no longer perform.

Creating ads through the Power Editor also allows you to insert more advertising copy in your ads themselves, especially Link Post ads that appear in the newsfeed. This greater flexibility allows you to split test ad copy that's not available through the Ads Manager.

The Power Editor also opens up a whole new world of targeting through partner categories supplied by Facebook's big data partners.

So let's get into how you use this powerful tool.

HOW TO INSTALL THE POWER EDITOR

If you're not a fan of Google Chrome, then you'll need to quickly change your loyalties if you want to use the Power Editor. As of this writing, the Power Editor is only used in the Google Chrome browser, which is an odd pairing, considering the sometimes hostile relationship between Facebook and Google.

The Power Editor is easily installed in the Ad Manager with just a few clicks. To install it, simply click on the left-side icon and install.

FIGURE 11.1–Installing the Power Editor

After you have installed the Power Editor, you'll need to download your ads from your account, which is done by clicking the top button that says "Download to Power Editor."

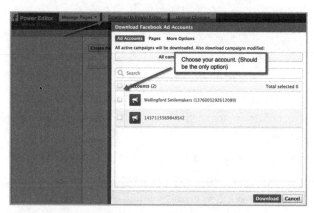

FIGURE 11.2–Download to Power Editor

Note: In some cases, if you are trying to add a client's account (that you are already an admin of) into your Power Editor, their account may not show up in your list of choices. You may have to add their account by their ID number, which you can get from the Ad Manager.

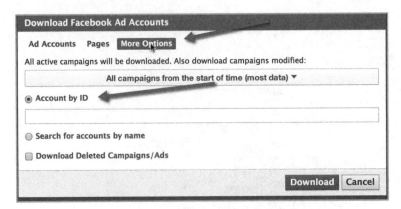

FIGURE 11.3–Adding Accounts by ID Number

A QUICK TOUR AROUND THE POWER EDITOR

As you'll see the Power Editor is quite a different animal than the Ad Manager, and not all of it is obvious. Once you start using the Power Editor, you'll quickly find out all its quirks and oddities.

Although creating campaigns and ads in the Power Editor is not intuitive and step-by-step easy as the Ad Manager, one of the greatest features of the Power Editor is that when you are working in it and don't finish a task, that task is automatically saved. This allows you to create campaigns step by step, and not all in one sitting. Nothing is worse than creating hundreds of ads, getting interrupted, and then coming back to your computer and finding all of them gone. This can happen quite easily in the Ad Manager. But in the Power Editor, this is far more difficult to do.

So let's take a look around.

Overall Layout

The first thing you'll notice is that everything is in a different place in the Power Editor versus the Ad Manager. All your controls over your campaigns are in a single screen with a minimum of scrolling.

The account name and download and upload buttons are arranged horizontally at the very top. The account name, or in many cases, just the account number, is prominently displayed so you know exactly which account you're in at all times.

The "Download to Power Editor" button is the one you've already used. This downloads information from the Ad Manager into the Power Editor. The "Upload Changes" button uploads any new activity from the Power Editor into the Ad Manager. So if you're working on a campaign, you don't have to set anything live or get approval from Facebook until you click the "Upload Changes" button.

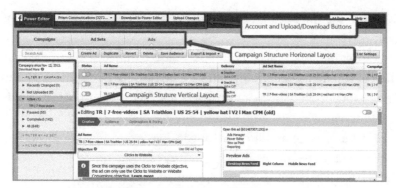

FIGURE 11.4–Power Editor Layout

You can access your campaigns, ad sets, and ads horizontally just below the navigation bar at the top. Or you can choose to access your campaigns or ad sets horizontally on the left sidebar.

The upper-right-hand corner is where you would access any images, custom audiences, conversion pixels, and reporting.

FIGURE 11.5–Power Editor Menu

If you're running huge campaigns, there's a very handy search box if you remember the name of the ad or ad set for the campaign you're trying to find.

FIGURE 11.6–Power Editor Search

If you're running campaigns with hundreds of ads sets and thousands of ads, this feature is a lifesaver.

Everything within the Power Editor is "click to affect," meaning that nothing happens unless you actually click and affect a certain part or feature. Nothing in the Power Editor happens on its own and triggers another part of the Power Editor. With the Power Editor, you need to do it yourself.

This is both a blessing and a curse, but it does avoid making mindless mistakes, especially when you're creating very large campaigns.

For example, if you want to create a campaign, you need to click the horizontal "Campaigns" button, and underneath it, just to the right, will be a whole set of new buttons for you to affect.

FIGURE 11.7–Power Editor Campaign

Once you've created a campaign, you'll then need to move to the right to click "Ad Sets," which has its own corresponding buttons below it as well.

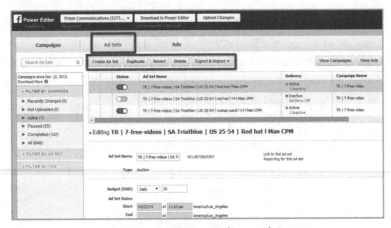

FIGURE 11.8–Power Editor Ad Set

Ads inside those ad sets inside those campaigns are then created using the "Ads" button with its corresponding buttons:

FIGURE 11.9–Power Editor Ad

This horizontal arrangement is extremely effective and logical when creating new campaigns, ad sets, and ads.

HOW TO CREATE NEW CAMPAIGNS IN THE POWER EDITOR

Using the horizontal left-to-right navigation described above, to create a brand-new campaign you would simply click on the upper-left-hand "Campaigns" button and then click "Create Campaign."

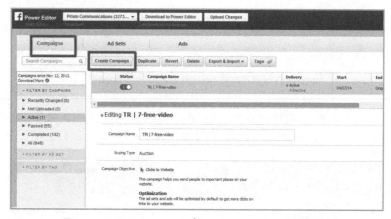

FIGURE 11.10–Power Editor Campaign Creation

A pop-up box will appear in which you can choose your campaign name, bidding type, and objective. We usually choose "auction" and either "Clicks to Website" or "Website Conversions." See Figure 11.11 on page 172.

The new campaign will then appear in the window in the center. Moving horizontally, then click on Ad Sets and then click the "Create Ad Set" button. See Figure 11.12 on page 172.

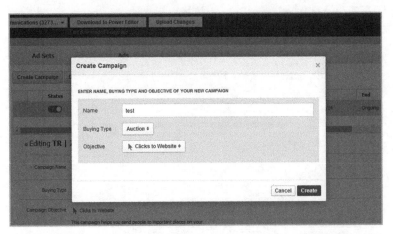

FIGURE 11.11–Power Editor Campaign Creation Tab

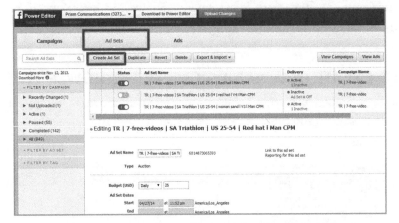

FIGURE 11.12–Power Editor Ad Set Creation Tab

This will immediately open a new pop-up in which you can choose the campaign for your ad set and then choose a new name for this new ad set.

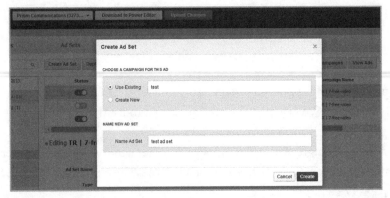

FIGURE 11.13–Power Editor Ad Set Creation Tab—Naming Your Ad Set

Then just move horizontally to the right again and click the "Ads" button to create your ad.

FIGURE 11.14–Power Editor Ad Creation Tab

Simply name your new ad using your existing campaign and your existing ad set.

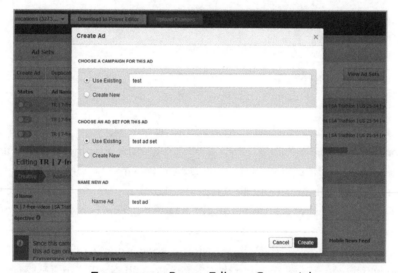

FIGURE 11.15–Power Editor—Create Ad

Congratulations! You've officially created your first campaign, ad set, and ad inside the Power Editor.

Now the real fun begins . . .

THREE SIMPLE STEPS TO CREATE ADS IN THE POWER EDITOR

The heavy lifting is over now, and this is where the real intelligence comes into play when creating ads inside the Power Editor. The real magic with the Power Editor is its targeting and conversion pixel capabilities.

Step 1: Create Your Ad

Immediately after you create your campaign, ad set, and ad, you'll notice that in the left-hand column you will suddenly see some changes that are important to know about and reference later on as you create multiple ads within your ads sets.

You'll see that the Recently Changed and Not Uploaded sections under Filter by Campaign in the left-hand column suddenly have numbers after them. This is your new campaign. If you click the "Filter by Ad Set" button below you'll see a corresponding new ad set.

You'll also see a horizontal blue shaded series of three steps that you'll become quite familiar with when creating your actual ad.

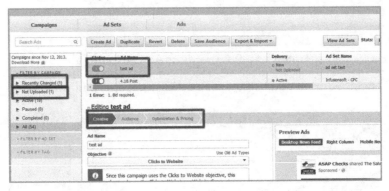

FIGURE 11.16–Power Editor—Ad Builder

Notice that the darker blue shaded Creative tab has your ad name in the box directly below the three horizontal arrows with the corresponding objective as we have previously chosen in the steps above as "Clicks to Website." So far so good.

We will create the number-one ROI type of ad on Facebook right now: the Page Post ad linked to your website, positioned in the newsfeed. This is the majority of ads that you'll be creating.

If you're managing multiple clients, simply toggle down to the client's Facebook page from which you will be creating the Linked Post ad. See Figure 11.17 on page 175.

The next step is one of the most powerful of all in the Power Editor. As you scroll through the "Creative" section, you will be faced with the choice: a post currently on your Facebook page or "Create an Unpublished Post." If you are simply promoting posts that you've already posted on your Facebook page, this is fairly easy. Just scroll through the posts that show and choose the one you'd like to promote, as shown in Figure 11.18 on page 175.

However, if you click "Create an Unpublished Post," this post will not appear on your Facebook page timeline and therefore can be used only for promotional purposes. These newsfeed Link Post ads are some of the more powerful ads on Facebook.

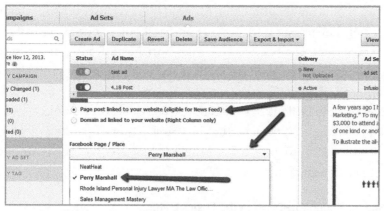

FIGURE 11.17–Power Editor—Create Unpublished Post

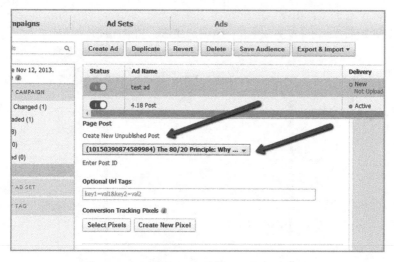

FIGURE 11.18–Power Editor—Select Post

The Most Powerful Tool in the Power Editor: The "Unpublished Post" (or "Dark Post)

Especially for agencies, and even for individual users, you don't want to muck up your client's timeline with bunches of ads that are geared toward promoting certain off-page content.

In the absence of true "A/B testing" in Facebook where each ad would receive roughly the same number of impressions and have similar placement (as opposed to Google where there is true A/B testing) and the click-through rate would then determine the winner, with Facebook ads this kind of testing can be best done through the creation of multiple "dark posts" that are not seen on the client's timeline and exist only for the purposes of promotion.

Note: You should always be looking for ways to let the user tell you what is working and what is not, but testing different ads on Facebook is not as scientific as it is on Google. Not even close! Facebook has too many variables affecting click costs and CTRs, such as social interactions, user feedback, Facebook's ever-changing algorithm, and dozens of other Facebook nuances!

Although this can be done in the Ad Manager as well, the best place to do this kind of testing and ad creation is from within the Power Editor. Regardless of which way you choose to do your ad testing, with both the Ads Manager and the Power Editor, they both needs to be done manually.

How to Create an Unpublished Post in the Power Editor

There are two ways to create an unpublished post in Facebook. (Please see page 191 for instructions on how to create a "Dark Post" Using the "Pages" section of the Power Editor.) Under the "Creative" section of the Power Editor, you simply click "Create Unpublished Post," and a box will appear that looks like this:

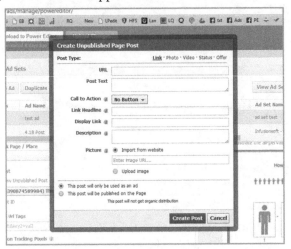

FIGURE 11.19–Power Editor Unpublished Post (Dark Post) Creation

You can then start filling in your ad information as in Figure 11.20 on page 178.

If you get confused, the nice thing about this pop-up is you can click the *"i"* at the beginning of each section for a full description of what the function of that segment of the ad is. It is always good to double-check which parts of the ad you are creating when inserting your ad copy and headlines.

The sections you'll need to fill in are as follows, starting from top to bottom:

URL: If you are using a straight URL, just insert that URL into this section. However, if you are using the Google Analytics URL builder, Infusionsoft, Improvely, or any

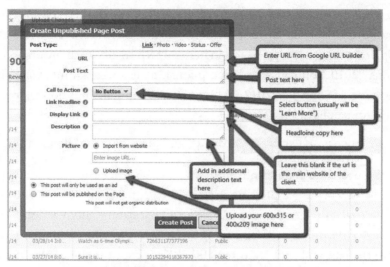

FIGURE 11.20–Power Editor Dark Post Labels

number of tracking link services, insert that raw link into this section. Your visitors will never see this URL in your ad.

To align your ads with your Google Analytics, most people will want to use some form of tracking link in this section so they can specifically track which ads convert best for them through an independent source outside of Facebook. Facebook does have the reputation of having inconsistent conversion pixel data. To remedy this, track your conversions and traffic through Google Analytics or some other tracking like Infusionsoft, Improvely, or any of the dozens of other tracking link creators.

The best thing about Google URL builder is it's free and it perfectly integrates into your Google Analytics data. To create your Google tracking URLs simply go to: https://support.google.com/analytics/answer/1033867?hl=en and insert the following:

> **Destination URL:** Enter the destination URL (this is the landing page or where you're sending traffic).
>
> **Campaign:** This should be your target audience group. An example would be M_25_54.
>
> **Medium:** This should be wherever in Facebook you're advertising. For example, news feed mobile would be "news feed_mobile."
>
> **Source:** This should always be "Facebook."
>
> **Content:** Describe the images you are inserting. For example: "girl_pink_Hill.
>
> **Term:** This should be the precise interests and any other overlay targeting such as friends of fans or similar audience targeting that you will be using for the ad.

For example if you are going to be targeting precise interests such as Ironman triathlon, 2010 Ironman world championship, 2011 Ironman world championship, Ironman 70.3, you can add in here something like this: "ironman grouping." (Note: "2010 Ironman world championship" is an actual interest that you can target inside Facebook. 2012, 2013, or 2014 championships don't show up at this point for some reason.)

Copy the Google Analytics encoded URL and place into the URL section.

Post Text: Post text should contain your main message as it's the heart of the post itself. As a general rule, the target URL (or shortened URL from the Google URL shortener) should be inserted at the end of the text along with a strong call to action.

To create a shortened URL, go to goo.gl, paste the URL from the Google URL Builder into the box, and click "Shorten URL." Then copy the shortened URL and paste it at the end of your post text copy.

The post text should then contain a call to action at the end, followed by your shortened URL, for example:

Click here to discover how: *http://goo.gl/KGx3wB*

Your post text should be no longer than this here:

Train Smarter NOT Longer
Tridot's Triathlon Training helps you beat your best time
and finish stronger than you ever have.
Give Feedback, Get the Program Free.
Click here to discover how: *http://goo.gl/KGx3wB*

Double-check your ad copy and make sure that it has proper spacing and doesn't look all mashed up together. If it is mashed together, cut out your ad copy, paste it into a text file, and reinsert it so it looks nice and neat.

Link Headline: The link headline is a very important section of your ad. Ideally, capitalize the first letter of each word and make it punchy and to the point. Examples may include:

- Train Smarter Not Longer
- Beat Your Best Time
- Swim Faster
- Want to Ride Faster?
- Get Your Free E-Book
- Who Else Wants to Flip Houses?

Display Link: We used to tell people to leave this alone, but what we've noticed is that if you have a tracking link from Infusionsoft or some other tracking link service, Facebook will display that URL instead of the URL for your website.

You can leave this section alone if you are not using tracking links, as your correct URL will show in the ad.

However, if the page you are sending your traffic to is on a URL that is NOT the client's main website URL, you'll want to insert your website URL in this section. For example, the landing page https://antares.leadpages.net/rqb-5-mistakes-ebook-fb-business-owners/ (this landing page URL is for example purposes and may not be active by the time you are reading this) is a subdomain from landing page provider Leadpages. For branding, you don't want your ad to have the subdomain "leadpages" showing in your ad.

To remedy this, insert your root URL instead of the actual landing page URL, and this takes care of this issue.

Description: The "description" is the link description and will be displayed below the image. This just gives you more area to add compelling copy to your ad. In this section, insert a description consistent with your post copy and name of your ad. You don't have a lot of characters to work with here, so keep it brief. (Facebook changes the character limits in this area very frequently so you will just have to try a few posts and see what you can fit in.)

Image: Images should be at least 600 x 315 pixels or Facebook's recommended size of 1200 x 627. If you deviate from these dimensions, make sure they have the same height-to-width ratio. You can certainly use larger images. Just keep it simple and use either one of those dimensions, or whichever is Facebook's latest specifications.

If the images you have are not the right sizes, resize them as follows:

1. Open up PowerPoint or Keynote.
2. Open up a new blank slide.
3. Insert the image into that slide.
4. Using JING, select the region of the image you want to capture.
5. Use the markers indicating to set the image size to 400 x 209 or 600 x 315.
6. Copy the image.
7. Save the image onto your desktop or some other file.
8. Click "Upload Image" in the Create Unpublished Page Post section and upload image you just created. With unpublished posts, you can upload only one image per post.

Final Checks on Ad Creation: Before you hit the big blue "Create Post" button, make sure you check all your spelling and grammar, *because with unpublished posts you don't get a second chance to edit them.* So check the post text to make sure it sits right, double-check for grammar or spelling errors, and then click "Create Post."

You'll now see this post in the drop-down menu for post choices to promote. Select this post and continue.

Select or Create Your Conversion Pixel: Conversion pixels, as discussed earlier, are simply a piece of code used to track certain actions people take on your website. If you are a direct-response marketer, these conversion pixels within Facebook are extremely important.

They can measure leads, registrations, additions to shopping cart, purchases, video views, or any other action you would like to achieve with your advertising. In this section you simply select the conversion goal previously created or create a new one and go through the steps for placement on your website.

Pick Your Placement: More Choices Than You Could Ever Imagine: At the very bottom of the creative section is one of the most dizzying arrays of choices any Facebook advertiser is faced with—namely, where to place the ad within the Facebook ecosystem. The choices are as follows:

- All Facebook (includes News Feed)
- News Feed (Desktop and Mobile)
- News Feed (Desktop Only)
- News Feed (Mobile Only)
- Desktop Right Hand, News Feed (Desktop Only)

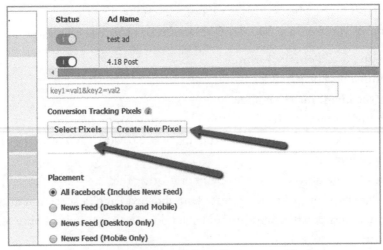

FIGURE 11.21–Power Editor Placement Choices

- Right-Hand Column (Desktop Only)
- News Feed Mobile Only in Right-Hand Column (Desktop Only)

Not to mention that if you click any of the mobile options, you have another array of choices on which mobile devices to advertise on, including:

- All mobile devices
- Featured phones only
- Android devices only
- iOS devices only
- All devices
- Specific devices, including smartphones and tablets
- Minimum version
- Only show on mobile devices when connected using wifi

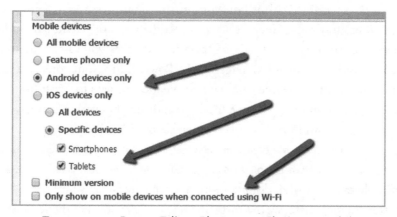

FIGURE 11.22–Power Editor Placement Choices—Mobile

All these choices are enough to make any Facebook marketer start to lose their mind.

But it's actually really not that complex if you just stop and think about what you are trying to accomplish with your ad. If you have a simple email capture in exchange for an ebook, you could probably just do News Feed (Desktop) or News Feed (Mobile).

If you are shooting for constant brand recognition but don't really want clicks to your site, then you may want to choose Right-Hand Column (Desktop Only).

If your goal is to get the visitor to download your iPad app, you'll want to go with iOS devices only, Specific devices, and Tablets.

Bottom line: when making these choices think of your audience and your conversion goal. In the vast majority of cases your ads will be either News Feed (Desktop Only) or News Feed (Mobile Only) as these are the most effective ad types. You can certainly test all the other variations, but those will be the most popular.

Now you're ready to move onto the next segment in ad creation.

Step 2: Create Your Audience

There are some big differences in this section of ad creation, compared to the Ad Manager, and these changes are super good for you—huge changes that make Facebook one of the most powerful advertising platforms on the planet.

With powerful targeting data and the ability to upload custom audiences from your email lists and create lookalike audiences with similar likes, interests, and behaviors, Facebook's profiling and matching algorithm create very powerful tools to laser-focus your ads and attract the exactly right potential customer for your product or service.

Custom and Excluded Audiences

If you've created a previous audience from a previous targeting segment, you can choose that existing targeting group through the Audiences section. This is very handy when you are creating multiple ads with similar ad copy but the same targeting group. It is a huge timesaver, especially if this is how your business operates.

The sections under that include Custom Audiences and Excluded Audiences. In this section, you can target your ads to specific audiences you've already uploaded in the Audiences section of the Ad Manager or the Power Editor, but you can also have the option of excluding other people who may not be ideal targets for your list.

Let's say you're promoting an ebook to a large audience, but you already have thousands of people who have downloaded that very same ebook from you through your Facebook advertising. To make your ads *even more effective,* you can target a specific audience but then exclude the audience of people *who have already opted in to your ebook.* That way, you're advertising only to people who are not opt-ins and who are *not* on your list.

So in this example here, we are targeting a specific custom audience and excluding specific other fans that we don't want to include because they are not good targets for this particular campaign.

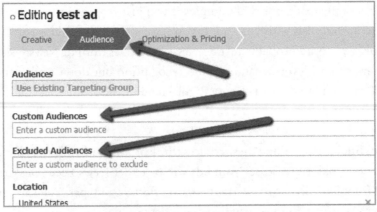

FIGURE 11.23–Power Editor Audience

The choices here are endless.

Perhaps you are doing a promotion for a paid product but don't want to target people who've already purchased that same product.

In that case you upload your custom audience or email list of all your leads but exclude your buyers list. This makes for a very targeted ad campaign in Facebook. You're spending money only on people who will buy, and you're not wasting any impressions on people who already have bought.

Location, Age, and Gender

Just like in the Ad Manager, you can target specific areas within countries all the way down to the zip code level or towns or cities within a mile radius of 10, 25, and 50 miles. In this section you can also exclude locations as well.

Age and gender are also targets in this section going all the way up to 64, but you can go even older by choosing "Any." You can also select specific languages to target.

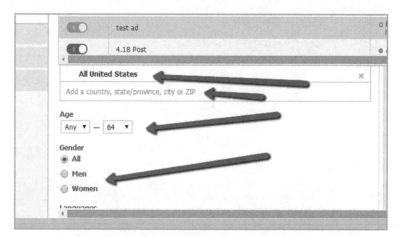

FIGURE 11.24–Power Editor Demographics

More Demographics

This is where big data (primarily from Facebook partner Epsilon) really makes the Facebook ad platform so powerful. Under the More Demographics section, the targeting choices are nothing short of amazing.

Targeting information can be stratified into its own subsections, which include an amazing array of personal and financial details unmatched on any advertising platform. Each section of More Demographics can be searched individually with auto-suggestions by Facebook, leading you to even more granular detail for your targeting.

Some of the sections in More Demographics include:

- *Relationship Status*: Interested in All, Men, Women, Men and Women, even "Unspecified"
- *Education*: Education Level, Fields of Study, Schools Undergrad Year
- *Work*: Employer, Job Title, Industries, Office Type
- *Financial Information*: Income Levels and Net Worth
- *Home*: Including Home Type, Homeownership, and Home Value
- *Ethnic Affinity*: Dominant Language, Bilingual English, or Spanish Dominant

Here is just a sampling of what kinds of *personal financial data* that can be targeted.

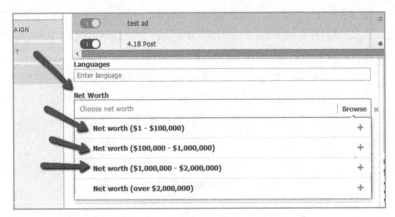

FIGURE 11.25–Power Editor Net Worth

Even income level can be targeted.

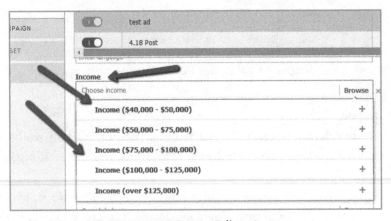

FIGURE 11.26–Power Editor Income

This is the kind of targeting ad data that in the past has been available only to huge companies with seven-figure-plus ad budgets, as they were the only ones who could afford to get this kind of data for direct-mail pieces and ad buys. No longer.

Now, it's all available to you, the solo advertiser, for the very first time.

So let's say you are marketing a high-end product to a specific group of customers and you know that your product resonates only with people who have a high net worth or are in a higher income category.

If this is the case, then why on earth would you waste your ad dollars marketing to people *who you know don't have the capability to purchase your product?* Now with Facebook advertising, you can target only those potential clients who have the means to purchase your product or service.

This makes your advertising more targeted and more focused than ever before. But of course, this does come at a cost to you, but the cost is relative. Facebook realizes that higher net worth individuals should be (and rightfully so) advertised to only by those advertisers who can afford it. Therefore, these types of category have typically more expensive clicks, and the customers are far pricier to acquire.

Interests

Although Facebook spoon-feeds you data, in this section that is far broader, as soon as you start typing in interests, you will see loads of other ideas instantaneously. This targeting is nothing short of amazing in its depth and breadth of scope.

Further, these interests can be overlaid with other precise interests. This is still a very effective way of reaching certain types of individuals. Interest can range from business and industry, to entertainment, to family and relationships, to what kind of food or drink or hobbies and activities your customers or prospects potentially have interests in. The possibilities are endless here as well.

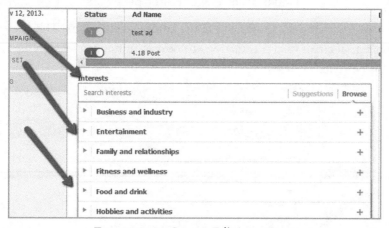

FIGURE 11.27–Power Editor Interests

We found that the general interests section that Facebook gives you in the drop-down menu is far too broad to target on its own. However, we will typically put in our own interests and let Facebook do the rest of the work by suggesting others to go along with the ones you already typed in. And if you pair these interests with other related precise interests or, even better, with a behavior, demographic, or age and gender within this section, you create massively effective and highly targeted ads.

Behaviors

Behaviors are also a place where you can find automotive purchases, charitable donations, digital activities, and financial information previously not available to the average advertiser.

Just like in the Interests section above, this section's real power is apparent when you start typing in a behavior you are looking for in your ideal customer. The program will show you amazing behaviors you never would have thought of, and they can be great interests and targets for your ads.

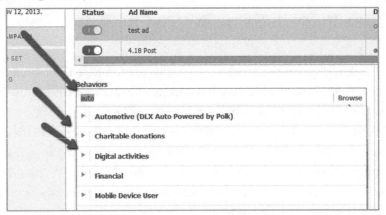

FIGURE 11.28–Power Editor Behaviors

Or let's say you are selling arts and crafts to do-it-yourselfers. There are behaviors based upon actual credit card transactions to bear in mind, provided by Epsilon, which matches this behavior exactly.

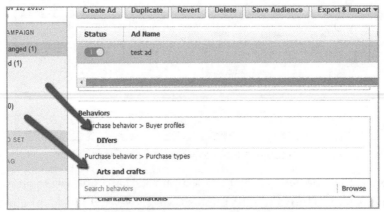

FIGURE 11.29–DIYs Purchase Behavior

Facebook Categories

If all this weren't enough, yet another section allows you to target specific subscribers, online spenders, or technology late adopters. The choices here are widespread and are typically used to create a perfect mosaic of your ideal customer in order to get even more precise targeting.

Facebook offers up some categories for you, but you can also type in the search box to search for your own as well.

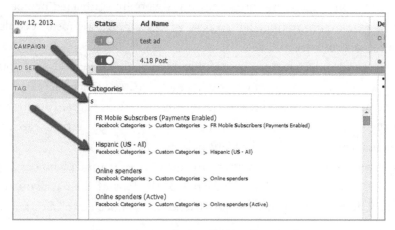

FIGURE 11.30–Power Editor Categories

Partner Categories

In addition to the big data demographic targeting and spending targeting in the previous sections, Facebook's Partner Categories take targeting to an even higher level through integration with big data providers Acxiom and Datalogix.

Epsilon largely provides the data in the sections before this section—and it's anticipated that the data and this section will likely be integrated into the advertising platform more coherently as has the Epsilon data.

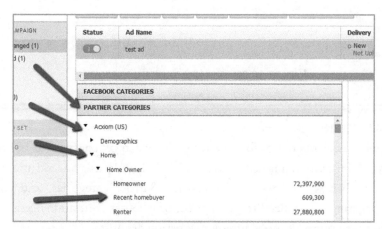

FIGURE 11.31–Power Editor—Acxiom

Nonetheless, the targeting data in this section is extremely powerful and includes such things as home ownership, recent homeowner, family composition including number of children and years of age, congressional district, senatorial districts, food consumption habits, job roles, and many, many others.

Connections

Last in this section is targeting for certain users who are connected or not connected to the pages you are promoting. This is how you can target friends of people who are connected to Facebook pages.

These sections can be extremely useful as targets all to themselves if you want to target fans of a certain page to which you have administrative access. Likewise, you can also exclude people as targets who are already fans of certain pages. This makes for very smart ad spending—larger agencies can use this as a very powerful targeting tool for specific clients while not to the detriment of other clients.

The bottom section is a great way to target the ideal customer who has a specific or precise interest and then "overlay" the friends of the fans of the page you are looking to promote. These are called "users whose friends are connected to" a certain Facebook page.

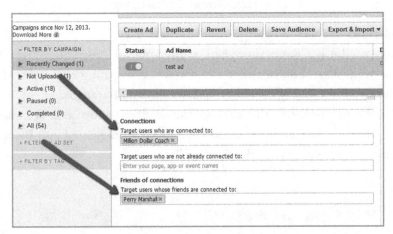

FIGURE 11.32–Power Editor Connections

Bringing It All Together

With a dizzying array of choices for targeting, it's easy to get confused as to how specific or broad your targeting should be. As a rule of thumb, as you add more interests, demographics, behaviors, Facebook categories, partner categories, and connections into your targeting, you'll need to be mindful of whether your audience is growing or contracting based upon all these different targeting groups.

To know whether or not you are increasing in size or decreasing in size your potential audience, simply look at the calculations in audience size once you select a new interest or demographic. This section is on the right-hand side of the screen and always tabulates whether your targeting is getting broader or more specific.

In this case here, we have targeting that is extremely specific, maybe *even too specific for effective advertising*. So as you keep adding on additional targeting, always look at this number to determine whether or not you are on or off base in your advertising targeting.

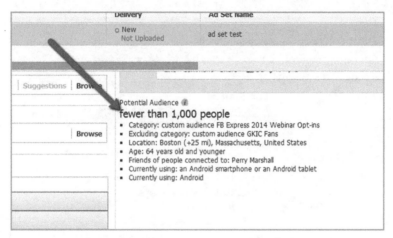

FIGURE 11.33–Power Editor Tabulation

A very handy tool in the Categories section is once you add more than one category into the search box, Facebook gives you the option to "target people who like ANY of these categories" or "target people who like ALL of these categories" to further refine your targeting. (See Figure 11.34.)

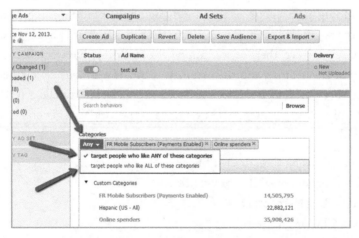

FIGURE 11.34–And/Or Option Categories

If you aren't sure if you're adding or subtracting targets, just look at your number totals to see if they are growing or decreasing, and you'll be able to make decisions more quickly.

Step 3: Optimization and Pricing

If making all those targeting decision weren't enough, when you finally click over to the Optimization and Pricing section, you are faced with another dizzying array of pricing choices.

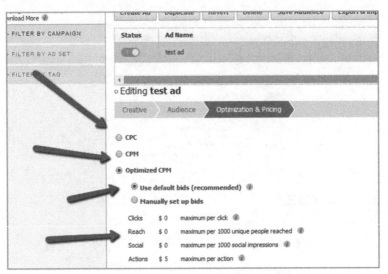

FIGURE 11.35–Power Editor Ad Bidding

One of the biggest decisions you'll need to make when you first start advertising on Facebook is determining what ad objective you want to use. And for each type, it has its own best type of bidding. Having said that, however, there are no hard and fast rules when it comes to bidding in Facebook, as they are changing their bidding algorithm and adding new ways to bid so often. (For more details on bidding strategies please see Chapter 9.)

But in our experience, there are certain types of bidding that work best for the certain types of ads you are creating, and the majority of the time it's either cost per click (CPC), optimized CPM (OCPM), or the new one, optimized CPM bid for clicks (OCPMC).

So the bidding is largely dependent on the ad type. And as a general rule, this is how you should bid:

- Clicks to Website: CPC or OCPMC
- Website Conversions: CPC or OCPMC
- Page Post Engagement: OCPM
- Sidebar: CPC or OCPM
- Likes: OCPM

So keep it simple.

If you are promoting a Link Post ad and are aiming for a conversion, go with CPC or OCPMC bidding. If you are just promoting helpful useful content you posted on your Facebook page, go with OCPM.

Regardless, it's always best to test different biddings and make your decisions based on results you see.

HOW TO CREATE AN UNPUBLISHED POST IN THE PAGES SECTION OF THE POWER EDITOR

Another way to create unpublished or "dark posts" is through the "Pages" section of the Power Editor. One way is through the Power Editor and the other way is through the Pages section. If you are creating multiple dark posts at once, we recommend you create those posts through the Pages section as it's most efficient and allows you to create multiple dark posts for multiple ad sets all at once in a single interface.

In some cases, when creating an unpublished post in the main section of the Power Editor, it may take a few hours for the post to appear for usage as an ad. This is one of the main reasons why we recommend creating dark posts in the Pages section of the Power Editor.

You create the post the same way as described earlier, but to get to this section you take a slightly different route.

1. Click Pages in the upper-left-hand section.

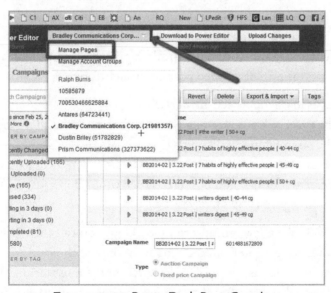

FIGURE 11.36–Pages Dark Post Creation

2. Select the Facebook business page you want to create the ad in, then click "Create Post."

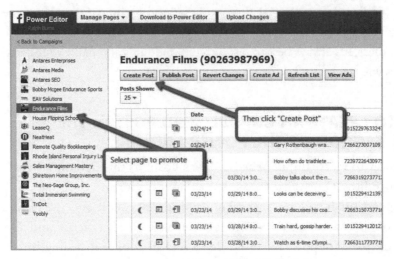

FIGURE 11.37–Pages Create Unpublished Post

3. Create your post exactly like you did in the "How to Create an Unpublished Post in the Power Editor" section on page 176.

HOW TO CREATE A VIDEO DARK POST IN THE POWER EDITOR

Video posts are some of the best-converting posts on Facebook. But to do it right you need to create video posts that are unpublished. The best way to do it is through the Pages section once again.

Although there are a couple of different ways to create video dark posts, this way is the most efficient and allows you to use the dark post as an ad as soon as it's created.

The steps to creating a dark video post are straightforward:

1. Click Pages in the upper-left-hand section.
2. Select the Facebook business page you want to create the ad in, then click "Create Post," shown in Figure 11.38 on page 193.
3. A new box will open up with multiple fields. Then simply upload your MP4 video file and create your title and post text. When you're done, just click "Create Post," as shown in Figure 11.39 on page 193 .

The video will take a few minutes to upload, but you can then switch back to the Power Editor and create an ad from the dropdown of post choices.

Congratulations, you just finished the chapter on the most technical and confusing aspect of the Facebook ads platform! Now onto the good stuff—the stuff that can make or break any Facebook campaign, no matter how good or bad your ads are: landing pages.

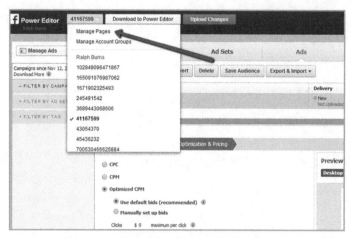

FIGURE 11.38–Select Page for Video Post

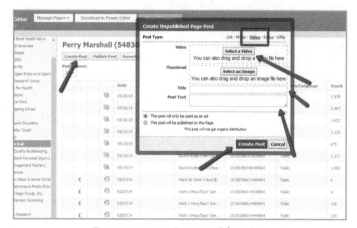

FIGURE 11.39–Create Video Post

Chapter 12

Landing Pages: Tiny Hinges that Swing Big Doors

SET SPECIFIC GOALS FOR LANDING PAGES

Even though he lived more than 2,000 years before landing pages were invented, Aristotle understood landing pages better than anyone. Technically, of course, he wasn't talking about successful landing pages—but why split hairs over amazingly good landing page advice?

A well-executed landing page is *the* difference between a successful Facebook ad campaign and a miserable failure. Getting a prospect to successfully click on an ad is only the first step of a relationship that can continue for days, months, or even decades. If you are going to establish a long relationship with a customer, you must first survive the first 15 seconds of his visit.

> "*First*, have a definite, clear practical ideal; a goal, an objective. Second, have the necessary means to achieve your ends; wisdom, money, materials, and methods. Third, adjust all your means to that end."
>
> —ARISTOTLE

Within 15 seconds (in many cases more like five seconds!) your prospect is deciding whether to stay with you or press the back button and abandon your presence forever. If you paid a dollar for a click and you lose your prospects in the first 15 seconds, you just paid $240 per hour to fail to engage the people who clicked on your ads.

You cannot afford to spend that much money on lost leads. Once prospects click on your ad, you have to capture their attention, trigger their interests, and not let them go. Your very livelihood depends on it.

This chapter is your crash course on landing pages. You will learn to build and execute a successful landing page on Facebook and on your website. You have no choice in the matter. Learn to do this well or go down in flames.

When you apply the technique of split testing to your landing page, you will—eventually—develop a stunningly effective page. It is hard work—but it is work that pays.

THE FIVE-SECOND LIZARD-BRAIN LANDING PAGE TEST

One of the best tests of any landing page is to show it to yourself or someone else for five seconds, then take it away. Then ask:

"After just five seconds, do you understand what itch this website is promising to scratch and what you're supposed to do next?"

If, after just five seconds, your prospect is confused or is still scanning the page trying to decide where his eyes should land, you're already in trouble.

Also, if after five seconds your prospect is still waiting for the web page to load, you're in trouble. Site and page speed are hugely underrated success factors. Fast websites sell. Slow websites don't. Fast websites have longer time-on-site, lower bounce rates, more page views, higher sales, and better opt-in rates. Slow sites drive people away. You should do everything humanly possible to ensure your site loads fast. You will find, for example, that all the lead generation pages on www.perrymarshall.com load very fast. When we doubled our site speed, the bounce rate improved by 20 percent overnight. Google's founders always obsessed about the speed of the Google home page, and that's one of their success secrets.

Your customer's "lizard brain"—his "inner Homer Simpson"—needs to instantly understand where on the page to look and what you're trying to say.

THE PAGE MUST HAVE A GOAL AND AN OFFER

First and foremost, you must establish a clear goal for your landing page. The goal must be measurable. In some cases, that goal will be to actually have the prospect complete an order. However, we always recommend an intermediate goal to capture prospects' information so you have more than one chance to connect with them and complete a sale. Landing pages are often called "lead capture pages." Remember that name because it implies the real goal of the landing page is to capture contact information.

It all begins with a compelling offer presented in your original ad. A quick way to establish credibility and build a relationship is to offer something in your original ad that you instantly deliver in your landing page. In a digital world, the offer and the delivery is frequently some form of information. You may deliver the information in videos, in papers, or on web pages. The benefit of delivering information is that it is easy to provide without incurring additional costs.

If your offer is to provide free information, it should be information that somebody who would buy your products would likely find interesting.

Note: In some cases, if you have your landing page inside Facebook, you can actually make a landing page a two-step process. You can hide some of your content so the visitor has to first "like" your Facebook page before he or she can see the rest of the content and opt in for your main offer. This is called a "like-gated page," an example of which is shown in Figure 12.1.

FIGURE 12.1–Step 1: Request a "Like" First in Facebook

After users like the page, we then request their names and email addresses in exchange for the lead offer. See Figure 12.2 on page 194.

In our experience, it is best to minimize the information and the steps you put in front of users before you collect their contact information. Focus your message and focus your prospect on providing you with contact information. Look at your Facebook ad and ask yourself if it has all the necessary elements. You ad should have the following elements:

- An eye-catching image
- A compelling headline

FIGURE 12.2–Step 2: Opt in to Get Your Coupon

- A specific offer
- A call to action, such as "click now" or "like this page."

Next, look at your landing page; it should have the following:

- A captivating headline.
- A compelling offer.
- A short description or video describing what it is you are offering and what's in it.
- Bullets can be very helpful in some cases.
- An explanation of how to get what you are offering. Do prospects fill in a form, make a phone call, or do something else?
- A promise not to violate trust. At minimum, include a link to your privacy policy.
- The opt-in form itself.

Don't stop thinking about your prospects' experience after they opt in. After the landing page, arrange for the following steps:

- Take them to another interesting page with an additional offer or a rapport-building video to make a deeper connection.
- Automatically follow up with interesting and engaging information.
- We sometimes call the page the visitor lands on after they enter their contact information and click submit the "thank-you page." However, you really want to be thinking about this page as more like the second step in your process. The

LANDING PAGE INSIDE FACEBOOK OR OUTSIDE FACEBOOK?

A common question we hear is: "Is it better to have your landing page inside Facebook or is it better to take people off of Facebook to your own URL?" The answer is neither one is best. It all depends on your specific scenario. In some cases you will see cheaper clicks taking people to a landing page inside Facebook because you're getting rewarded for keeping the user inside Facebook. In some cases you may see better conversion rates keeping people inside the "safe Facebook environment."

However, in some cases you may see higher conversion rates taking people off of Facebook, because there are fewer distractions like Facebook notifications, other Facebook ads, etc.

You may have better success taking people off of Facebook to your site because your site has a nice professional feel to it that gives you credibility and increases conversions. You may have a second and third step in your process that goes much smoother if it begins on your site instead of inside Facebook.

There are a ton of different factors that can affect which place is best for your landing page, so my advice here is to just test and see what works best for you.

"money page." We call this the money page because this next step is really where the money is made.

To achieve the maximum results from your ad, you design the entire user experience from ad to final purchase.

APPROACHES TO LANDING PAGE COPY

Different people will provide dramatically different suggestions on what constitutes a good landing page. We will review several different approaches you can test, including:

- Minimal
- Long Copy
- Squeeze

Minimal

A minimal landing page may not have much more on it than a restatement of the original promise in the advertisement, an opt-in form, and a request for a "like." Our favorite description of a minimal page is "a message in a vacuum." The prospect is not distracted by other offers or lots of text. Just a simple call to action.

The thinking behind this is straightforward. If someone clicks on an ad that makes a specific offer, then he or she has already expressed his or her interest in that offer. Don't keep selling after the prospect is ready to buy. Instead, provide the simplest opt-in form imaginable to complete your delivery.

If you enticed your prospect with an ad that promises "Avoid embarrassment. A simple test to discover if you secretly have bad breath," then, on the landing page, you may not need to do much more than say, "Enter your name and email address and we will send you the simple test!" Perhaps add some bullet points for just a little emphasis.

Or if your landing page is on Facebook, you may say, "Like this page to get access to our free video: 'How to know if you have bad breath!'"

It is highly likely that anything more than a minimal opt-in page will decrease your subscriber opt-in rates, not increase them. Of course, you should split test this claim.

Long Copy

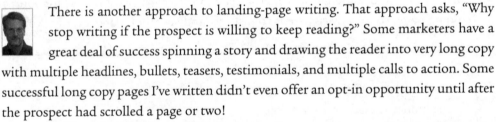 There is another approach to landing-page writing. That approach asks, "Why stop writing if the prospect is willing to keep reading?" Some marketers have a great deal of success spinning a story and drawing the reader into very long copy with multiple headlines, bullets, teasers, testimonials, and multiple calls to action. Some successful long copy pages I've written didn't even offer an opt-in opportunity until after the prospect had scrolled a page or two!

Now you might ask, "Why would you ever write an opt-in page with the first opt-in scrolled off the page?" Our answer was simple: We didn't want a long list of prospects; we wanted only prospects who were clearly emotionally attached to the message. We wanted prospects who read to the end of a long page of copy and finished by saying, "I want to learn more."

What type of business might want to do this? A high-end consulting business with limited delivery capability would. If your delivery system doesn't scale, then you really do want to focus on finding the best customers—best for them and best for you. Prospects who read your long copy and then request a white paper are really interested in what you are saying.

They are investing their time and their energy in reading your messages. They are much more likely to be better consulting clients than those who refuse to read more than 25 words.

If you are selling a complex product that requires deep understanding from your customer to make a purchase decision, test long copy messages. Even if the long copy is not in your original landing page, it may be appropriate in your emails, videos, articles, white papers, and blog posts.

In long-copy landing pages, the prospect may be given multiple opportunities to respond. The page may tell a bit of a story, provide some testimonials, and then provide an opt-in. If the user doesn't opt-in, then the copy continues offering more stories, more testimonials, and more opt-in opportunities. This could go on forever.

There is another benefit to long copy for some customers, especially corporate ones, which are looking for a specific solution to a specific problem. They may be wary of providing their contact information unless they are convinced you have something they want.

Long copy can convince them you have the answer they are looking for.

Long copy provides prospects with an opportunity to stand on your front porch and find out what you have to offer. They need to read and think about your long copy in order to become comfortable enough to trust you with their name and email address. These customers would likely never be captured with a short-copy landing page, and they can be some of the most lucrative customers because they control multimillion-dollar budgets.

Although short copy may convert to more opt-in leads than long copy, it may not convert some of your best leads. Therefore, it may be wise to test both short-copy and long-copy landing pages to catch both ends of the spectrum.

THE LONG AND THE SHORT OF IT

Long copy and short copy are not an "either or" proposition. Selling on the front porch offers an infinite number of landing page opportunities. Your original Facebook ad may lead to a short landing page with an opt-in offer. In your follow-up emails, you may send messages that link back to long-page sales copy. It is perfectly OK to have both.

I suspect that it is much harder to do a successful long-copy landing page in Facebook. There are multiple reasons for this, including:

- The user gets distracted by Facebook ads and navigation.
- You have limited width for your long copy text.
- Facebook users are relaxing and may have a mental predisposition away from long copy.
- Facebook users are not searching for answers and don't really want to read yours.

My suggestion: If taking a long-copy approach on a Facebook page, then replace text with a longer video.

SQUEEZE PAGES

You may have read or heard the term "squeeze page" in your study of online marketing. Squeeze pages are single web pages designed only to capture an opt-in response. Frequently, a squeeze page is the only web page clearly visible on an entire URL, and it can have long copy.

The squeeze page typically has no additional navigation and no external links. The goal is to focus the attention of the user on the opt-in offer only. It makes the user feel like the easiest way to leave the page is to provide an email address. The page squeezed visitors until they finally relented and gave up their email.

Highly aggressive squeeze pages display pop-ups asking for an opt-in even if the user tries to leave the page without opting in by using a back navigation button.

Google considers "hard" squeeze pages (opt-in pages with no links) to be counter to good user experience. It no longer gives those good ranking in Google search and may even refuse to run your ads if you direct your customers only to a hard squeeze page.

Facebook was clever. By allowing for the "like" relationship between your visitor and your Facebook page, Facebook provides a friendly method for you to capture some of your visitors' information in a friendly way so you do not need to squeeze them nearly so hard.

Facebook does have rules about what can occur on a landing page pointed to by a Facebook ad. Make sure your landing page is following these rules or risk having your account banned.

EXAMPLE LANDING PAGE RULES

Facebook has a series of reasonable requirements around landing pages and destination URLs.

If you include a URL in the ad text or image, then the landing page must be at that URL. Landing pages cannot generate a pop-up, pop-over, or pop-under when a user enters or leaves the page.

Landing pages cannot disable the browser back button or in any way try to trap the user on the page, aka "mouse trapping." Landing pages cannot use "fake" browser behaviors like offering a close button that should close a window but instead opens another window.

YOUR LANDING PAGE IS ONLY THE FIRST STEP

One way to think about the experience you are engineering for your visitors is to realize that you are creating for them a series of linked-together landing pages—a chain of landing pages. An example chain is shown in Figure 12.3.

The first link on the chain may be a "like." In order to provide free information and services to your user, they must first "like" your Facebook page. Only after they like the page are they even offered the second link in the chain, the opt-in form. Many sellers think that once the user has opted-in and provided their email, the job is done. Wrong. This is actually the best place to now close your first sale.

The visitor has committed to at least one action. They may have liked your page, and they have submitted their email or contact info to you. They are in the habit of saying yes, so don't stop asking now. After they have completed your opt-in form, they should be taken to another page that contains a video further describing your products and services.

If they like the video, it is perfectly reasonable effort them to make an even bigger commitment in the relationship. Like buying now!

If they buy, you can take them to yet another page with yet another offer. Perhaps on this page there is a request for them to contact their friends on Facebook to tell them about this great new product they just purchased. This chain of pages and offers, as seen in Figure 12.3, can continue on and on. If they want to keep the conversation going, then there is no reason for you to stop.

Figure 12.3 is an example of the first three steps of Perry's *80/20 Sales and Marketing* one-cent book offer sales funnel. In this case we send Facebook traffic to the landing page that tells people about how they can get the book for just one penny plus shipping. They have to opt-in (with their name and email) to get to the order form, which contains a $6.99 charge for U.S. shipping and $13.99 for international. On the order form there are a couple of one-click upsell offers. After this order form is processed, the new customer is then taken to a thank-you page, which includes another offer made via a sales video.

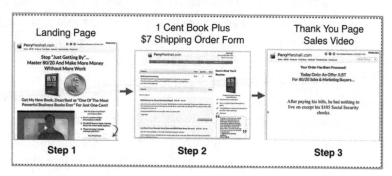

FIGURE 12.3–A Chain of Landing Pages and Offers

This process may not be appropriate for all businesses and offers; still, if your potential customers are willing to keep reading or watching, then you should keep writing and showing. As long as the visitor is on your front porch, offer them more ways to amuse themselves, more ways to learn about your products and services, and more opportunities to interact and buy.

AUTORESPONDERS

The vast majority of successful Facebook marketing campaigns we have seen include an autoresponder. It's a huge mistake *not* to use email marketing in conjunction with Facebook. We've seen *very* few successful Facebook ad campaigns that do not collect email addresses.

Think about it: Facebook was actually built through viral email marketing. When you signed up, Facebook invited you to supply your Gmail or Yahoo! login so it could "spam" all your friends and invite them to join you on Facebook. Many, if not most, people get email notifications every time something happens in their Facebook account.

Email is still the chassis that online marketing is built on. This is unlikely to change any time in the near future.

An autoresponder is a program that automatically sends emails in sequence. These emails are almost always written and scheduled in advance. The forms on your landing page should lead directly to an autoresponder that sends the initial package of free information and also a series of well-written follow-up messages. All of these messages should be packed full of value, great conversation, and great ideas so they are not perceived as spam.

Simple autoresponders you can use:

- *iContact*. If you are looking for an inexpensive autoresponder that's basic and easy to use, consider iContact. It does not try to force you to use double opt-ins.
- *AWeber*. There are a lot of things we like about AWeber, and both Tom and I use it extensively. But AWeber almost forces double opt-ins, and we really hate double opt-ins because a third of your opt-ins never confirm. AWeber has good phone support, and its support team will help you set up single opt-ins if you wish.
- *Infusionsoft*. If you have a sophisticated business, or if you're going to have a sophisticated business, I recommend that you just go to Infusionsoft. You can go to www. ManageProSoftware.com and sign up. I have a video that outlines my own autoresponder strategy at http://www.perrymarshall.com/buildingthemaze/.
- *Ontraport* (previously named Office Autopilot, at ontraport.com). This is very similar to, and is a direct competitor to, Infusionsoft. I know lots of happy customers using Ontraport, and you should also check them out if you are not using a CRM.

If you sell an ecommerce product, or virtually any kind of product on the web, you're likely going to find more success by targeting people, connecting with them, starting a conversation, and building a relationship with them first, before you try to monetize your clicks. This is why autoresponders are a central part of our marketing.

MAKE A COMPELLING OFFER

A lot of people want to offer a raffle or a contest to capture initial contact information. Although this technique does work and can generate a lot of leads and activity, I do not think it is as effective as using a compelling free offer or compelling low-priced offer that compliments your business. Something that gives you the ability to smoothly transition that prospect or customer to the next level on the thank-you page or via your automated email follow-up system.

Why? Because a raffle or contest is a short conversation. "Here. Enter my contest. Done." Not much else to talk about. But a well-written piece of information, in print or video, draws the prospect onto the front porch and into a conversation. It is the beginning of a relationship. In most contests, most people lose. Not really the best way to start a relationship.

So what is your compelling offer? Well, it will be unique to you. Describe your customers, who they are, and why they would buy from you. Then ask yourself this question: Is there something these customers would like to know that I could tell them? If there is, then make that your offer. By the way, there is always something your customers would like to know that you can tell them. If you can't think of it, then simply ask your customers. They will let you know.

Chapter 13

High-Speed Page-Generating Software: Game Changer

THE STONE THAT TAKES DOWN GOLIATH

Any time a marketing guru doesn't know the answer to a question, he can usually save face simply by telling you to test it.

How many books, courses, seminars, webinars, coaches, etc., have told you the landing page is everything? You need to be split testing headlines, landing page layouts; split testing with video and without video. Testing. Testing. Testing.

Yep. And the only problem is, all of that takes time. Customization. Money. If you tested everything it would take 250 years. Which, of course, is why you sought out the marketing guru, to hopefully save you from some of that.

So what do you do?

Nothing. Well, maybe nothing more than driving traffic into your original sales funnel without doing any real testing. You focus on creating ads, targeting, and keywords. And you focus on fulfilling your product or service.

Sound familiar? Or maybe you have done some testing using software like Optimizely, Visual Website Optimizer, Crazy Egg, or another solution. Hopefully so.

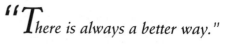

"There is always a better way."

—Thomas Edison

Whether you have your own team of badass web designers and developers to help you with this or not, stick with me.

My biggest peeve working with clients is *inability to be nimble*. Lethargic, clogged with bureaucracy and indecision. Unable to test different funnels' headlines, offers, layouts, videos, non-videos, etc., without huge delays every time we set up something new. And this is not even close to the only reason I love the tools in this chapter, so even if this isn't you, read on.

Imagine being able to quickly create new landing pages, thank-you pages, and sales pages that are *empirically proven* to work.

Welcome to the wonderful world of collaborative design. Yet, in this case you don't need to hire a team of designers and developers to do this for you—you have some of the best designers and marketers in the world at your fingertips designing pages *for* you and testing these designs with *their* own money. Not yours! And it takes less than five minutes to create and publish one of these formulaic landing pages for your own business.

HIGH-SPEED PAGE-GENERATING SOFTWARE PLATFORMS YOU CAN CHOOSE FROM

At the time of this writing, LeadPages has 72 different proven landing page templates and have just launched a new Marketplace for more designers to submit their templates that we users can have instant access to and see how they are performing in the marketplace.

LeadPages is generating almost three million email opt-ins per month right now within their system from dozens of different industries, and they are tracking and ranking the performance of every single template. And to top it off, they are tracking the performance of every customer's published page in accordance to its specific industry.

You can even sort the templates in order of highest conversion rates! For a demo of LeadPages in action please visit www.PerryMarshall.com/lpdemo.

The convenience of LeadPages is there is absolutely no design or coding necessary. All you do is choose a template you like and start swapping out the dummy copy with your own copy and upload your own images or logos to replace the placeholders.

LeadPages has complete hosting on ultra-fast servers and gives you the option to use their own hosted URL, use a WordPress plugin, install your page inside Facebook, or download the HTML to use within your own server.

Every page is mobile responsive, which is an absolute key in today's environment, especially since 70 percent of Facebook traffic is mobile.

Here are some of the types of pages you can quickly execute:

- Sales pages

FIGURE 13.1–LeadPages Overview

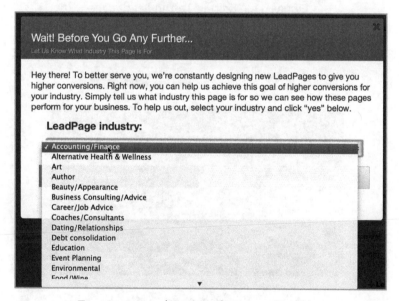

FIGURE 13.2–Industry Performance Tracking

- Opt-in pages
- Webinar pages
- Thank-you pages
- Upsell pages
- Launch pages
- Pre-cart pages
- And many other custom pages

Customizing new pages is as easy as clicking on the section you want to customize and changing the text or uploading your own image.

FIGURE 13.3–Editing Text in LeadPages

FIGURE 13.4–Custom-Designed Buttons Integrate with Email Software

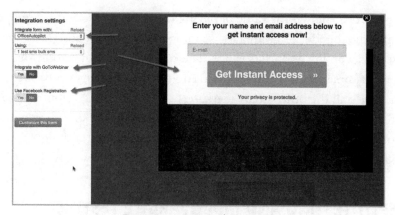

FIGURE 13.5–Email Settings

You can scroll through all of the templates and click to choose which one you want to customize.

FIGURE 13.6–Templates

I cannot stress enough the value of having the marketplace and having people like Clay Collins, the founder of LeadPages, sending out weekly videos giving insights and tips on what is working and what is not. The conversion optimization tips alone that you get as a customer are worth the subscription to the LeadPages software.

Then there's all the other smart marketers out there trying to outdo everyone else and create the highest-converting template in a given group. For example, they'll offer a competition and give a prize to the person who can submit a design that beats the existing highest-converting webinar registration page template.

EASY SPLIT TESTING AND MULTIVARIATE TESTING

It is super easy to create split tests with LeadPages. You can easily duplicate a page and change one major factor on that page to test the differences. Or you can use an entirely different template and test one against the other.

In fact, as I am writing this right now I am in the middle of a new test with a new client who was averaging an 11.7 percent opt-in rate for his free video series that leads to a live workshop and eventually into his high-end $18,000 per year coaching program.

After looking at his page and knowing a little about his market, I knew if I could get inside his LeadPages account I could probably get that conversion rate up to at least 20 percent and hopefully even higher. After the first couple days we are on the right track, up to over 19 percent. In this case we went to a simpler layout (without a video) and created a more compelling headline that was much more specific and tangible than the original.

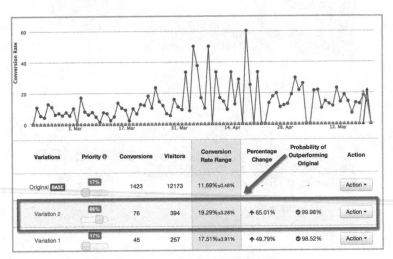

FIGURE 13.7–Split Test Results

Here is the original page (the control) they were using, which is converting at 11.7 percent.

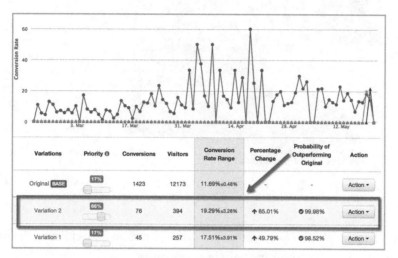

FIGURE 13.8–Split Test Results

Variations	Priority ❶	Conversions	Visitors	Conversion Rate Range	Percentage Change	Probability of Outperforming Original	Action
Original BASE	17%	1423	12173	11.69%±0.48%	-	-	Action ▾
Variation 2	66%	76	394	19.29%±3.28%	↑ 65.01%	✔ 99.98%	Action ▾
Variation 1	17%	45	257	17.51%±3.91%	↑ 49.79%	✔ 98.52%	Action ▾

FIGURE 13.9–The Control

Figure 13.10 on page 214 is the variation I created that is up 65 percent.

FIGURE 13.10–Variation 2

Then a few days later Taki created one with the webinar checklist as the main offer, and we got another 20 percent increase in conversions!

FIGURE 13.11–Webinar Checklist LeadPage

In some cases you will be better off using video on a landing page, and in other cases you will be better off with a much simpler page. In Taki's case he has a wonderful series of training videos that deliver tons of value and training that visitors get immediate access to after they opt in, so I am not as worried about making that vital connection with video that's necessary in many cases on Facebook. He is able to do that with his videos right on the next page.

LeadPages also has some other useful features, including one of my favorites called LeadBoxes. With LeadBoxes you can create a quick and easy opt-in opportunity on any page, just by turning the text or image into a hyperlink. When the visitor clicks the link or clicks the banner on your sidebar, an opt-in pops up almost like a light box, so they can very quickly and easily opt in without leaving your site or having to go to another page and make a decision. This boosts conversions. Please visit www.Leadpages.net to see a demo of how this works.

Please go to www.PerryMarshall.com/lpdemo to watch a demo of LeadPages in action.

OTHER LANDING PAGE BUILDERS

There are definitely some other great resources you will want to check out, and in many cases you may use multiple builders like this with your sales funnel. LeadPages may work great for your opt-in page, and OptimizePress 2.0 may work best for your sales page. Or you may use Unbounce.com for your landing page and use LeadPages for your webinar registration page and thank-you page. Every situation is different.

OptimizePress 2.0

For more flexibility within the page builder OptimizePress 2.0 is a great option. OptimizePress 2.0 is built for WordPress and is excellent for building sales pages, membership sites, launch funnels, and more. With OptimizePress you can completely change the layout of each template, or you can start with a blank page and just start adding widgets like video placeholders, opt-in forms, text blocks, testimonial blocks, bullet point widgets, and more.

You can customize the background of each individual section throughout the page. You can easily add exit redirect pop-ups, conversion codes, and so much more. OptimizePress 2 can be used as a WordPress theme or it can be added to an existing theme via a WordPress plugin.

Unbounce

For the most flexibility and functionality with your landing pages or sales pages you may want to try Unbounce. Unbounce is another great solution that we use for some of our own campaigns and client campaigns. Unbounce is a true drag-and-drop page builder, with many different templates you can choose to begin with and customize.

Unbounce also has great split testing and multivariate testing right inside their platform, similar to LeadPages.

10 Minute Pages

10 Minute Pages is very similar to LeadPages. However, it does have a drag-and-drop functionality similar to the way OptimizePress 2 works. We are not currently using 10 Minute Pages, but I know other companies using it and are happy with it.

In the next chapter I'm going to show you how to "warm up" your cold traffic that you bring to your landing pages, so you get better conversions!

Chapter 14

Merging Direct Response with Content Marketing

MARKETING BEFORE YOUR MARKETING

What if you could spend just pennies, or even micro-pennies, advertising to large numbers of people, then spend your *real* dollars only on people who paused to find out just a little bit more?

With Facebook, you can do that. You can "market before you market" and extend your advertising reach to even wider audiences. Before the technique I'm about to describe was developed, this was impossible. Now you can do it with ease.

> *"Give samples to interested people only. Give them only to people who exhibit that interest by some effort. Give them only to people whom you have told your story."*
>
> —CLAUDE HOPKINS, *SCIENTIFIC ADVERTISING*, 1918

THE PROMOTED POST RETARGETING LOOP

The change that social media brought to the world of marketing—the feature that really made brands look up and reach for their keyboards—wasn't the massive audience or the demographic data. That stuff all helps, of course.

But what really stood out was the "social" aspect of social media.

Facebook allows marketers to build a relationship with their audiences *before* they make their pitch. This is huge. It's the difference between buying from someone you know and trust and being pitched to by someone you've just met—who's shown no interest in you, your goals, or your priorities.

Facebook isn't a sales tool. It's a relationship-building tool that smoothes the path to the close.

In this chapter, I'm going to discuss a very strategic process that you can engineer with Facebook and ensures you're always making your offers to people who have *already* met you or connected with you somehow.

You're not walking up to them for the first time with a product in your briefcase and your hand out for their money. You're walking up to them with a smile on your face and your hand out to shake theirs, and they are shaking your hand with a genuine, trusting open hand because they know you aren't trying to pitch something on them.

You'll then meet them for a second time. Your hand will be slapping them on the shoulder like a friend—and they'll be ready to listen to you as conversation turns to the benefits of your product.

That's what the Promoted Post Retargeting Loop can do.

It sounds complicated. It isn't. It's actually a very simple process but an incredibly effective one.

HOW THE PROMOTED POST RETARGETING LOOP GOT ITS NAME

This process is a loop because your marketing efforts loop back to the people you've already met. But you can also think of it as part of the three-layer funnel. And the reason it is called the "Promoted Post Retargeting Loop" is because when Facebook first introduced news feed page post ads they were commonly referred to as "promoted posts." You don't hear the term *promoted post* as much as you used to, as they changed the term to "boost post," and this really relates only to when you boost a post right from your Facebook page itself.

The Promoted Post Retargeting Loop is my own term. So for the purpose of this strategy, a promoted post is any post that you ignite with Facebook ads, whether it's from your Facebook page, the Ads Manager, the Power Editor, or anywhere else.

THE THREE-LAYER FACEBOOK FUNNEL

Remember the "Three-Layer Facebook Funnel from Chapter 5 (page 69)? Well, before we get into the details of this tactic I want you to understand that this strategy should be just a portion of your overall Facebook ad spend. This will not be your only strategy. This is just one key piece of the puzzle.

Facebook campaigns begin with audience building. You create posts, promote them to nonfans, and keep building up those likes and audience figures.

As the audience builds, you work on engagement. You promote your posts to existing fans, encouraging them to like, comment, and share so that they're interacting as well as viewing.

The last part of the funnel is conversion. This is when you take the audience you've built and engaged with on Facebook, and you drive it to your landing pages and sales pages.

In general, I expect to spend about 20 percent of my campaign budget on the first two layers of the funnel and the remaining 80 percent on conversion. (Of course these ratios may change depending on the time of year or promotional schedule.)

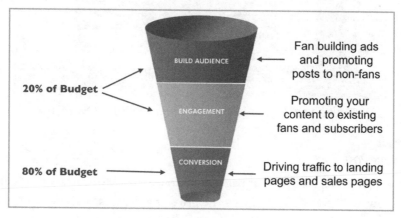

FIGURE 14.1–Three-Layer Facebook Funnel

The Promoted Post Retargeting Loop is really using all three phases of that funnel, expanding the audience and building engagement until your leads are ready to convert.

Start the Loop

The loop begins very simply: You publish a piece of content on your own website or blog. It could be a blog post, a video, or anything else that your future customers will find useful and interesting.

That's the handshake and the smile. It's selling from the front porch, but you're paying to get sidewalk traffic. It's the opening of a conversation. No one has to opt in or take any action to consume that content.

Around that content, you can place share buttons, make some offers, and add some calls to action. You might use a "Hello Bar," request email addresses in return for a checklist, or make any other offer you think will persuade some of your users to act.

Most won't click "share" or "like," although if the content is good enough, some will. (People don't share landing pages, but they do share good blog posts.) And most won't opt in. You might get an opt-in rate of anywhere from 5 to 20 percent on that page, which is fine for now.

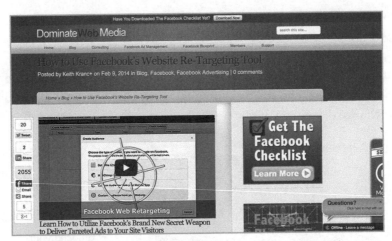

FIGURE 14.2–Post a Piece of Content on Your Own Site

Amplify Your Post

But first, you have to promote that page. You can do that with Facebook ads and with a budget as low as $5 to $7 a day. That's the price of a daily cappuccino and pastry—and the ads contain far fewer calories!

You should be using newsfeed ads, targeting the demographics that you know have responded in the past to your direct response ads or those that through your research you have found to be the best target audiences. See Figure 14.3 on page 221.

Those people move right into your funnel. They're becoming part of your audience, and some of them are starting to engage.

Even in the best-case scenario, though, around 70 or 80 percent of the people who click on your $5 per day Facebook ad and reach your blog post will click away without taking action.

They're not lost. In fact, you don't even need them to take action. If you've installed a retargeting pixel on your page, you'll still be able to call them back by using a second ad.

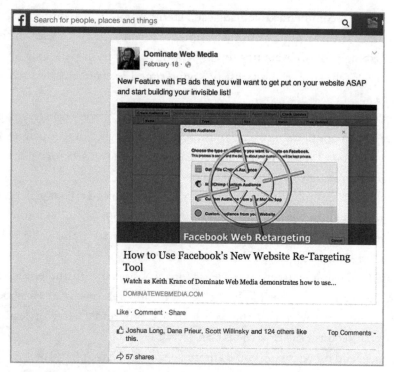

FIGURE 14.3–Amplify Your Post into the Facebook News Feed

This ad will be linked to your landing page and be aimed at those people who have already visited your site.

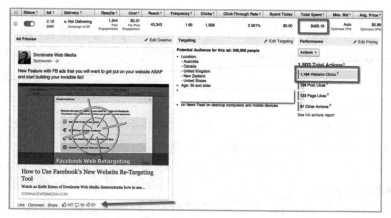

FIGURE 14.4–Blog Post Amplification Analytics

In Figure 14.4 you will see the Facebook reporting data for this specific post. The specific interests I targeted in this ad are blocked on this screenshot, but in this case I was targeting ten of my best interests all in one ad.

Normally we recommend separating each interest or audience into a separate ad set so you can track the performance of each audience much easier. However, in this case of promoting a blog post, we were not driving traffic to an opt-in page and watching the data quite as closely, so in the interest of saving time I just put my best ten audiences into the one ad.

I already know these audiences work for my business; they have already proven to in other lead generation, webinar registration, and other types of campaigns. If you are new to Facebook ads, I would recommend creating separate ad sets for each audience so you can track more carefully.

I spent $420.19 promoting this blog post with Facebook ads. That generated a reach of 43,343 (the total number of unique users who saw the post), 71,286 impressions (not shown in this report but is in the main reporting), 1,164 clicks to the website, 1,344 post engagements, 127 likes, 10 comments, and 57 shares.

Because I am using retargeting and Facebook website custom audiences, this added 1,164 new people to my "invisible list" that I can now retarget with Facebook ads or other banner ads on the rest of the web with a promotional offer or lead magnet—something that requires the user to take an action.

Once they land on your site, you want make sure you have plenty of strong calls-to-action (CTA) throughout your site in order to turn a good percentage of these visitors into subscribers or customers right away. You will see in Figure 14.2 that I have several CTAs above the fold, visible in that screenshot.

I have a banner on the right taking people to my Facebook Checklist squeeze page, I am using a www.Hellobar.com call-to-action bar at the top of my site taking people to the same place—my Facebook Checklist squeeze page—I have social share buttons, I have a live chat box people can leave a message in even if we are offline, and a few more throughout the page and the site.

Close the Loop . . . and Convert the Lead

You can use Facebook's own retargeting platform (Faeebook Website Custom Audiences) to close the loop or you can use a third-party provider like Perfect Audience, AdRoll, or one of the other Facebook Exchange partner retargeting companies. When you enter the details into Facebook's Ads Manager or Power Editor you'll be able to place your ads in front of those people who were interested enough to look at that first piece of content but have not taken action with you yet.

Example targeting: "All Website Visitors" with negative audiences of "Facebook Checklist Opt-ins" and "Facebook Ads University Purchasers." In this situation my retargeting ads would display to only visitors who have visited my site but not opted in or bought yet.

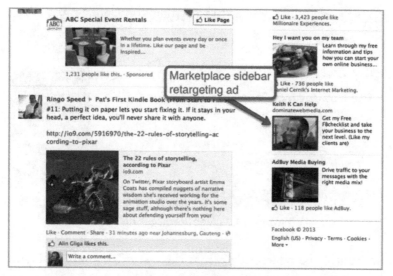

FIGURE 14.5–Right-Column (Sidebar) Retargeting Ad

In Figure 14.5, you can see how one of my ads looks when it's retargeted to someone on Facebook. This is a right-column ad, but you can, of course, use the news feed as well.

Note that the ad contains a picture of me. That's partly to help brand myself, but it's also because it reminds them who the ad is coming from. Because they've been on my website and watched at least part of a video of me in it, I'm now a familiar face. When they click on that ad, it takes them to a landing page to download my free Facebook Checklist.

Of course, after they opt in they will be taken to a thank-you page that will have an additional paid offer on it. They are now in my sales funnel.

FIGURE 14.6–Facebook Checklist Landing Page

FIGURE 14.7–Web Retargeting Ad

You also want to be retargeting across the rest of the web. In Figure 14.7, you can see a 300 x 250 banner of me promoting a three-day live in-person workshop I put on. This ad can be created using Google's retargeting platform, Perfect Audience, AdRoll, ReTargeter, or another retargeting platform. Google has the most options Perfect Audience and AdRoll are much easier to use and also have partnerships with Facebook and are rolling out some really cool new features, such as retargeting other sites' visitors.

It sounds a little complicated. It isn't. The process is as simple as an email autoresponder:

1. Post content on your own site, with subtle calls to action.
2. Amplify that content on Facebook.
3. Use retargeting banner ads and news feed ads to bring nonconverting visitors into your sales funnel, already warmed up and ready to take action!

It's simple—and it works.

We've seen fantastic ROIs using this method. Just take a look at Figures 14.8 and 14.9 for a few snapshots of the ROI generated from retargeting campaigns (from 11:1 to 20:1 ROI).

To get the most up-to-date recommendations and tutorials of web-retargeting platforms visit www.PerryMarshall.com/fbtools. This stuff is changing too fast to put our recommendation and a detailed tutorial in this book.

That we've seen such great figures using this method shouldn't be too surprising. After all, it allows marketers to return to the basics of marketing. People do business with people they like. The Promoted Post Retargeting Loop gives people a chance to like you—and it then gives you a chance to go back and sell to them when they're ready to buy.

FIGURE 14.8–Perfect Audience Retargeting Campaign

FIGURE 14.9–AdRoll Retargeting Campaign

FACEBOOK WEBSITE CUSTOM AUDIENCES

Facebook's internal retargeting feature is called "website custom audiences." With website custom audiences (WCA) all you do is place Facebook's WCA pixel onto the pages you want to track visitors. If you are using WordPress, any similar content management system, or a decent ecommerce platform, you can place the pixel "site-wide" very easily. You can also place it on pages you create using LeadPages, Unbounce, or any other landing page builder.

As long as the pixel is showing up on every page, you can then create individual pages inside Facebook to track visitors. For example, you may want a separate list for lead conversions, sales conversions, and shopping cart abandonment.

When you create a Facebook WCA, your custom audience will be growing every day, assuming you have visitors hitting those pages every day. If your list is not growing, then something was not set up correctly. See Figure 14.10 on page 226.

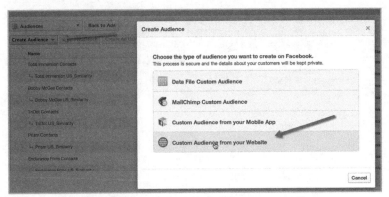

FIGURE 14.10–Create Website Custom Audience

You will want to create a sitewide audience (Figure 14.11), then create as many individual page audiences as you can think of (Figure 14.12). The earlier you do this the better—you are not getting charged for tracking these visitors; you only get charged when you start to run your ads!

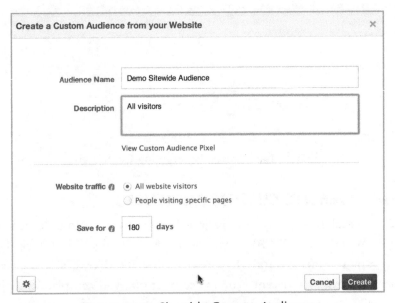

FIGURE 14.11–Sitewide Custom Audience

Facebook Retargeting on Mobile

The way retargeting works when using Google, Perfect Audience, AdRoll, or another platform is that it is browser based. You are placing an invisible "cookie" onto the browser of the user who visits your site. So if they are using the Firefox browser when they visit your site today, then later on using the Chrome browser or Internet Explorer,

FIGURE 14.12–Individual Page Audiences

or if they get on a different computer or device, then your retargeting ads will not display to that user. They will only work if they are on the same computer and the same browser.

Facebook doesn't work this way. Facebook's retargeting is not cookie based; it connects to the user's logged-in Facebook account. So someone can visit your site on a desktop computer, and you can serve that person retargeting ads the next day on his mobile device. This is powerful.

ENGINEERING YOUR OWN SEO

Using this strategy you can now be completely in charge of what type of visitors come to your site. No more stressing about the next Google algorithm change. Bring your own hypertargeted traffic to your site and have systems in place to transition them into subscribers and customers.

One Simple Video Can Turn a Loser into a Winner

ONE VIDEO TESTIMONIAL CAN MAKE A CAMPAIGN

Great testimonials persuade. Even for the toughest of products.

Testimonial videos don't even have to be professionally shot or polished in editing. We once had great results using a testimonial from a customer who sat too close to the camera in bad light and produced a very low-quality clip. It didn't matter. Because the testimonial was absolutely genuine, it delivered great results. The opt-in rate among those who had seen the testimonial was 40 percent higher than among those who came from a different type of Facebook ad and hadn't seen it.

> *"Dialogue should simply be a sound among other sounds, just something that comes out of the mouths of people whose eyes tell the story in visual terms."*
>
> —ALFRED HITCHCOCK

We once had a client who was selling a $3,000 training program from a live webinar. Webinar sign-ups are always hard. They're even harder if the audience hasn't already consumed your content. They're particularly tough when you're pitching something. And even if people register, most don't show up.

I wasn't convinced the landing page was strong enough alone to deliver high conversions so I asked the client if he had any testimonial videos.

He had a great testimonial, so we added a call to action to the lower third of that video, encouraging people to click the link in the post to register for a webinar. The response was fantastic, much higher than we would have expected without that video.

Using video ads like these on Facebook brings all sorts of benefits. First, you get variation. Instead of running your link post ad or an image linked to your landing page again and again in front of the same audience, you'll have a new powerful piece of creative to display.

You'll also be able to do some really interesting split testing, and what you'll find is video ads generate much higher engagement than other forms of ads. You'll get more likes, more shares, and more comments, and those comments will be more positive too, especially if you come across as genuine and friendly. It's easy for people to be negative and critical about someone they haven't seen, who they feel distant from. If they've watched you and listened to you, they'll find it much harder to criticize you.

Best of all though, a video ad is the perfect warm-up act for your landing page. People will watch the video on Facebook, and when they click through, they'll know what to expect and they'll already be interested.

There is a downside, though. Facebook charges for clicks on the video, not for clicks through to the website. Not everyone who watches the video will click, so you'll pick up less traffic to your page even though you'll be paying for the views. But you'll also get a higher opt-in rate among those who do click through and, most importantly, a higher sales conversion rate. People won't just have seen the copy on the landing page; they'll also have seen the content in the video so they'll be more ready to buy. You'll have created one more level of trust.

For strengthening the power of your landing page, it's hard to beat a Facebook video ad.

VIDEO: AN ESSENTIAL FACEBOOK MARKETING TOOL

Facebook can display all sorts of different content, but brands have long discovered that when it comes to winning reach and engagement, visual content always delivers the highest performance. That's why if you look at the pages of any leading brand, from Nike to Coca-Cola, you'll find almost every post carries a photo.

When it comes to *marketing* on Facebook, though, the most powerful form of content is videos.

You'll still be posting photos and writing posts, but nothing builds trust and value more than video. That's not just true of Facebook, of course. Whether you're using video in a Facebook video ad, on a landing page, or on a thank-you page, you'll be connecting with your prospects on a much deeper level when using video.

On Facebook, video is doubly important. You're trying to take someone from a social environment—a place where they're writing a comment to a friend or uploading pictures of their family picnic—and move them into a sales process. They're having fun, trying to avoid making difficult decisions about their business or their shopping, and you're trying to pull them into your sales funnel to make a decision.

To do that, you need something that has emotional gravity. Videos—whether they're presentation screen record videos, white board videos, animated clips, or my favorite, direct-to-camera video—they make a deeper impact.

In this chapter, I'm going to discuss five different ways in which you can use videos to boost your Facebook marketing performance. Please understand these five strategies are general, and the purpose of this chapter is to get you thinking about how you can use video for your specific situation.

1. Facebook Video Ads

The ability to host video ads inside of Facebook is a huge benefit, and it's also very simple. You don't have to do any more than upload a video file as a Facebook post and then promote it through Facebook's Ad Manager. You can place it in the sidebar or you can put it in your audience's news feeds. Both are very effective.

You don't even have to create a completely new video for this strategy. If you already have a video on your landing page you can just change the call to action slightly to reflect the fact that the viewer is on Facebook and not on your web page.

So when you shoot the video for your landing page, you create two endings. One says: "Enter your contact details on this page"; the other says: "All you have to do is click the link in the post." A quick edit and you'll have one video that you can use both on your landing page and in your Facebook ads.

2. Retargeting Your Videos

You should be working your video ads into the mix as part of your ongoing Facebook marketing campaigns, but there's one place where they can be particularly effective: in retargeting.

We use videos on Facebook in some cases to target people who have opted in on a website but haven't yet bought. They might have completed half an order form, then abandoned it and not returned. Or they could have downloaded a free checklist but not placed an order. We know they're interested; they just need another push. This can be done by using custom audience ads or Facebook website custom audience retargeting.

Present a video ad to those people focused on the product in which they've shown an interest, and you place a very powerful hand on their back.

We've seen huge ROIs using this one strategy: as high as 10:1 or even 20:1.

The volumes may be low because you're targeting only people who have visited your website but not bought. But the results are fantastic.

In Figure 15.1 we have a video ad that is displayed only to people who have opted into a free video series on triathlon training but have not yet bought the core product. In this campaign we run ads to offer a free training and then move the user to a sales page inviting them to a paid, live three-day intensive training program. The video in this ad is a testimonial video of former students talking about the amazing results of the program being offered on the sales page. And the link in the post is taking the user directly to the sale page.

FIGURE 15.1–Facebook Video Ad Taking Users Right
to the Sales Page

3. Video Ads on Sandwich Pages

The key strategy for marketing on Facebook—the single most important thing you should be taking away from this book—is that you need to prepare your audience *before* you present them with that order button.

Facebook provides great tools to do that, but even when you manage to pull your prospects off Facebook, you should still be preparing them for the purchase.

Sandwich pages come between Facebook and whichever action you are looking to get the visitor to take, and videos work very well on them.

Let's say, for example, that you were promoting on Facebook a product that you'd placed on Amazon. It might be a digital book or a physical product. Maybe you're looking to make sales directly on your Amazon product page. Maybe you're looking to bump up your Amazon rankings by increasing the traffic to your product page. Maybe you're looking to get more reviews. If you simply run a Facebook ad on Facebook leading to the sales page, many of your prospects still won't be primed enough to buy yet. They need more nurturing.

So instead of sending them directly to Amazon, you send them to a sandwich page that features a video. It could be a training video that shows people how to use the product, or a testimonial video, or any other content that adds to users' knowledge, builds trust, and increases their willingness to buy.

Beneath that video they'll find a button that takes them the Amazon page, where the reviews and product images should add the final touch that pushes them to buy.

By the time they're looking at the order button, they'll have seen a video ad on Facebook, a more detailed video on the sandwich page, and reviews on the Amazon page.

And here's the thing—because you'll have placed a retargeting pixel on the sandwich page, you'll be able to hit them up again on Facebook. Even better, if they click through as far as Amazon and don't buy, Amazon will be retargeting them as well, so they'll be getting hit from all directions.

This is a hugely powerful strategy that makes sure that buyers are primed before they're asked to buy and persistently pulled back if they don't.

But it won't work for every product. The item has to be cheap enough for prospects to purchase without too much hesitation. For products that cost $500 or $1,000 or more you'll probably need to use a different strategy.

4. Videos on Landing Pages

So far, I've discussed video ads that send users somewhere else: to a sandwich page, for example, or to an Amazon page. But usually you're going to be sending them to a landing page, and it goes without saying in many cases that that page should have a video.

It could be a testimonial—or even more than one testimonial. It could be an explanatory video, shots of the product, or a sales piece that explains the features and highlights the benefits.

5. Thank-You Videos

Finally, the result of all these videos and marketing will be an order, and that deserves a show of gratitude. A last video on the thank-you page won't be something you need to promote directly, but it will build more trust, goodwill, and authority. It will deepen your relationship with your customers, and make sure that they're more likely to come back to you and buy again in the future.

VIDEO-MAKING IS NOW EASIER THAN EVER

Creating videos has never been easier or cheaper. The technology has improved so much over the last few years that even propping up your iPhone on your desk or using a webcam that costs less than $100 can produce a video at a quality that would have required $3,000 worth of specialized equipment a few short years ago. Anyone can now shoot quick, authentic videos and edit them on their desktops.

For publishing on your own websites and landing pages, I recommend using the Wistia player. Wistia is both a video player and a video hosting company. It works very well with a broad range of customer relationship management software (CRMs) and all the major email marketing software providers, and it's hugely flexible. It has amazing statistics for user action and engagement, and more importantly, you can set up some pretty badass marketing automation that is all based around which videos people watch and how long they watch each one. For example, you can set a follow-up email to be sent *only after* the subscriber watches 75 percent of a specific video. If the subscriber doesn't watch the video, he or she can be sent reminder emails until they watch it.

Wistia does have a monthly subscription fee, though, so people looking to pay a one-time payment might be better off with the Easy Video Player. And you can use YouTube too. It's not great, but if you play with the code you can clean up the page on which the video sits. Please visit www.PerryMashall.com/fbtools to see our most up-to-date recommended video tools, players, editing software, video template-creation software, etc. Some amazing tools have been released lately that allow you to create professional, 3-D animated videos all on your own, without having any video editing skills, and much more.

However you create and publish your videos, the important thing is just to do it. The first few videos you shoot are always a bit uncomfortable (and the results are often discouraging), but the more you do it, the more natural it will feel and the better the results you will get.

You should have seen how bad my first few videos were. I sounded like robot! In fact, I still make bad videos sometimes. But I will tell you right now that videos have been the biggest game changer for me the past ten years. By far. And the same goes for many of my clients.

Soon, you'll find that you've got exactly the right content to deliver the best results on Facebook.

Chapter 16

Split Testing on Facebook

MY FIRST CRACK COCAINE-LIKE EXPERIENCE

I will never forget the day I discovered how easy it was to split test on Google AdWords. It was 2002 and after I was done creating an ad, the "Create a New Ad" button was still there. I clicked it and wrote a different ad.

"Is this going to do what I think it's going to do?" I asked myself.

I went to Google, typed in my keyword and refreshed the page. Sure enough, it was flipping back and forth between "A" and "B."

> *"If you can't accept losing you can't win."*
>
> —Vince Lombardi

Sure enough, the next day, both ads had their own stats.

Oh, my goodness, this is going to change the world! I thought. And I was right. It did. I discovered tiny changes made huge differences. For example:

Popular Ethernet Terms	Popular Ethernet Terms
3-Page Guide—Free PDF Download	Complex Words—Simple Definitions
Complex Words—Simple Definitions	3-Page Guide—Free PDF Download
www.bb-elec.com	www.bb-elec.com
2 Clicks— CTR 0.1%	**39 Clicks— CTR 3.6%**

Notice what happened: All I did was reverse two lines, and the clickthrough rate jumped from 0.1 percent to 3.6 percent!

I split tested landing pages, and now I was multiplying my traffic. Any improvement in traffic then multiplied again in sales leads. Then we tested sales pages and got another multiplier. Ari Galper, founder of Unlock the Game, enrolled in our coaching course and grew his sales from $5,000 per month to $100,000 per month in ten months.

The results of this simple testing were like crack cocaine!

A/B AND SPLIT-TESTING BASICS

The practice of pitting your ads against each other to determine the winner is called A/B or split testing. Without question, split testing is one of the most important tools in the direct marketer's toolbox to best optimize advertisements, increase ROI, and lower overall ad spend.

The concept of A/B split testing is quite simple: Create two ads, offer them on the ballot of public opinion and let the voters decide which one is more effective.

All things being equal, both ads have an equal chance of winning, especially when they have the exact same audience targets and the exact same advertising budget.

In A/B testing, you allow the public to decide who wins and who loses. Once you determine the winner—based on statistical significance—you dump the loser and scale the winner. You can then split test another ad against the winner to determine your next winner.

Rinse and repeat.

Split testing has been around since the late 1800s—many years before the internet. Direct-mail marketers with mail flyers with different department numbers and phone number extensions in order to measure which direct-mail piece converted the best workflow with the most inbound phone calls. Split testing is nothing new, except that online, it's far easier and more elegant to do with the multiple tools we have available to us today.

Online, there are many ways in which to test landing pages, ad copy, and many other useful data to determine your lowest cost per lead and lowest cost per sale ranging from complex split testing software to simple A/B testing on advertising platforms like Facebook.

So all you really need to do a simple split test is create your ad set, create two separate ads with two separate sets of copy, images, and headlines, and pit them against each other: the ultimate form of democracy by simply letting the voters decide which ad is the best one.

You'll then measure conversions, CTR, CPC, and impressions, factor all those pieces of data into your analysis, and then pick your winner.

Not so fast . . .

The problem is that if you create two ads within the same ad set, Facebook will never give your ads the exact amount of equal impressions. In fact, they will favor one over the other, largely devoid of your influence. They *could* show your ads equally, but they simply choose not to.

SPLIT TESTING, FACEBOOK STYLE

You want your best ads to be shown to the best audiences with the highest clickthrough rates and the lowest cost per click.

All you need to do is let the voters decide in your campaign as to which ad they click, like, and ultimately take action on. In the end, the votes are counted and the winner declared. Just like an election.

In Google AdWords, this is easy. But with Facebook, not so simple.

The problem is that the "political system" in Facebook is not a level playing field.

Seems simple enough when you "let the people decide"; after all, there are 1.3 billion active users in Facebook as of this writing, so why wouldn't this work?

It works in political elections, right?

Two candidates are placed on the ballot, and the people go to the polls and vote to determine who wins and who loses. Our electoral system seems simple enough, but as we all know, there's far more to the political process than just individual voter ballots. And anyone who is familiar with the American electoral system knows that there are multiple other influences outside of the voting process that influence our outcomes on Election Day.

Political action committees, smear advertising campaigns, lobbyists, campaign contributions from wealthy individuals—the list goes on. On Election Day, it's not quite as clear as to the actual influence of the individual vote.

So when it comes to split testing, think of Facebook as the very large and powerful PAC or special interest group that seemingly influences every national election.

You, as the individual advertiser like you as the individual voter, have very little control over this electoral process as Facebook decides which ad they like more instead of you allowing the public to decide on your behalf.

Facebook simply doesn't make it easy for you as the advertiser, because instead of equally dividing impressions for your advertisements, Facebook plays favorites.

So in order to be successful split testing ads in Facebook, you just need a strategy to get around this whole political process to level the playing field in order to get a clean election devoid of PACs, special interest groups, lobbyists, and big-money private campaign contributors.

You can confuse Facebook even further by throwing in four or five ads and split test those against each other, doing an A/B/C/D/E test. This strategy unfortunately makes the situation even worse.

Multiple ad creation confuses Facebook so much that your entire campaign receives *fewer impressions overall*, largely because Facebook simply doesn't know what to do with your maniacal (although highly logical) five-way split test.

But now with the new structure within Facebook of campaign, ad sets, and ads, you now have a split-testing friend in the ad set.

The Best Way to Split Test in Facebook: The Ad Set

So, how do you know which ad works best in your campaigns? How do you get a clean election without the influence of big corporate money and PACs?

Your friend is the early 2014 release of the Ad Set in the new Facebook advertising structure:

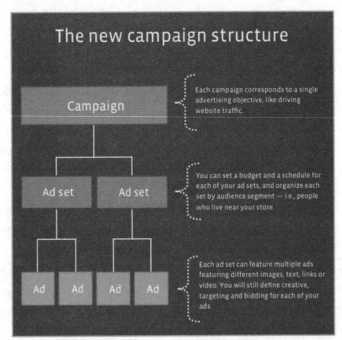

FIGURE 16.1–Facebook Campaign Structure

The ad set, which up until recently did not exist, is the Facebook split tester's friend. In order to get a good split test prior to the invention of the ad set in Facebook, you would really need to create two separate campaigns and then create individual ads in each campaign. This solution, although workable, is a far too messy and makes your Ad Manager unwieldy and extremely inefficient.

Let's say you want to split test two separate ads with two distinct images in order to determine which will convert the best. You can also do this by many other types of data such as desktop news feed versus mobile news feed or any other of the myriad different data points to ideally optimize your ad.

You can try to do it the old way by creating two ads that compete against each other for impressions. Sometimes—depending on your targeting—this does work. However, the impressions for each ad will be different in 99 percent of cases, so you need an alternative strategy.

This is why utilizing the new ad set format is so effective.

Let's say you want to test the exact same audiences and interests but simply want to figure out which ad copy and image converts best.

The new ad set will allow you to do this, especially for news feed ads.

Here's the four-step process, most easily done inside the Power Editor:

1. Create a campaign; if you have a campaign already, even better—use that.

FIGURE 16.2–Create Campaign

2. Create an ad set within that campaign, and choose your targeting.

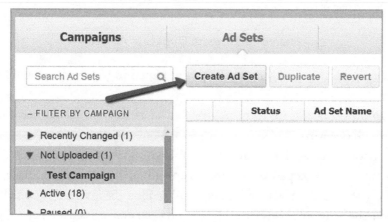

FIGURE 16.3–Create Ad Set

3. Create an ad within that ad set; this will be the "A" of your A/B split test.

FIGURE 16.4–Create Ad in Ad Set

4. Create another ad set within that same campaign. This is most easily done by using the Facebook "Duplicate" button. This button then creates a new ad with the same targeting and the same copy. You can also duplicate ad sets and ads inside the Ads Manager. (Facebook changes the location of this function very frequently so please check your Ads mManager to see where that function is.)

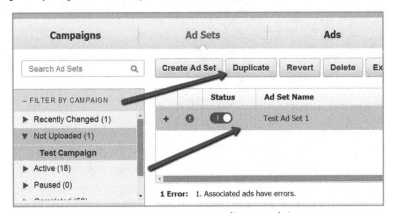

FIGURE 16.5–Create Duplicate Ad Set

Just rename this new ad set and the ad contained in it so you remember which is which.

You can now split test (so to speak) the two *ad sets* against each other with a single ad to see which one wins.

This is about as close as you can get to a formal split test in Facebook.

You now have two copies of the exact same ad. In the second ad, make one thing different from the first ad. You could change the headline, the image, the capitalization, the punctuation, the body text, or even the destination URL. Having said all that, the image you choose is the biggest factor that sways your CTR, so we suggest you change the image first.

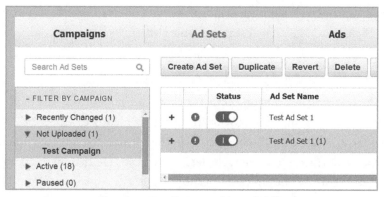

FIGURE 16.6–Rename New Ad Set

At some point Facebook may have the capability of doing proper split testing, but as of right now, Facebook does not currently support automatic, formal split testing. But using the ad set can get you around this issue, and it's far easier to manage than creating separate campaigns, which is what we would previously do before the invention of the ad set.

As there is no indicator of statistical significance within this type of A/B testing, you need to use your best judgment as to which ad is the clear winner. If your budget permits, 4,000 to 5,000 impressions and 100 clicks should at least give you a good sample size.

If after 5,000 impressions you still don't have a clear-cut winner for conversions, CTR or lowest CPC, then simply pause one of those ads and create a new split test.

As with all true, statistically significant split tests, the key is to not stop—if budget permits—before you get an ample sample size.

Here's an example of two ads we ran alongside each other in two separate ad sets. We were testing the exact same ad and the differences between desktop versus mobile for conversions. After 7,000 impressions, there was an obvious and clear-cut winner.

Oftentimes, however, the winner is not as apparent. This is when you need a tool that can determine if there is statistical significance. Brian Easley and Perry Marshall have an online split-test algorithm that tells you how confident you can be in declaring

		MDC BB Seminar LA 6.8 California I Coaching BB SA I Desktop	● Active 6 Inactive Ads	19 Conversions	$15.23 Per Conversion	11,581
		MDC BB Seminar LA 6.8 California I Coaching BB SA I Mobile	● Inactive	0 Conversions	--	7,082

FIGURE 16.7–Split Testing Desktop vs. Mobile Placement

your winner. Although this tool does not factor in conversions, it's very effective when measuring clicks and CTR. The test is available at http://splittester.com.

Measure the Most Important Conversion in Your Split Test

Provided you are using conversion pixels for your lead generation, sale of your product, or whatever other type of metrics you are using to measure success, those numbers should be your ultimate determinant as to whether or not you have a winner.

Since your advertising cost is largely determined by CTR, this metric is an important one to look at and study but not nearly as important as a conversion. Yes, CTR matters, but not merely as much as lead acquisition and conversion. And with the Power Editor giving you the ability to measure multiple conversion pixels in your advertising, you'll need to focus on which of your conversion pixels is making you the most money. Those conversion pixels can include:

- Leads
- Registrations
- Add to Cart
- Checkout
- Key Page Views
- Other Website Conversions
- And more . . .

In many cases you may have far more leads generated in one ad but you may have fewer Checkouts or Add to Cart conversion pixels that are triggered when someone

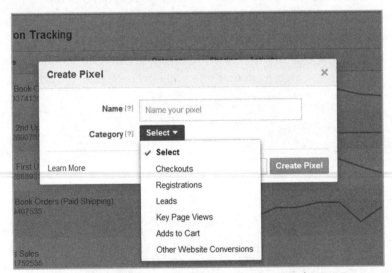

FIGURE 16.8–Create a Conversion Pixel

purchases your product or service. If you are split testing two separate ads and one is getting more leads but fewer sales, look carefully at these different conversion metrics to determine your ultimate split-test winner.

To show this you can very easily look at the Reports section to determine which part of your sales funnel is converting the best per each ad.

FIGURE 16.9–Facebook Reporting

Run your reports and check off the different conversions to show which specific ad is converting on your ultimate advertising goal. In this case, we had multiple ads split testing against each other with many creating registrations, but the ultimate goal was the conversion on their Add to Cart pixel.

To show this, you set up your reports to show both Leads and Adds To Cart.

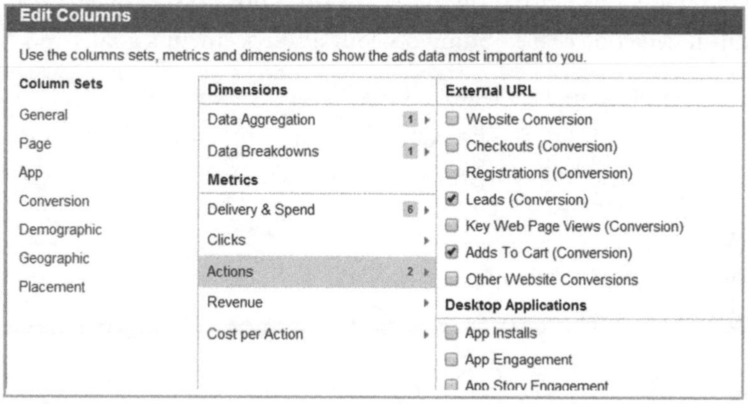

FIGURE 16.10–Choosing Your Conversion Data to Report

The report will then show your winner. In this case we ran a two-week test and, after about 30,000 impressions, declared the winner. After the winner was chosen, we gave the winning ad more advertising budget while cutting back the ad budget on the loser.

Impressions	Clicks	Registrations (Conver	Adds To Cart (Conver	Spend
34,908	481	76	53	$266.67
82,228	2,263	134	119	$547.90

FIGURE 16.11–Analyzing Your Conversion Data

Oftentimes when you run your split test, it's not a zero-sum game; you may just reconfigure your budgeting to the ad that's doing better while still giving some impressions to the ad that's not doing quite as well. It all depends on the goal of your ad campaign or—if you're managing ads for clients—the goal of the client.

What Should You Split Test?

It can get a little overwhelming to try to figure out which part of your ad you should test. Do I test my description? Should I test my image? Do I test my headline?

It can get pretty overwhelming with so many choices in Facebook . . .

When split testing news feed link post ads, it's paramount you test three factors first, listed here in order of importance:

1. *Image.* Far and away the image you choose for your newsfeed ad is the biggest factor that affects CTR and ultimately conversions.
2. *Headline(s).* The ad headline below your image as well as the first line you use in your news feed link post ad are both extremely important to test.
3. *Buttons.* Facebook started offering "button" choices in early 2014, and they have a half-dozen choices depending on your advertisement's goal.

But to be complete, make a list of all the factors you may change for your split tests, and work your way through the list, doing one at a time. In addition to the list above, you can also change the following during split tests:

- Offer
- Headline word choice
- Body text message
- Call to action
- URL
- Facebook destination page

The choices and variations are nearly endless, but if you focus on the first list and concentrate on those three factors, you'll find a winner quickly.

FIGURE 16.12–Areas Good for Testing

Important tip: Always A/B test BIG ideas and big differences before you bother with small ones! Fear vs. desire is a big idea; uppercase vs. lowercase is a little idea. Bright colors vs. dark is a big idea. Font choice is a little idea.

Multivariate Split Testing

In our split testing above, we changed only one thing at a time. When you're first starting out, this is very smart to begin with, but as you and your advertising gets more and more sophisticated, you may want to start testing multiple variables called multivariate testing.

In most cases, testing one ad against another for differences in conversions for images or headlines will suffice in getting you to your goals. But in some cases, it may be appropriate to test both at the same time using multivariate testing. In Facebook, this is much harder to do, which is why we stick primarily with A/B testing first and then move on to multivariate testing later.

For example, if you determine the clear winner in your split testing that favors one image over another, you can then start testing other factors at the same time using the same strategy as outlined above.

This can get complicated fast if you're comparing multiple ads from multiple ad sets. As soon as you start creating more ad sets inside a single campaign for the same exact audience, you may unwittingly get penalized by Facebook and start losing impressions overall. To counter that, you may need to create *separate campaigns* and not just separate ad sets.

In the last section, your goal was to determine one factor that affects your conversions. Nine times out of ten that most important factor will be the image you choose for your news feed link post ad. So when you start to multivariate test, you are in essence fine-tuning what is already working.

The issue is that by the time you finish all your tests, your ad may have run its course through your entire audience and you may be losing impressions because of ad fatigue.

Although many others advocate multivariate testing as the key to advertising success, with Facebook advertising its best to keep things simple with A/B tests, unless you are targeting very large audiences that are less prone to ad fatigue. We'll address ad fatigue shortly.

When All Else Fails, Manually Split Test

Everyone likes automation and to "set it and forget it"; I know I do. But sometimes the manual way is simply the best way.

In most cases, it's far more efficient to dig a trench with one guy in a backhoe instead of ten guys digging that same trench with hand shovels. Sometimes, however, the trench is more carefully and more precisely dug the manual way. Of course, this all depends on the skill of the backhoe operator as well as the collective skills of the trench diggers.

It's unfortunate but true that Facebook does not treat all ads on their platform equally. And if you split test ad sets against each other with a single ad in each ad set, Facebook may sabotage you by not giving you equal impressions. This doesn't always happen and depends on the audience you are targeting. When this happens, this is precisely the time when you need to go manual.

In some cases—and depending on the breadth and scope of your campaign—it may be easier just to set up multiple ads with multiple variations within one set, then manually swap them out as they start to gather more and more data.

Figure 16.13 is an example of an ad set where we did just that:

Although sidebar ads are certainly not our favorite ads, they do have their place and can oftentimes be split test automatically within a single ad set. In the case above, we had a clear-cut winner testing the same exact ad copy but with a different image.

In that ad set, there actually were four separate ads, which we manually changed every three to four days.

After about two weeks, two ads emerged as the clear winners. To finalize the test, we set the remaining two ads live within that ad set to face off against each other.

Remarkably, Facebook gave each ad similar impressions.

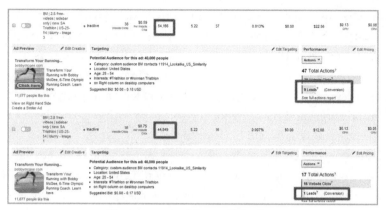

Figure 16.13–Manual Testing

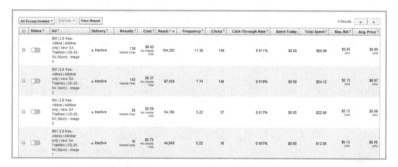

Figure 16.14–Manual Testing Sidebar

Why? Probably because they had pre-existing impressions on Facebook, which gave them the knowledge that each ad was in fact effective.

If we had started this ad set with all four ads running simultaneously, there would not have been enough impressions for each ad to determine a winner; Facebook would have given impression to one over the rest.

What we found was that by manually testing multiple ads, each ad seemingly *gained Facebook's trust* and then we could split test the best two out of the four directly against each other.

Although this does create more work for you, manual split testing works extremely well but does require manual effort initially.

How to Fight Ad Fatigue with Split Testing

As with any other advertising medium, ad fatigue occurs on Facebook as well. Ad fatigue is simply when the targets in your audience see your ad so much they tire of it. A worse scenario is called "banner blindness," when the audience fails to notice the ad at all. CTR falls and ad costs soar in these cases—not an ideal scenario for an advertiser.

Ad fatigue is not much of a problem in Google AdWords, for example, where your audience is usually a "passing parade." Ad fatigue is worse on Facebook. Generally, in Facebook you're always in the business of coming up with something new, not so much to test as to keep things fresh and interesting for your audience.

You'll have less trouble with ad fatigue when you have a very large targeted audience. The more impressions and more frequency you have with a particular ad to a specific audience, the more ad fatigue will likely occur.

Ad fatigue was a huge issue when Facebook only had sidebar ads largely because those ads were constantly shown as you scanned your news feed. Ad fatigue for newsfeed ads is far less of an issue than for those running in the sidebar, but it is something you want to be aware of.

In cases where your audience is very small and you have a healthy daily budget, ads will become less effective on your audience more quickly. Here's an example of an ad with a very small audience, which is probably nearing the end of its useful life, before it needs to be swapped with another:

FIGURE 16.15–Small Target Audience

To calculate ad fatigue, it's a simple formula:

$$\text{Potential Audience Size / Reach} \times \text{Frequency} = \text{CTR Decline} = \text{Ad Fatigue Factor (AFF)}$$

In the ad shown in Figure 16.15, we have an audience size of 320 with a reach of 211 and the frequency of 1.74.

This means that 211 people saw our ad on average 1.74 times. Since our audience is 320 total, only about 109 people have not seen this ad as of yet.

Fortunately, the ad has been running a short period of time and the audience has not grown weary of it yet. How do we know? Because the ad has a relatively high CTR of 5.707 percent, which on Facebook is very healthy, indeed.

That CTR will decline over time; probably within the next week it will be half if not one-quarter of that 5.707 percent. At that point, we will then switch the ad manually as just described.

Manual swapping and split testing is a common solution to the ad fatigue problem. The only difference with this audience targeting is that it is a website custom audience that is growing each day. Since the audience is growing each day, we may actually "outrun" the usefulness of this particular ad.

Regardless, ad fatigue will play a major role in this small campaign at some point, which is why we have eight other ads in that campaign we can choose from when the ad gets tired.

In some other cases, you may have a very large audience size and ad fatigue may be less of an issue. Regardless, you do need to switch out your ads on a regular basis to prevent this from occurring.

In the ad set below, our clicks to this ad have steadily decreased over the entire time it's been live—at this point, nearly four weeks. The reason the ad continues to perform well is because of the large audience size and the AFF mathematical formula outlined above. The frequency is only at 1.33, but this is a newsfeed only ad so Facebook will typically never let the frequency get much higher than 1.5 or so.

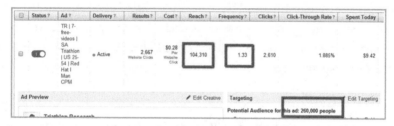

FIGURE 16.16–Newsfeed Ad Fatigue

As you can see, there's an audience of 260,000 with 104,310 having seen the ad 1.33 times. The clicks are on the decline over the past four weeks, but still the ad performs well, having accrued 2,667 website clicks in that time.

Using AFF, we know we have more than half of our audience yet to see the ad, before it truly runs out of steam, at which point in time, the CTR will drop off considerably. Regardless, the ad's CTR has remained very consistent, as shown in Figure 16.17 on page 250. You can look for "CTR Trend" in the lower-right-hand side in the Ads Manager, directly under your individual ad.

The bottom line is this: Ad fatigue occurs regularly in Facebook, less so in the newsfeed. You should still switch your ads as much as possible but balance this with your overall objective. For direct-response marketers, this is lead generation and purchases of services or products. If you see these drop off, you are likely suffering from ad fatigue and need new ads to inject new life into your campaigns.

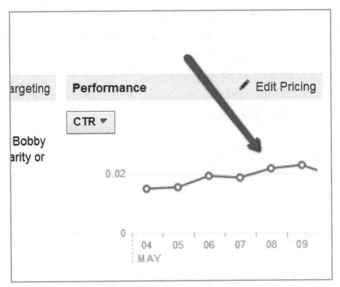

Figure 16.17–Monitoring Click-Through Rate Trend

However, never change out an ad because you're *fearful* of ad fatigue. Do it only if you see your conversions dropping or your CTR declining and your ad costs increasing. If your CTR starts going south, your conversions will likely do the same, so it's something that you need to keep an eye on.

> **Go to www.perrymarshall.com/fbtools for the latest updates & to get valuable resources for more clicks from Facebook for less money.**

Chapter 17

Nobody Ever Regretted Mastering this $10,000-Per-Hour Skill

YOUR $10,000-AN-HOUR JOB

How would you like a job that paid up to $10,000 an hour? The good news is, you may already have that job. The bad news is, to have an hour's worth of effort return $10,000, you have to write absolutely killer ad and sales copy. In the ad business, this is called copywriting, and great copywriting can make or break a business.

"If you don't like what's being said, change the conversation."

—Don Draper

Give me a so-so product with the world's best copywriter, and I will sell millions of dollars' worth of the product. Give me a great product and a bad copywriter, and the company may go bankrupt. This is not fair, but it is true. There is a reason top copywriters are among the best-paid professionals on the planet.

In advertising, copywriting is king. And if you can write an ad that gets the world to stop and take notice, you are worth your weight in gold. If you write a landing page that leads to a sale, then you have created an online money machine.

This is not necessarily easy. Getting John Q. Public to pry open his wallet and give you his credit card is challenging. It may well be the most difficult task you have ever undertaken, especially if the transaction is online. Your customer is at home, sitting at his computer, bored, and probably lazy, and getting him to do anything is a chore. Getting him to pay you is a miracle.

By the time a Facebook user gets to your message, she has already been exposed to as many as 3,000 advertising messages that day! Advertising from radio, TV, newspapers, billboards, placards, store signs, and websites have all tried to catch her attention.

Logos on T-shirts, cups, and boxes; sexual images, sensual images, happy images, funny images, and cute images have already been used to try to attract your prospects' attention. Each one of them has been assaulted by direct mail, telemarketers, network marketers, nonprofits, and more—3,000 have already been fended off.

There is a reason corporations spend more than half a trillion dollars (trillion with a "T") annually trying to make their products seem attractive, interesting, and worthy of buying. This is the fray you choose to enter when you run an ad: to get John Q.'s attention in a world saturated with advertising.

There is a reason that good copywriting is the hardest skill to hire out. There is so much work in copywriting that some people make a living writing ads without ever really getting very good at it. And those who do get really good at it will eventually figure out they can make the most money selling something of their own. Some retire. And if they work, it is as much for the challenge as for the money.

In addition, copywriting, for those who are truly masters at it, is not always that much fun to do for other people. Even when the world's best copywriter writes the world's best ad, more than likely the client will want to change it. The world's best copywriters get tired of defending their ideas to people who do not, and cannot, recognize great copy. So, if they have already bagged their cash, they give up and go home. Too painful to try to consult.

This puts the typical entrepreneur in a bit of a pickle. You find you have to acquire another skill. You need to learn how to write your own ad copy. You need to learn how to write it, test it, and measure it.

Because copywriting is so essential, even if you choose to contract this work out, you still need to know how to objectively evaluate the results, at least. It is OK, even recommended, that you write *bad* ads at first. The key is, how fast can you recognize the ad is bad and replace it with one that works? I actually recommend that you write bad ads because if some of your ads are not bad, it means you are not trying enough different approaches.

Another reason you should at least try to write your own copy is because nobody else will ever be as insightful, passionate, or interested in all the fine nuances of the business as you, the entrepreneur. Your passion and insight leads to great copy.

Your job is tricky. It is to get Jane Q. Public so interested and engaged in your message that she ignores the 3,000 other messages coming at her this day. Instead, she focuses on yours. She gets so excited, engaged, and interested that she can't think about anything else. She has to have what you sell. She has to have it now!

DIFFERENT GOALS AT DIFFERENT TIMES

Different copy has different goals at different times. Do you know the goal of writing a resume? The goal of writing a resume is to get the interview. That is it. In most cases, the resume doesn't get you the job, the interview does. However, to get the interview you need the resume.

If you forget the goal, you make serious errors in writing the resume, like making it too long.

Your Facebook ad is like the resume. It is not trying to close the deal; it is just trying to get the click. What can you say in your ad to get the click?

CAPTAIN HOOK

Your ad may have all of a quarter or a half of a second to try to capture your prospect's attention—to hook the user. A half of a second is how long it takes for your prospect to see your image and read your headline.

Facebook describes your ad as a *headline* and *body text*. This is likely how the ad is read. If the image is interesting, they read the headline. If the headline speaks to them, they read the body text—all of this process is incredibly quick.

Your entire ad itself is also a headline. It is a headline to the experience readers will receive if they click! Your ad is a headline that makes a promise to the user. When they click on the ad, they get to experience the story told on your landing page.

Your ad needs to be so compelling that it draws those who read it to continue to experience your story on your landing page. If they don't click, they feel bad. They regret not clicking later. That is a true hook.

INSANELY GOOD TITLES

Insanely good titles have one thing in common—they all trigger emotions.

If the image is the lure drawing wandering eyes over to your ad, then your title is the hook. Give it a slight jerk and try to catch your prospects' thoughts. Connect a word or phrase in your title to the emotional trigger in your readers. Something they love or hate. Something of deep interest or importance to them. The easiest way to do this is to have the title contain the psychographic target word. If that word is the name of someone famous they admire, it is really very easy.

Targeting members of the Jaycees service organization? *Jaycees* is probably a good word for the title.

Targeting Saint Bernard lovers? *Saint Bernard* is a good candidate too.

Targeting fans of Van Halen? Hard to go wrong with *Van Halen* somewhere in the title. In fact, for something with such strong affinity, it is hard to beat "O U Love Van Halen 2?" To riff off of their most famous album, OU812, you could even replace "Love" with a heart symbol.

You get the idea. It is actually amazingly simple to create a great headline in Facebook once you know the psychographic target.

When I (Tom) target homeschooling parents, the vast majority of my best-performing ads have the word *homeschoo*l in one form or another in the title. Why? Because it is a trigger word for that psychographic. The ad in Figure 17.1 performed amazingly well for months with a silly picture, a three-word headline for ADHD parents, and body text that made an interesting promise.

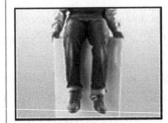

FIGURE 17.1–Psychographic Trigger in the Headline

COMPELLING BODY TEXT WITH A CALL TO ACTION

Make an offer in your ad that you deliver on your landing page. If you claim "Scientific research ends tooth decay," then make a call to action (read it now) and offer immediate access to a white paper, audio, or video on your landing page. A call to action is always best when it is explicitly stated.

Include the image from the ad on the landing page, and conversion rates will improve even more! The repeated image offers greater comfort and consistency to visitors and lets them know they are in the right spot to continue the story.

The body text in the ad is the start of the story you continue on your landing page. Make it as interesting of a story as possible. Make a compelling offer—click to save 50 percent!

The massage seen in Figure 17.2 triggers pleasant memories in anyone who has ever enjoyed a massage. The headline implies a great present to give or receive. The body text begins the story, "A soothing massage can relax you like a summer vacation." It has a very clear call to action—click to save 50 percent on your next massage!

FIGURE 17.2–A Very Clear Call to Action

The body text makes a compelling offer with a call to action. The offer is why the user clicks. The call to action encourages "click."

If you are an auto mechanic, offer a coupon for a "Free Brake Inspection." Deliver the coupon on your landing page or immediately after a user clicks "like."

Immediately delivering on the offer builds credibility and begins the front porch relationship. No matter what you are selling, always find a way to make an attractive offer in the body text of your ad.

If You Are Selling	You May Offer
Cupcakes	A Free Cupcake
Training	A Free Lecture
Dental Services	A Free Teeth Whitening
Tires	A Free Tire Inspection
Restaurant Experience	A Free Birthday Meal
Marketing Services	Free Tips Video
Printer's Ink	A List of Seven Ways to Save Money on Printing
Software Development	A Free Guide on How to Stop Projects from Failing

Do you see a pattern here? Marketing on the front porch is about giving things away. Lemonade, snickerdoodles, or free advice. If you are a dentist trying to find a lifetime customer, you may want to give away something bigger.

The *free* word is a powerful word.

We frequently give away free information such as a "Free Guide" or "7 Secrets to" where you can fill in the blank based on your business. People like lists, people like secrets, and people like free.

POWER WORDS TO TRIGGER EMOTIONAL RESPONSE

Set your hook with powerful words. If you search for "words that sell," you will get hits on all sorts of different power words used in advertising. Take a look at these lists. Get your mind flowing with words that have the power to trigger emotional responses.

See what emotional response you have to the words. "Amazing" makes me want to smile. "Lifetime" make me feel more secure. How do these words affect you?

Words do not have to be positive to trigger emotional response and interest. "Defeat" is a powerful word that may be negative or positive depending on the phrase.

There is a reason you see certain words over and over again in ads—they work. *Sale* captures almost everybody's attention. A compelling ad appeals to the prospect's emotions, needs, desires, and dreams. A single word in your headline can dramatically improve your ad's effectiveness if it captures your prospect's attention, and excites, motivates, and compels the user to click.

Here are some words to get your juices flowing when writing headlines and copy. These are words that advertisers have had luck with in the past. Slowly read through the list. Say each word out loud. What—if any—emotions does each word trigger in you?

A—Absolutely, Achieve, Act, Amazing, Anybody, Astonishing, Automatically

B—Bargain, Believe, Benefit, Best, Bewitched, Big, Bigger, Biggest, Bonus

C—Creative, Clouds, Colorful, Colossal, Competitive, Confidential, Conquer

D—Dream, Defeat, Delivered, Demand, Desire, Direct, Discount, Dominate

E—Easy, Easily, Endorsed, Enchanted, Enormous, Excellent, Exciting, Expert, Explained

F—Famous, Forbidden, Forever, Fortune, Free, Full, Fundamentals

G—Guarantee, Guaranteed

H—Health, Healthy, Heart, Helpful, Hidden, Highest, How (How to), Huge

I—Immediate, Immediately, Improved, Informative, Inspire, Interesting

J—Join

K—King

L—Launching, Lifetime, Like, Limited, Love, Luxury

M—Magic, Mammoth, Money

N—New

O—Obsession, Outstanding

P—Passionate, Perspective, Pioneering, Popular, Powerful, Practical, Professional, Profitable, Proven

Q—Quick, Quickly

R—Rare, Reliable, Revealing, Remarkable, Revolution, Revolutionary, Reward

S—Safe, Safely, Sale, Save, Scarce, Secret, Secrets, Secure, Sensational, Simple, Sizable, Skilled, Special (Special Offer), Strong, Sturdy, Successful, Suddenly, Super, Superior, Surging, Surprise

T—Tasty, Temptation, Terrific, Tested, Tremendous, True

U—Ultimate, Unconditional, Unique, Unlimited, Unparalleled, Urgent, Useful

V—Valuable, Virgin

W—Wealth, Weird, Wild, Wonderful

Y—Yes, You, Your

As you work in your business, make your own list of words your audience is specifically attracted to. Keep both lists handy when writing new ads. If you are blocked, just pick a word from each list and see what happens when you put the words together. You are seeking to create powerful word combinations to trigger an emotional response.

How many power words can you spot in the ad in Figure 17.3?

FIGURE 17.3–How Many Power Words Can You Spot in This Ad?

A need is stated clearly in the headline. An attractive woman looks up toward the headline statement with a bit of whimsy and contemplation. The body text makes a simple promise with power words sprinkled liberally throughout the text.

Here is a quick test. So what is missing in the ad in Figure 17.3? Did you say a clear call to action?

It is implied in the text but could be made stronger. Test different calls to action with your ads to see what converts best. *Click now. Free guide. Click for free guide. Click for free video. Click for list. Like.* Test them all. See if one outperforms the others.

PLAIN, CONQUERING, ENDEARING, HEROIC, SARCASTIC, HYPED, COMPASSIONATE, AND SENSUAL COPY

Men often do not discover until they are married that their voice has a tone. They need their wife to tell them—and she does. Everyone has a tone, and in ad copy you should actively choose to create a tone. Name your tones in terms like *romantic, sensual, endearing, conquering, heroic, hyped, compassionate, sensual,* and *friendship* to help give them meaning and identity when you write.

When writing ad copy, select a tone you believe may be appropriate for your targeted demographic. Write an ad in that tone and write an ad in an opposite tone. See which ones your users like better. Or put multiple tones into rotation since a different tone may appeal to the same person on a different day.

Certain words lend themselves to different tones:

- Sensual: love, kiss, caress, magic, moon, heart, secret, forbidden, virgin, lover, lure, forever
- Conquering: destroy, decimate, achieve, conquer, smash, crush, extract, overthrow, beat, skunk
- Endearing: cute, puppy, kitten, adorable, pretty, sweet, poignant, affection

Other tones require more than one word to pull off:

- Hyped: world's lowest prices; make money now; crazy discounts; limited time offer
- Compassionate: I feel your pain; find relief

Here are some examples of writing a headline using different tones.

- Boring: Lose 10 Pounds
- Conquering: Destroy Fat Forever
- Sensual: Love Your Body Again

SELL A BENEFIT, NOT A PRODUCT

Write a headline that features your benefit, not your product. Feature what you plan to deliver to your customers to make their lives better and more exciting. If possible, be specific. "Flatten your belly" is a good headline. "Lose 10 Pounds in 5 Days" is a better headline. It tells the prospects exactly what you can do for them. If you could follow "Lose 10 Pounds in 5 Days" with the phrase "without ever being hungry," now you would really have people's attention.

Benefit-delivering headlines:

- Magical 6 Percent Monthly Return
- Grow CTR 29 Percent in 5 Minutes
- Sleep Like a Little Baby
- Land a $100,000 Dream Job

These headlines are not selling a system or a product; they are selling a dream. If you are selling a dream like a "Magical 6 Percent Monthly Return," you can even feature the benefit of the benefit. What do you get if you make all that money?

- Retire Early with Millions
- Travel the World with No Worries
- Create a Financial Legacy

COMMIT TO STUDYING COPYWRITING

If you want your business to be a success, commit a few hours every month to studying copywriting. We can only scratch the surface of the subject of copywriting in a book on paid Facebook advertising. This topic can and does fill volumes. Some of the best copy on copywriting is actually quite old and can even be found for free online.

- *The Robert Collier Letter Book* by Robert Collier
- *Advertising Secrets of the Written Word* by Joe Sugarman
- *On Writing* by Stephen King
- *Scientific Advertising* by Claude Hopkins

SUCCESSFUL ADS MAY FAIL

Successful ads do fail the CTR test. That sounds a bit strange, but it's true. There are multiple measures of success. The one reported by Facebook is CTR, clickthrough rate. Unfortunately, CTR is a very poor measure of true success. To succeed, you need people to do a lot more than click. You need them to purchase. An ad that gets me a lot of clicks but no sales is a failure. It is that simple.

One of the hardest things to learn how to do is to turn off an ad that is driving you a lot of clicks. You turn it off because it isn't giving you any sales.

Always remember your ad is just the first step of a more complex "ecosystem." A good ad compliments the landing page and leads the prospect to an eventual sale. If no one ever buys from the ad, then something is broken.

Your landing page is the story behind your ad. It is a mistake to create your ad without first building your landing page, because the ad is the headline to the compelling offer you deliver on your landing page.

The ad provides:

- An image
- A headline
- A compelling offer

The landing page provides

- A short description of what you provide (bullets are a good idea here if using text);
- An explanation of how you get it;
- A promise not to violate your trust (privacy policy, no spam);
- The opt-in form itself.

The Power of Hidden Psychological Triggers

WRITE IN THOUGHTS

Deciding to write ads puts you into a unique and new category—a thought writer. Your writing puts thoughts in other people's heads. You change what they think, what they believe, and what they do. If you do it correctly, they don't even notice that your thoughts have become their thoughts. They don't even notice as they bend to your will.

Do it well, and you join Don Draper and the other *Mad Men*—influencing for better or for worse the hearts and minds of the people of the world.

> "*A*dvertising is not a science, it is persuasion, and persuasion is an art, it is intuition that leads to discovery, to inspiration, it is the artist who is capable of making the consumer feel desire."
>
> —BILL BERNBACH

If you choose to take on this new role in *The Matrix*, you are choosing to take the red pill. Your eyes are about to be opened. You can no longer be blissfully unaware of the nature of the advertising around you. You can no longer be a passive consumer of advertising. You must now become its master.

Have you ever heard people say "Advertising doesn't affect me" as they drink a Coke and chomp on a Big Mac, their feet clad in Nikes?

Neo, if you take the blue pill, you wake up in your bed and believe whatever you want to believe. Go ahead, dear consumer, keep thinking that advertising doesn't affect you.

You can no longer afford to be so naive. Take off the blinders, open your eyes, and learn to take a deep look at the world of advertising.

Begin to look at the messages around you. Ask yourself: Where do they come from? Why are they placed here? How are they measured? Are they effective?

You are now asking yourself these questions. You are a marketing maniac.

Specifically examine direct-response advertising where the customer has to complete an action "now" for the ad to be effective. Watch to see if those same ads continue to run over time. If they do, there is a good chance they are actually working. Time to understand why, so you can do it, too.

DIRECT ATTACK ADS

Type "weight loss" into a search engine and instantly see ads for weight loss products. In fact, you only see ads for weight loss products. Same with arthritis; type "arthritis" into a search, and you see ads for pain medications and clinics.

When you do an internet search, you type in your immediate need and interest. You are looking for it "right now." Ads that speak directly to what you are searching for "right now" are direct attack ads. There is very little nuance to this. Search advertising comes at you head-on and at full speed. None of the ads catch you by surprise.

RIGHT-ANGLE MARKETING

But here is a secret the masters of marketing understand. Ads do not have to come at you head-on. They can also approach from the side—from a right angle to your direct line of vision.

Visible only out of the corner of your eye.

Right-angle marketing, originally a concept for masters of search and print advertising, is especially powerful on Facebook. Right-angle marketing is advertising a product or service based not on users' immediate needs but on **who** they are, **where** they hang out, and **what** they believe, *regardless of what they happen to be doing right this minute.* What makes the sale a right angle? Selling a product that is not "obvious" to sell to your target customers.

For example, a group of people love the tiny dog breed Shih Tzu. Advertising veterinary services to someone who likes Shih Tzus is direct attack marketing. A good direct attack at a Shih Tzu lover for a veterinarian in Facebook is an ad that says you "specialize" in the needs of this specific breed. Great ad. But not a right angle.

So, what might be a right-angle ad to a Shih Tzu owner? That is the problem. You don't know. It isn't obvious.

It may be the case that Shih Tzu owners are five times more likely to purchase a Caribbean cruise than the average American. This would be a right angle. If it were true, you would run Caribbean cruise ads to people who own Shih Tzus—but how would you ever know that?

Maybe Shih Tzu owners are often Jewish women in New York City. If that's true, how would you figure that out?

Most people treat Facebook as another method of search advertising. They only come at their prospects head-on. Facebook demands a bit more finesse. Facebook requires more right-angle marketing. A hidden power in Facebook is that it can help you discover these right angles.

Facebook will help you discover ways to connect to your prospects that you never imagined. Discovering ways to increase CTR and conversions that are only obvious in hindsight.

Does this really happen? All the time.

 ## CONNECTING PEOPLE TO MARITAL BLISS

Before the internet took off, people mainly dated and married people who lived in the same town. Only a few pioneers embraced the idea of dating and marrying strangers. Only a few hearty souls were relationship pioneers. One was my friend, whom I'll call Bob. Bob ran a mail-order bride service for Christian, single men. He helped connect Christian, American men to Christian, Filipino women.

Bob ran advertisements, did lead generation, and sent letters to guys talking about how it was hard to find a woman who shared their values. "Wouldn't it be nice to find a woman with character who wasn't just after your money and wouldn't leave you when the going got tough? Are you sick and tired of our decadent society where people are so disloyal and divorce is so common?" This message resonated with his audience.

Bob advertised in all of the easy-to-spot locations. Specifically, in magazines read by Christian men. The business was a success. Connections were made, and marriages resulted. Bob, of course, wanted to figure out how to grow the business even more.

We were in a group with Dan Kennedy, and Dan asked the right-angle question, "Are there any idiosyncrasies that your customers have in common? Where they

CONNECTING PEOPLE TO MARITAL BLISS, continued

hang out? Hobbies? The type of work they do? Something other than just being Christian men?"

Bob said "Well, I don't know." Dan said, "Why don't you find out?" So he did.

When we got together again Bob had discovered something significant. Over half of his customers had the same job: 50 percent of them were *truckers*!

Bob had never noticed this before. In hindsight it made sense. Driving over the road is a hard and lonely job. Lots of time away from home, making it hard on existing relationships and even harder to start new ones. Truck drivers, as an occupation, needed relationship help. The need was so acute that these men were willing to try brides from overseas.

Advertising to truckers was a right-angle approach to reach potential customers. A right angle totally changes your approach to a market.

Bob could now put ads in trucking magazines and fliers and signs at truck stops.

Bob could write new ads in the language of trucking, making his prospects feel immediately at home. His business skyrocketed.

Most customer bases have something in common that is not initially obvious, just like Bob's. Once you learn this new connection, a whole set of new opportunities emerges. Not only can you place new ads in new locations, but you can write ad copy to appeal to the specific psychographic. You, just like Bob, can leverage right-angle knowledge everywhere in your business.

RIGHT-ANGLE IMMERSION ASSIGNMENT

Today I (Tom) am going to give you a right-angle advertising immersion assignment. Make a trip to your local library, newsstand, or bookstore where you find many different magazines. There are thousands of magazines available on specialty interests—knitting, horses, history, cars, guns, cooking, and more—and a selection of the more popular ones should be easy to get your hands on.

Grab a stack of these magazines and head to a location where you can sit down and study them.

Take a magazine like *American Civil War History* and flip through it a page at a time. Look at each advertisement in the magazine. Ask yourself one question: Is this advertisement *obvious* or a *surprise*?

An obvious advertisement in an American Civil War history magazine is an ad for Abraham Lincoln DVDs, because the ad is "on topic." If the ad comes straight on at the interest being represented by the magazine, it is obvious. In our Civil War history magazine, obvious advertisements would include:

- Civil War re-enactor gear
- Civil War history books and videos
- Any history books and videos
- Tours of Gettysburg

It does not take marketing insight or genius to target selling Civil War costumes to people who buy an American Civil War history magazine. This is obvious.

So what is a surprise? A surprise is: "Why are they advertising a *manure vacuum* in *Civil War History*?"

Now that you know a manure vacuum exists, would you be surprised to see it advertised in a horse racing magazine?

When you review *Civil War History*, you might be surprised to see ads for watches and men's jewelry.

It was a surprise. I would not have guessed in advance that a direct-marketing ad for a watch or a pendant was a good fit for *Civil War History* magazine. The watches were tied into the theme as historic "re-creations," but the jewelry was, well, jewelry.

This is right-angle marketing.

The jewelry advertiser discovered the demographics and psychographics of *Civil War Magazine* readers made them more inclined than the average man to purchase jewelry. Jewelry has a permanence appreciated by people who study history.

BUT I SELL CHECKS, MUGS, PENS, AND T-SHIRTS

If you sell commodity items, you can still market at right angles. In fact, it is probably easier to market at right angles. While reviewing a magazine on dogs I was surprised to find an ad for checks. Printed checks, with pictures of dogs. A commodity item in a dog magazine targeted, of course, to dog owners.

If you sell commodities, one solution is to target a niche. A niche that is technically at a right angle to your commodity but easily accessible. It is hard to get people to switch from their normal check-printing service to your discount check-printing service. Even if you save them money, it is probably not enough money for anyone to care about.

But imagine if you find somebody who totally loves their Saint Bernard and you offer them beautifully printed checks featuring world famous prints of Saint Bernards. Now you have targeted their love. You have connected emotionally. Tell a good-enough story, and they will purchase your checks, even if it costs them more.

Don't focus on the low price, look for right angles. There's a million of 'em!

Right angles can be inexpensive to target on Facebook. It costs a lot to put a full-color check-printing ad in a dog magazine. You can add free tabs to your Facebook page and test ads selling to Saint Bernard owners, and 20 other specific breeds, all for $400.

SEARCHING FOR RIGHT ANGLES

 Not all right-angle opportunities show up automatically in your Facebook reports. In fact, if you are selling a commodity item, you will have to do the homework yourself to find right-angle or niche opportunities.

Search on "magazine categories" and look at all of the various categories of published magazines. One website sells more than 1,500 magazines across 75 categories. Magazines are a great overview of people's likes and interests. Think about what it means for a magazine to be written, published, and delivered to your local newsstand. There must be enough interest in these categories to support an entire publishing industry. Here is just a tiny sample of magazines in the "A" category.

- Animals and Pets
  - Birds
  - Cats
  - Dogs
  - Fish and aquariums
  - Horses
- Art and Antiques
  - Antiques
  - Art
  - Dance
  - Painting
- Auto
  - Auto news
  - Auto repair
  - Classic cars
  - Hot rods

- Motocross
- Motorcycles
- Off-road vehicles
- Trailers and motor homes
- Trucks

Remember: Your product doesn't have to automatically intersect with these likes and interests to target them. You can craft a message to relate any like or interest back to your core product.

What is more interesting to discover is whether your customers already disproportionately relate to one of these topics, like "hot rods." If they do, you can emotionally appeal to and target them based on a "seemingly unrelated" interest.

I (Perry) was surprised to find checks advertised in a dog magazine. But after getting over that initial surprise, I would not be surprised to find them advertised in a cat, horse, fish, or bird magazine too. Why? Because I now see the natural connection between the product and enthusiasts wanting customized checks. They use checks to emotionally connect to a pet or companion.

I found a couple of Alaskan cruise ads in an arthritis magazine. What do Alaskan cruises have to do with arthritis? Nothing—except that many older people are highly interested in both curing arthritis and going on cruises. Right-angle marketing.

Here's another example: If you pick up a magazine like *Black Belt,* in the back you will frequently find ads for business opportunities, real estate, etc.

What does martial arts have to do with real estate investing? Obviously there is no direct connection. But martial arts enthusiasts are ambitious and competitive. They also relate to authority in a certain kind of way. So an ad for a real estate investment course that talks to them in alpha male language stands an excellent chance of doing well.

At my Maui Elite Master's Summit, a $5,000-per-person marketing seminar, I asked for a show of hands: "How many people in this room are brown belt or above in martial arts?" Out of 100 people, 8 raised their hands; 8 percent of my high-end customers are accomplished in karate, tae kwon do, or some other similar sport.

That's probably five times the percentage of accomplished martial artists in the general population. Right-angle marketing once again. My best are highly competitive, achievement-oriented people.

THE RIGHT-ANGLE SEARCH IN FACEBOOK

Use Facebook's Graph search (as described in Chapter 7 on page 87) to find right angles. You can get really creative when searching for right angles. (See Figure 18.1 on page 268.)

FIGURE 18.1–Right-Angle Searching

Keys, Not Keywords

Do not think of the likes and interests listed in the responder profile report as keywords. If you think of them as keywords, then you miss the real opportunity. They are not keywords to improve a search. They are keys to unlocking your prospect's mind.

The real opportunity in the likes and interests common to your prospects is improving how you target and talk to those prospects. It is to incorporate the most common likes and interests of people who click on your ads directly into your ads, your landing pages, and your follow-up copy.

The more you know about your prospects, the more you can speak to them in words they understand. You can reference books they like to read, TV shows they like to watch, movies they love, and celebrities they like to follow. If you are having front porch conversations, is it better to talk about Dan Brown's *The Da Vinci Code* or Aldous Huxley's *Brave New World*?

It will make a difference.

The more you reflect and connect to your prospects' personal interests, the more comfortable they feel standing on your front porch. They respond more frequently to your status messages, they read your copy with more passion, and they purchase your products with more confidence. Why? Because you connected with them.

ONE RIGHT-ANGLE SENTENCE GROWS THE CONVERSION RATE 11 PERCENT

You get the idea that "likes and interest" may uncover a key concept you hadn't thought of, such as, "I should advertise directly to truckers." But you are not convinced that mentioning the right novel on a landing page will improve conversion. You are pragmatic. "Does this stuff really make a difference?" you ask.

Bryan Todd was driving traffic to the website CosmicFingerPrints.com. This site discusses the intersection between science, astronomy, and religion. Bryan was running ads on Facebook driving traffic to the page and seeking an opt-in to "Learn the Secrets of the Universe."

After a while, Bryan ran a responder profile report and noticed that his responders had an interest in science fiction, history, and really liked the books *Brave New World* and *1984*. So, he split tested two landing pages that were identical, except one page inserted the following two lines:

> This ultimate question touches the distant past, and—with the forewarnings in Orwell's 1984 and Huxley's *Brave New World*—it touches the distant future as well.

Bryan recognized that people who like science fiction think about the distant future and the distant past, and he already knew specifically that his prospects liked these two books.

In hindsight, like most right-angle marketing connections, they all go together. If you're inclined to click on an ad that says, "Where Did the Universe Come From? Did It Come from God?" you probably do all of these things. Bryan added the sentence to the page.

It's hard to anticipate the effect on your landing page, but we know it has some value.

The conversion rate for the page increased 24 percent immediately with the addition of the two lines. Over time, that conversation improvement settled down to a steady 11 percent.

ONE RIGHT-ANGLE SENTENCE GROWS THE CONVERSION RATE 11 PERCENT, continued

Do you want an 11 percent improvement in your landing page? Relate better to your readers.

Reach inside their heads and reflect their secret thoughts back to them.

It really is a Brave New World.

If you find someone who loves the same books you love, doesn't that person become more interesting to you?

Of course. It works for you, and it works for your prospects.

Of course, unearthing this level of detailed information about your customers is nothing special. It's not like you couldn't do this before. You would build a survey, hire the Gallup organization, and call two or three thousand customers on the phone and see what they told you.

You'd ask them about their education, family, and job. Ask them their hobbies and interests. Ask them what they are watching, reading, doing in their spare time. And who they hang out with.

You'd ask them what organizations they belong to and what they believe. You'd ask them hundreds of prying questions and hunt for patterns. Not hard at all. Perhaps now you see why Facebook is so special. Advertise on Facebook—and collect this information automatically, for no extra charge.

RESPONDER PROFILE REPORT DEFEATS AD FATIGUE

Facebook keeps the specific users anonymous in the responder profile report. You receive data in this aggregate form even from people who have protected their profile. This is great for you and the users. You get data from everyone, and the users keep their privacy.

The privacy, however, comes at a price. You must have a large enough group of people clicking on your ad in a relatively short period of time for Facebook to generate this report for you. If you are not getting enough clicks for this report to be generated, increase your ad spend for a two-week period, and if your total clicks are high enough, you will obtain the report.

Save a copy of the report immediately. This report goes away and cannot be regenerated from past data.

Did your ad fatigue? Look at your responder profile report, and test a new right angle.

A successful ad is something to celebrate—it cannot run forever. If everyone in your target has seen your ad 20 to 30 times and you received a great CTR, then give yourself an advertising award. The ad was great. Ad fatigue is a signal to try a new right angle. It is the clue to change the subject in your front porch conversation.

Facebook says its most successful advertisers change their ads about every 12 days. Here is an amazing secret. You can also change them back.

If an ad fatigues after 12 days, it will probably come to life again in another 90 to 120 days—sometimes even faster. As you create more successful ads, finding more right angles, put them into new campaigns. Eventually, you have more campaigns to put into rotation. Ad fatigue will have helped you test and build hundreds of tiny conversations. Keep the ones that work and use them over and over again. You will be so intimately connected to your target audience that you will have customers for life.

This responder profile report is your new best friend, making ad fatigue an adventure, not a chore.

Chapter 19

Free Traffic and Free Impressions vs. Paid Advertising

FREE CLICKS CAN BE DEADLY

 Bill McClure, founder of www.Coffee.org, is a serial online entrepreneur, going all the way back to eFlowers.com and FlowersDirect.com, which he sold in 2002. He also did a stint as a member of my elite roundtable group.

When Bill investigated the coffee market, he considered several existing websites that were available for sale.

One of them was doing $3 million per year in sales with a tiny staff and strong profitability. On paper, it was a superb business.

Only two problems.

> "*The small businessman is smart; he realizes there's no free lunch. On the other hand, he knows where to go to get a good inexpensive sandwich.*"
>
> —Adam Osborne

1. Almost all the traffic was from free, organic "search engine optimization" (SEO) traffic. The left side of the search results. Now that *sounds* really great. Free search traffic? Great SEO? What's not to like about that? The problem with it is this: What happens when the free traffic goes away? Notice that I said "when" it goes away, not "if" it goes away. It's an eventuality that there will be some Google dance,

and one sad morning, the guy will be showing up on page 6 of Google search results instead of page 1. The traffic dries up, and suddenly a $3 million business becomes a $300,000 business.

2. There was no benchmark of being able to buy traffic *at will* (i.e., with paid advertising) and convert that traffic to sales profitably. Which is to say: That business, even though on paper was worth several million dollars, was not even a real business. It was built on the availability of free customers, which is a foundation of sand. Temporary success at best.

As a matter of fact, the business owner was afraid to even touch the website, which was clearly out of date, because he was afraid changing something might ruin his great SEO rankings.

Instead of that business, Bill bought the domain Coffee.org, and has built it into a traffic-conversion machine and an established brand, Miss Ellie's coffee—a southern twist on America's favorite morning beverage.

Facebook has been a major part of Bill's strategy for Coffee.org and their fan page is a study in effective social media, at https://www.facebook.com/CoffeeDotOrg.

If your business is dependent on free customers, you do not have a business. You do not have any kind of "real" business until you have the ability to buy advertising from a variety of available sources and transform that traffic into sales and profits.

The kicker is, once you have solved the conversion puzzle, ALL forms of qualified traffic convert. You dominate your market in multiple dimensions, and you become nearly impossible to displace by other competitors. You are feared in your market. A force to reckon with.

Bill is feared in several markets, not just coffee. Once you've mastered this concept in one market, you can take it to others.

I am always and forever totally wary of free advertising because eventually too many people try to join in, and your message risks getting diluted and lost in a flood of poorly conceived spam.

Make no mistake about it. The primary reason to create Facebook pages that get "likes" by your visitors is to have the opportunity to hit your "likes" with **paid** advertising.

It is always better to learn how to make a paid ad work and then, while the opportunity is available, apply those skills to make a free ad work, too.

This chapter, however, is about free impressions in Facebook. I would be remiss, in a book on Facebook advertising, not to provide additional suggestions on how to take advantage of those amazing, free Facebook ads: status updates.

STATUS UPDATES AS FREE ADS

When you post a status update on your Facebook page, everybody who liked the page *may* potentially receive a copy of that message in their news feed along with a thumbnail image. Your brand is instantly in front of hundreds to thousands of customers free of charge.

Let's do the math. If you work hard and get people to like your Facebook page for your business, you can probably get up to 5,000 fans just from your existing customers walking in your Facebook front door. If you craft a status update for your customers 365 days a year, with just a measly 5 percent organic reach, you would receive around 100,000 impressions free of charge.

Improve your front porch experience just a little and add a few more status update per day, and you can turn that 100,000 into 500,000 or a million or more.

Do you find this interesting yet?

These are 500,000 impressions reminding your existing customers you are in business and providing them with a reason to return.

If, just once a year, each of your customers repost just one of your status messages to their own Facebook walls, you will be introduced to as many as 200,000 new customers— free of charge.

(By the way, Coffee.org has 250,000 Facebook fans. It gets traffic from a dozen different places. It is not perilously hanging by the fingernails of any one traffic source.)

Unfortunately, if you have 5,000 fans, very few of them may ever receive your status updates. Why? Because not every one of your status updates is a turbo-magnetic social media magnet! You'd have to be superhuman to make every one of your updates good enough to get 100 percent traction.

Facebook does not want to feed uninteresting status messages to their users. They don't want to overwhelm users with too many status updates.

Facebook will not automatically feed every status update to every eligible user because it would be way too many messages—a mighty Niagara Falls of messages. Facebook doesn't want its users drinking directly from the Niagara and risking going over the falls. So they dam the river of messages, filter the water, and route it to a tap where it can be dribbled out safely.

If you want your updates routed to your users for free, you need to learn to write good messages and include rich media (while realizing that you will still need to amplify them with Facebook ads to get even more reach out of each post).

ENSURING YOUR STATUS UPDATES REACH YOUR USERS

Which status updates get displayed to a user? Facebook hopes it is the status messages the user wants to actually see. How does it calculate this? Well, it is a secret. But if we ask ourselves "How would we calculate this?" we may be able to glean some insight on how to write better messages so that Facebook will forward them to more users.

If you were Facebook, filtering the news feed, you would be inclined to forward messages to users from pages where they:

- Regularly like status updates,
- Answer questions,
- Regularly comment on status messages,
- Sometimes repost the status updates to their walls.

There are probably more ways for Facebook to determine if users like a page, such as watching how many times your fans actually visit your page, how much time they spend on the page, whether they respond to multiple messages at one time, and on and on.

But for the moment, we will suggest it is those actions listed above that primarily reflect a user's interest in your status updates. If you write status messages that entice fans to engage in one or more of these four activities, then Facebook will be dramatically more likely to send them your status updates.

You can also surmise that the more the fan interacts with a response, the more Facebook values that response. Reposting a status update to a fan's own status indicates higher interest in a status message than simply liking the message. However, any of these activities provide positive feedback to Facebook about a fan's enjoyment of your page and your status updates.

With Facebook Insights—data that you can easily access right from your Facebook page's admin area—you can access a ton of data on all of your individual posts, your fans, etc. And the great thing about this is that you can take a post with high engagement and amplify that post even more with some paid traffic behind it!

DON'T SPAM—NEGATIVE FEEDBACK

If you keep striking out sending status updates, then take the hint. Your status messages are likely being considered spam by many of your fans. Watch your fan count to see how many people "unlike" your page. If the number is high, you may have problems.

Facebook provides its users with the ability to actively provide negative feedback on your messages as well as positive feedback. We suspect the feedback number it reports is only positive feedback.

At the upper-right corner of your posts, when they appear in your news feed, you may click on a dropdown and leave negative feedback. You have a few different choices here, and Facebook is changing these options regularly.

FIGURE 19.1–Types of Feedback on Posts

One last thought about negative feedback: I (Perry) believe that the surest way to be loved by some is to be willing to be hated by others. This is true not just in marketing but in all spheres of life.

Take a look at any influential, famous, or successful person you care to name. Bill Clinton. Mick Jagger. Gandhi. Britney Spears. Nelson Mandela. Christopher Columbus. Lady Gaga. Gloria Steinem. Steve Jobs. Mother Teresa. Ralph Nader.

Every one of these people has (or had) a polarizing effect on the world around them. People either love 'em or hate 'em. These are people who have boldly presented themselves, their ideas, and accomplishments to the world and ignored the naysayers.

My question for you: What bold, controversial, and decisive stand can you take that will polarize people—that will repel some and attract others?

Success lies on the other side of your answer to that question.

That said, from the standpoint of Facebook's system, it does you no good to make people mad *after* they've become your fans. Of course, there are always going to be some disgruntled folks in every crowd. But the more precisely you target your traffic to begin with, the less mismatch there's going to be.

A WHEELBARROW OF CREATIVE IDEAS FOR DAILY STATUS MESSAGES

 It can be a challenge to come up with great status updates to keep the front porch conversations going, especially if you are doing this 200+ days a year. To make this challenge easier, get yourself a series of good sources for articles, quotes, and ideas. Specifically, find sources that offer RSS feeds. Then direct these sources into a single location where you can quickly review the ideas and come up with each day's status messages.

There are several steps to setting up this process.

- Find good sources for new ideas. This is usually done by using Google to search for your keywords and then finding the best blogs and sites that provide articles on those topics.
- Use Google Alerts to follow your favorite topics and thought leaders in your industry.
- Post that inspiration into your Facebook status.

There are multiple things that can inspire good status messages, including:

- Quotes
- Articles
- Funny and educational videos
- Blog posts
- Websites
- Events that happened on this day in history
- News

In many of these cases, you post links to these ideas with just a brief introduction by you. In other cases, use these sources to spark a conversation on your page.

It is more important to spark conversation than to just repost interesting stories. It is really important to share front porch conversations and not to continually be selling. Unless you sell fun adventures or events, only the rare post should be directly about your product or service—as rare as one in ten posts.

In addition, automatically reposting from your own blog or your Twitter account is not really a good idea. Sure it's quick, but reposting directly from a blog or a Twitter account feels like a repost. It doesn't feel like a warm and friendly front porch conversation.

Also, Facebook knows they are reposted. If you were Facebook, would you treat a repost differently from original content? We would. And we bet Facebook folks do, too. Facebook status updates are a fundamentally different form than a tweet or a blog post.

Take the time to reformat your message specifically for the Facebook environment. It is worth the extra minute or two of effort.

Almost Always End with a Question

Of course, we could still do even more. Our fill-in-the-blank question invites a short-term response, but we could also ask another open-ended question. To invite front porch conversation, you can add the following to your post:

"Jonas Salk was famous for inventing the vaccine.

Press "Like" if you know the answer. Did you vaccinate your kids? Why or why not?"

You are aware there is some controversy around this subject, so you invite your fans to speak to the controversy; however *you* take no position. Now you have a combination trivia question, like request, and front porch conversation starter, all in one status update. I bet this gets you at least a 1 percent response rate.

In some way or form, almost all of your Facebook status messages should end with a question. Ending with a question invites conversation from your fans, and conversation is positive feedback.

If you are running a Facebook page that features children's books and you run across a great list of 100 books every child should read, you may be tempted to just post a link to that list as a status update. The problem is, posting a link to a list of books doesn't really invite feedback. This list could be used instead to inspire a Facebook message that invites feedback.

"My favorite book when I was growing up was: _____."

And now, instead of posting a link to a long list, you have posted a simple question that invites immediate feedback. Users can quickly respond, have a bit of fun, and go on their way.

If you really like the book list and really want to post it, then you can always add the list as a link in a comment after several people have replied with a comment. Another approach is to attach and post the list to your status update but to also write a message that invites participation.

Make People Feel Good about Themselves

The world has got enough bad news already. Right? People go to Facebook for some form of escape. It you want people to like a message, then send a message that makes them feel good about themselves. We call these types of status updates "love-your-mother" messages. Basically, the post is some version of "press like if you love your mother."

On a page dedicated to parents of homeschoolers, I (Tom) posted the following status update:

Did you know that on this day in 1887, Anne Sullivan began teaching six-year-old Helen Keller? Press "Like" if you think everyone who teaches six-year-olds is a "Miracle Worker" in their own way. :-)

It is not a surprise that this status update received a home run, with a response rate over 2.5 percent. It is positive, affirming, informative, and makes people feel good about themselves and what they have accomplished.

Free Cupcakes

There is another type of status update that several small businesses have built entire marketing business models around. We call these "free cupcake" messages, inspired by Sprinkles Cupcakes. Sprinkles, which had surpassed 500,000 fans the last time I checked, frequently posts this style of status message:

The first 25 people to whisper "make my day" at Sprinkles of Palo Alto will receive a free special cupcake.

> Every business should give away cupcakes. Cupcakes are awesome! If you are a storefront, what is your cupcake? If you, as a coffee store, give away 15 free lattes a day but in return collect 250,000 fans, those fans will become the least expensive marketing operation you have ever done.

Might we suggest you go one step further than Sprinkles? Occasionally offer someone who posts a funny comment a free coupon as well. It is a subtle way to encourage likes without violating Facebook's terms of service, which forbid using "likes" to officially enter contests.

Remember, Facebook needs to see responses to keep sending your feed to your fans, so you need to get responses on your post. Our recommendation for anyone using a free cupcake strategy is to write a status post like:

The first 25 people to whisper "make my day" at Our Store will receive a free special cupcake. Press "Like" if you love our cupcakes, and tell us why!

Now you have the people coming to the store for free cupcakes, and everyone is encouraged to press "Like" and add a comment. Give someone who makes a funny comment a free cupcake at the local store, and post that person's picture back on the page to demonstrate that you sometimes give free cupcakes just for funny comments. (Be careful asking for a "like" in your status updates, as Facebook now discourages this. Just focus on engagement. Ask for comments and responses, not just a like.)

If you have a local store, you should have some sort of free cupcake offer connected to Facebook status messages.

Pictures, Videos, and Links

Funny pictures, emotionally moving videos, or really valuable links are great status updates for your page. However, they frequently do not get as many responses as simple fill-in-the-blank trivia question posts.

Why does this happen? The first and most obvious reason is that people are sharing your media content on their profiles and you are getting credit for posting the content.

Clearly, there is another measure of a successful message we may want to create. We offer you the following:

If you get 50 percent more impressions than you have fans when you post media, then you have hit a single. If you get 100 percent more impressions than you have fans when you post media, then you have hit a home run.

The best way to score these points with your status updates is to post items that get reposted. In our experience, funny or emotionally moving videos top that list. (Especially stuff that's drippy, sentimental, or inflammatory. But be very cautious of inflammatory!) Of course, you can always do a call to action in your post as well and request that fans share the video.

Please, let's get the word out. Repost this video to your wall—tell your friends!

JOINING THE CONVERSATION

After you post your original status message, you may also want to occasionally participate in the follow-up conversation by posting in the comment stream and liking comments from your fans.

When you like a comment, the person who made the comment gets a message that their comment has been liked! It closes the loop on the conversation and makes them feel good. If you are the administrator of the page and they see you liked their comment, it makes them feel especially good. So, like lots (but not all) comments. Like the comments you really like. If you like them all, it may trigger Facebook to recognize that you are trying to game the system. Be genuine. Be real. Use these tips to generate real interaction and conversation, not to game the system.

We strongly encourage you to allow your customers to freely comment and post to your walls. You have the ability to delete comments, but this function should be used sparingly. Specifically, delete only:

- Spam

- Inappropriate language
- Unfair or attacking comments

Some conversations get heated. We like to stay out of those conversations and allow them to burn themselves out. We are not here to fight or argue with our customers or to convince our customers to think like we do about every issue. If two customers are arguing with each other and keep posting comments, think of how you must have convinced Facebook that they really like spending time on your page. We bet they count every single comment as a deep and abiding interest in your status updates.

If a user is spamming or otherwise behaving inappropriately, you can remove the comment, ban the user, mark the comment as spam, and report the comment as abusive as seen in Figure 19.2 and 19.3. To do this, click on the X that appears when you hover over the upper-right corner of the comment.

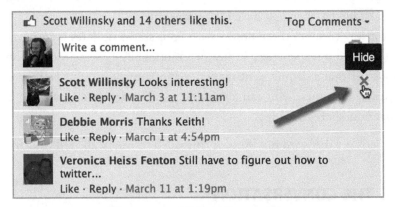

FIGURE 19.2–Hiding Comments

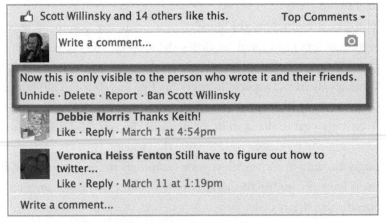

FIGURE 19.3–Deleting Comments, Reporting Spam, and Banning Users

Syndicating Your Status Updates

It is possible to directly reference people, pages, events, and groups in your status updates. If you are responding to someone in a comment or posting a status message to someone who has "friended" you, put the @ character before you type the user's name, and you will have the opportunity to turn that name into a link to the user's profile. The message will also be posted on that person's home page, visible to the user and his or her friends.

If you reference another page, event, or group in your status message, you can also place the @ character in front of the name of the page, event, or group, and those names will become links in your message to the page, event, or the group you referenced. In that way, your status update will appear on the wall of that page or group.

This is a powerful method of syndicating your status message to multiple walls all at once. However, it should be used with care so that you are not perceived as spamming. Use this feature:

- When you want to respond directly to a specific comment by a specific person, and
- When you want to have your message appear on the wall of another group or page.

Harvest Spontaneous Testimonials

Testimonials are your greatest friends. People are dramatically moved to action by testimonials. This effect is why testimonials are so frequently faked and why many governments are cracking down on the use of testimonials in advertising. It's because they work.

Give someone scientific evidence that your product helps people lose weight, and they yawn as their eyes glaze over. Have a hot, young woman testify that "I lost 15 pounds in 10 days on this diet, and I loved it," and suddenly you have everybody's attention. When fans of your page post messages featuring their love of you and your products, it is clear to everyone that a real person is speaking—not a canned testimonial. Facebook page testimonials take testimonial credibility to an entirely new level.

So encourage your users to talk about your products. To testify! Try status messages such as:

- Click "Like" if (your product) has helped you. What do you like most about it?
- Click "Like" if you love (your product). What do you love most?
- Click "Like" if you use (your product). Why did you choose us?
- Click "Like" if you've ever recommended (your product) to a friend. What did you say?
- Click "Like" if you are a customer. What product do you like most?

(Note: Facebook has recently adjusted their algorithm to penalize pages for asking people to like a post. By penalize, I mean to decrease the organic reach or EdgeRank of that particular post. Please do a little research on the most current trends of Facebook's EdgeRank system and how they are treating post content.)

Not only do these messages elicit conversation, they also deliver great insights into how your customers are thinking about your products and services. Of course, there is a little risk associated with asking this type of question—you may receive negative feedback as well.

However, negative feedback is important for you to hear, too, so you might as well hear it now. Plus, you control the delete button!

If a customer leaves an especially great testimonial, send them a private message asking for permission to repost the testimonial on your website and in your outside marketing literature. You now have a nice, clear record for where the testimonial came from and how it was solicited in case anyone ever asks.

Commenting on Other's Walls—Another Reason to Have a Page

Facebook allows pages to behave, to some degree, as if they were users. If you are the administrator of a Facebook page, you may select to "'Use Facebook" as that page. If you select that option, you receive "likes" for the page and "notifications" for the page as if you were a normal user.

If you are using Facebook as your page and you post a comment or a status message on another page's wall, then your post includes your page name, your page thumbnail, and links back to your page.

It is perfectly reasonable to identify 50 to 100 additional, active pages whose visitors may also be interested in your page. You may post comments on these pages from time to time that add to the conversation on that page and complement your page's offerings. Spend some time reading each page and learn what types of comments are common and well received. Your goal is to blend into the conversation and to occasionally say something so interesting or insightful that readers of those other pages decide to click on your profile and learn more about your page, too.

This is a great way to generate some free publicity for your page. However, be careful; Your posts should actively add to the conversation of the page you are visiting or that page's administrator may mark your post as spam.

Some people simply don't pick up on subtle social clues as to what is proper behavior and what is rude behavior. Rude behavior is likely to get you marked as a spammer and abuser on Facebook, and it may kill your ability to syndicate messages.

So here's some frank advice: If you are the type of person who talks loudly on your phone in a restaurant or in a coffee bar, then you probably should not be posting on other people's pages. You are not good at picking up on subtle social clues as to what is proper social behavior and what is rude, and you should not be trying to execute this strategy. We are totally serious.

Keeping Up with Comments on Your Page

People may make comments on new and old stories all over your Facebook pages, in old status messages, and on other tabs such as discussions.

If users are making comments in a discussion, it can be easy for you to miss them. However, if you "Use Facebook as Your Page," you can select to receive a notification email that a user has posted a new question or comment to your page, even in an obscure discussion section. You can then click on that notification and go directly to the point where you need to respond to your user's comment or question.

You may also elect to have these notifications sent directly to your email. If your users are asking questions on Facebook, your support team can be very responsive without actually having to log in to and look at Facebook. Given how distracting Facebook can be, this is a real win. You can respond in almost real time to customer questions and comments, creating an active community feel to your Facebook page without having to be actively scanning your page.

PAGE INSIGHTS

Facebook has created page "Insights" to provide you with summary information about how your pages are being used. Check on your insights every few days to look for unexpected trends.

To find this information, click on a link called "Insights" on the top of your Facebook page.

FIGURE 19.4–Facebook Page Insights

Then click around in the Insights reports. There are a lot of interesting hyperlinks and controls on these reports that do not necessarily look like hyperlinks and controls. So click on everything!

Insights on page visitors include:

- New and lifetime likes
- Daily, weekly, and monthly active users
- Unique page and post views
- Likes and comments on posts
- Page fan age and sex demographics
- Page fan country and city geographics
- Page fan language
- Total tab views
- External referrers

Insights on posts include:

- Impressions
- Reach
- Engagement
- Post clicks, likes, shares, and comments

Insights also provide nice trending graphs like page likes, net likes change, where your likes came from, post reach, likes, comments and shares, total reach, and more.

The labels "Daily Active Users," "Weekly Active Users," and "Monthly Active Users" on this graph are controls. Clicking on the label "Weekly Active Users" turns that part of the graph on or off.

Make sure you read on to the next chapter to find out what Perry's new predictions on the future of Facebook and what things to watch out for to keep you from getting the "Facebook slap."

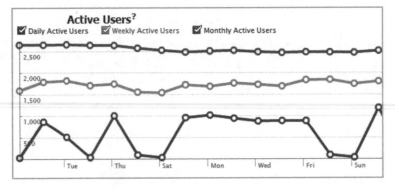

FIGURE 19.5–Active Users Graph

Chapter 20

A Brief History of Google Advertising—and Some Facebook Predictions

THE SMART STUDENT OF ANYTHING IS ALWAYS A STUDENT OF HISTORY FIRST

This chapter will put money in your bank account and add years to your life.

When you understand the history of Google, not only will you position yourself to avoid a bunch of blunders in Facebook, you'll also be able seize very big opportunities. Vast treasures are buried in the shark-infested waters of internet advertising.

Hint: You often find these treasures in sunken sea vessels.

> *"Those who don't know history are destined to repeat it."*
>
> —EDMUND BURKE

I (Perry) started using AdWords when it was little more than one month old. Today my books on Google AdWords are the most popular in the world. I've had a front-row seat to Google's zero-to-tens-of-billions smash, business success story. It was exhilarating to experience it.

I knew exactly what was going on long before Google went public at their audacious opening price of $85. I've witnessed the birth and growth of the biggest and most successful advertising machine in history. It's been flat out amazing.

Along the way, I also consulted with thousands of people in hundreds of industries. I have close, personal connections with hundreds of solo entrepreneurs and roundtable members who have grown businesses from zero to millions of dollars of sales. Google advertising gave birth to entire new industries and niches that did not and could not have existed before.

Not only have I observed the pay-per-click industry evolve, I've also watched business owners fight their way from zero to raging success. I've walked with them through their personal nightmares and victories.

This is a vital chapter for you to read and understand. First and foremost from a Facebook perspective, but more broadly for perspective on any kind of online advertising. Even for forms of online advertising that we never discuss in this book. Please pay close attention.

FROM GOTO.COM TO OVERTURE TO GOOGLE

The first time I ever heard of pay per click, I thought it sounded perverse. You're going to sell search engine listings to the highest bidder? Only whores would do that. How are you going to achieve any kind of honesty with that kind of system?

I gave it little thought beyond that. It didn't occur to me that the highest bidder is often the company that does the best job of giving lots of people exactly what they want (which is why most large shopping malls have Sears and J. C. Penney and every city has a Walmart). Even if you only grudgingly believe in the power of capitalism, you have to admit that what people spend money on, they value.

That was 1999 or so. GoTo.com had started a bidding system, which it then syndicated to search engines like AltaVista, Yahoo! and MSN. I was scarcely aware during the next two to three years that it was fast becoming a billion-dollar company.

GoTo.com changed its name to Overture and continued making money hand over fist.

My mentor Ken McCarthy encouraged me to attend his System Seminar in April 2002. He introduced his colleague Jon Keel who was one of the first people on earth to figure out how to make pay per click work.

Jon gave a stunning presentation, explaining Overture's system in detail, the psychology of keywords, the importance of tracking conversions; and he revealed what to me was a bombshell: the Overture inventory tool. It displayed what search terms people were typing and how frequently.

Tools like this are pretty familiar today. Then it was earth shattering. It was like peering *behind* the internet curtain for the very first time. Seeing exactly how many people were searching for paintball or plumbers or airline tickets to Philadelphia.

Having the ability to endlessly explore human desires and eavesdrop on the conversation inside peoples' heads.

INSIGHT NUMBER 1

The cornerstone of all internet advertising is market research. *Everything* starts with understanding your market. In online marketing you *never* just sling mud against the wall to see if it sticks. You always start with at least some knowledge of what's already going on—otherwise you'll get murdered.

(Dr. Glenn Livingston offers an excellent free series of tutorials for online market research at www.LivingstonReport.com.)

INSIGHT NUMBER 2

The internet is *rifle shots, not shotgun blasts.* This is especially true if you're new. Keyword research tools have been telling us that for ten years. Facebook likes and interests tell you the same thing. The more narrow your focus, the easier it is to speak to your prospect in the exact language she wants to hear. Selling to large audiences with broad interests is a game for ninjas—not beginners.

In Jon Keel's seminar presentation, he explained the huge difference between two keywords that amateurs might assume are similar: "weight loss" and "bariatric surgery," a procedure that shrinks your stomach.

Jon explained that "weight loss" is very general; it's something people search for when they're just poking around on the internet. "Bariatric surgery" is a much more serious term for people who have something exact in mind. It converts to sales much better, and it's a lot more expensive.

Even back then, Jon was painstakingly measuring sales from clicks. He was years ahead of everyone else. Jon insisted that if you weren't tracking conversions you might as well be driving down the expressway at 85 miles per hour flinging $100 bills out the window.

At this time, AdWords had existed in its current form for only a month or two. I went home and decided to try AdWords instead of Overture. It only took a day or so for me to get hooked. Most people weren't using Google yet, but I thought it was a great search engine. I fast discovered Google had built the coolest direct marketing machine ever.

Overture simply gave the top listing to the highest bidder. AdWords had an extra twist—Google multiplied the bid price times the clickthrough rate (CTR) to score your rank. It favored advertisers who wrote better ads, because an ad that doesn't get clicked on doesn't make Google any money. It also doesn't serve the advertisers, and it doesn't serve the end customer either.

This was a stroke of genius on Google's part.

Google execs had another rule: Ads had to achieve at least 0.5 percent CTR or they would get disabled.

Eventually Google replaced the 0.5 percent rule with more sophisticated mechanisms. But at that moment, this rule meant AdWords was only easy for people who were good at writing copy. It added a barrier of entry that favored people like me who already understood direct marketing.

Google had four other major advantages compared to Overture.

1. It allowed you to split test ads. I'll never forget—I created an ad and noticed the "create a new ad" link was still there. I clicked on it again and made a new ad, different from the first one. I went to Google and searched for my keyword and clicked refresh a few times. Sure enough, my ad flipped from A to B and back to A. And yes, sure enough, Google gave me statistics for both ads! Dang. I can now test copy as easy as clicking a "submit" button! And I discovered that even tiny differences made *huge* differences in response.

   Get the Ethernet Basics
   Simple Tutorial on Ethernet, TCP/IP
   5-Page Paper, Free Instant Download
   www.bb-elec.com
   0.2% CTR

   Ethernet Basics Guide
   Handy Tutorial on Ethernet, TCP/IP
   5-Page Paper—Free PDF Download
   www.bb-elec.com
   1.2% CTR

   WOW. What a tremendous advantage for Google! They gave advertisers incentives to write better and better ads, pulling eyeballs from the left side to the right side. A copywriter's dream. I was in heaven. Overture did not have this feature. You could run only one ad at a time. *Massive* disadvantage for Overture, as time would tell.

2. Google ads showed up instantly; Overture's took three days to get approved. When you submitted a Google ad, it started showing right away. You could submit more ads, test them against each other, and three days later on Google you might have a winner out of four ads you'd tested. Meanwhile your first ad was

just getting started on Overture. And you couldn't test. This advantage accrued compound interest over time. In a month, you could test ten things on Overture. But could test 100 on Google because it provided so many more feedback loops than Overture. This meant that Google's revenue engine was improving its effectiveness daily and Overture's was not. It also meant that the innocent endeavor of managing a Google AdWords account became an adventurous, addictive, profitable game of human psychology. *Massive* disadvantage for Overture. Oh, my goodness. Kiss of death.

3. Most people didn't know this then, and most still don't today, but Google applies the same culture of testing to everything they do internally. Not only do they give their advertisers immense ability to test things, they test everything themselves. The number of characters allowed in a Google ad? It's the result of billions of clicks of testing. The colors, fonts, and images of the Gmail sign-up page? Exhaustively tested. Google researchers probably tested 47 shades of green. At Google, every dispute is settled by testing. Overture did far less of this than Google. Once again, *massive* disadvantage!

4. Overture's interface was clunky and hard to use. Google's was easy and intuitive. Add that to all of Google's other advantages, and it was hard to see how Overture could possibly stay in the lead. Overture's customers begged for better tools. Overture ignored them.

   Later, Yahoo! bought Overture. And it still ignored its customers. In only two to three years, Google became a juggernaut and beat its competitors by miles. Google left Yahoo! in the dust. Today, Yahoo/Bing lags far behind AdWords with no hope of ever catching up.

Why am I telling you this? Because in *any* form of online advertising, you're going to succeed for the same four reasons:

1. Testing
2. Speed
3. Testing
4. Ease of Use

As you experiment with different ads, landing pages, and offers, you will find it's devilishly difficult to predict what people want. Heck, I've been indulging in the sport of direct marketing for 15 years. But when I try to guess winners on A/B tests, I still get only 50 percent of the answers right. Even with all my experience I just don't know.

You don't guess, you test.

One more thing about speed. The reason YouTube passed up Google Video and all other video-sharing sites—and the reason why Google eventually had to buy

YouTube for $1.65 billion in 2006—was because Google Video was bureaucratic just like Overture.

It took three days to get videos approved. YouTube was instant. Again, more feedback loops and more opportunities for addictive behavior on the part of content providers.

My friend, if you're online, you got to strip the bureaucracy out of whatever you're doing and build your business for speed.

ON THE INTERNET, ONCE A SITE ESTABLISHES DOMINANCE IT'S VERY DIFFICULT FOR RIVALS TO CATCH UP. SOMETIMES IMPOSSIBLE.

Why? Because size gives you more speed, speed gives you more size, size attracts audience, audience builds size, and a snowball effect always kicks in.

Also, please notice that it's not about "first mover advantage." It's about speed and testing advantage. Most of the "coulda, woulda, shoulda" stories are about internet companies that couldn't get out of their own stupid way.

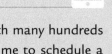

HOW GOOGLE KICKED YAHOO! IN THE ASS

A few weeks ago, a very large Wall Street investment firm with many hundreds of millions of dollars invested in Yahoo!, and Google called me to schedule a consultation.

They wanted me to help them understand "how the sausage is made" and share my views on Google and Yahoo!'s long-term prospects for growth.

Back in the day, GoTo (oops, I guess they're called Overture now) (oops, I guess they're called Yahoo! Search Marketing now) had the tiger by the tail.

They built the world's first pay-per-click money machine, and they had it made in the shade. They organized all the chaos of the internet and started selling clicks. Now search engines could finally start making some money.

And baby, did they ever make money. They thought they were making a lot.

But then Google came along. Google showed 'em how it should REALLY be done. I'm not sure any company in the history of the world has ever made so much with such apparent ease.

HOW GOOGLE KICKED YAHOO! IN THE ASS, continued

You can ask any guy on the street why Google has done so much better, and they'll tell you it's 'cause Google is just a better search engine. And that's true, but that's only half the story.

The other half of the story is that they designed AdWords to maximize the amount of money they make on every search. Advertisers have great incentive to lure people from the left side of the page to the right side to click on those paid ads.

And yes, this has a LOT to do with you, as I shall explain shortly. If you're going to succeed in this game, you're going to succeed for the exact same reasons Google succeeded. So pay close attention as I tell you what I told the guys at the big investment firm.

You may know that Yahoo! just changed the size of their ads from 190 lines of description to 70, just like Google.

Know why they did that? Because Google figured out before Yahoo! did that they'll make more money showing ten little ads than three or four big ones. Yahoo! finally figured it out, too.

How did Google know that? By testing.

Yahoo! didn't test. Shame on Yahoo!. (Shame on everyone who doesn't test, for they shall share the same fate.)

Well, then there's the clickthrough-rate formula. You should know by now that Google multiplies your bid price times your clickthrough rate to figure out where you belong on the page. Yahoo! doesn't do that. Which means Yahoo! ads that get clicks don't rise to the top, and Yahoo! makes less $ from every single search than Google.

Now let's say they make 10 percent less. Does that mean they get 10 percent less business? NO, it's worse than that. Because they have syndication partners (MSN, AltaVista, etc.) and thousands of individual sites who share the profit.

If their partners get a piece of the action, they make 10 percent less, too. Which means they'd rather run Google ads than Yahoo! ads. Which means Google

HOW GOOGLE KICKED YAHOO! IN THE ASS, continued

gets more clicks and Yahoo! gets less. The 10 percent disadvantage becomes 25 percent.

But it gets still worse. Because if you've got 25 percent less traffic, advertisers are 25 percent less interested, which means there's fewer of them. So the bids are lower, and now you're 40 percent behind, not 10 percent.

In the real world of business, 10 percent is really 40 percent.

(You should write that on a piece of paper in big fat magic marker and tape it to your wall.)

I'm not done yet. Yahoo's software is five years old; it's clunky and horribly bureaucratic. Every time you want to change something it takes three days, and it's a nightmare.

I told my friends who manage those hundreds of millions of dollars that heads should have been rolling at Yahoo! a LONG time ago, because this should not be news to anybody!

Heck, I knew this back when Overture was still ahead of Google. Sad. Very sad.

To our friends at Yahoo! Search Marketing—who will no doubt see this email—I say: You better accelerate your plans to fix your stupid broken system, because you're losing ground every single day.

I say this as someone who has not the slightest interest in the Wall Street side of this equation. I own no Google stock (that would create a conflict of interest, given the work I do). I own no Yahoo! stock. What I'm interested in is me and my customers getting the most bang for our advertising buck. And I know that pressure from Wall Street just makes it tougher on advertisers.

Plus I'd like there to be at least one company besides Google who doesn't have its head stuffed in a cloud. I want just ONE good PPC alternative to Google. How about you?

(Need I mention that MSN has a program in beta right now? Yahoo!, you'd better watch out, Bill Gates is coming to plunder your house.)

HOW GOOGLE KICKED YAHOO! IN THE ASS, continued

OK, all this Wall Street stuff is fine for analysts and pundits. But what does this have to do with YOU?

A LOT. The lesson here is: 10 percent is really 40 percent. 20 percent is really 100 percent.

Because there's always a feedback loop. What goes around comes around—how effectively you use every single click on your Google ads, your website, your emails, your upsells; how well you're able to pay your affiliates or JV partners—multiplies and multiplies. On tiny hinges, big doors swing.

A 10 percent improvement on your sales page today may very well be the difference between you being #1 or #2 in your market one year from now, or being totally out of business. I am not exaggerating. And folks, we can all point fingers at Yahoo! for being #2 instead of #1. That's easy to do. Next weekend at the Super Bowl, the winner will take it all, and the loser will slink away in shame.

But this is your website and your business, and you're not an armchair quarterback. You are THE quarterback. Woe be unto you if you fail to apply to your own business the lesson that Yahoo! is learning right now—that every one of those clicks count, and they don't just add up, they multiply.

SPEED SPAWNS ANOTHER JUGGERNAUT—AFFILIATE MARKETING

I wrote the first edition of *The Definitive Guide to Google AdWords* in the summer of 2003. At this point, AdWords hadn't quite caught on, but then a young surfer dude named Chris Carpenter wrote a book called *Google Cash*.

Google Cash explained how you could sign up for an affiliate program, sign up for Google AdWords, give Google five bucks, and start sending traffic through your affiliate link. You could be an invisible traffic broker, pocketing the difference between your click cost and your affiliate commission.

All you had to do was find a combination of keywords and affiliate programs that was profitable and you had an instantly profitable business. You were now an invisible traffic broker.

Google Cash caught on like wildfire. Within six months, hundreds of thousands of people all over the world were bidding on every conceivable word and phrase in the English language—and quite a few other languages—and driving traffic to eBay, Amazon, ClickBank, and thousands of other sites.

It was a massive, underground gold rush.

The thing about it was, it *worked*.

Honestly, I thought it was stupid at first. (Remember, I also thought pay per click was perverse, too. I was wrong.) To me it was just too simple.

Well it *was* too simple, as I shall explain later. But actually it was too simple *not* to work. Some percentage of the time, it was bound to succeed. A lot of people were making a lot of money with this, and there were a lot of keywords available for 5 or 10 cents.

This is what made Google go supernova. Because after a while, no matter what you typed into Google, you saw ads. Every company president, every marketing and sales manager, every webmaster saw somebody showing up on Google, and it wasn't them.

This sucked 'em into Google AdWords against their will. You think clicks should be free? Too bad, 'cause your competitors are buying space where you ought to be showing up. Google hit the tipping point and exploded. I had customers making $100,000 a month brokering clicks.

The genius of *Google Cash* was: You have zero commitments. It's way easier to go find another product to promote than it is to own a product or change your own product. Or even change your website, for that matter. The name of the game is speed and testing.

Google cashers embraced speed and testing overnight. So a new, billion-dollar industry—pay-per-click affiliate marketing—sprang up out of nowhere. At light speed.

THIS IS WHERE THE HISTORY LESSON KICKS IN

The history lesson has everything to do with Facebook and pretty much anything else you do in marketing or advertising. Because this speed/testing combo was like crack cocaine. It was addictive, and it was shallow. It created lots of problems, including the following:

- *An invisible affiliate business is extremely fragile.* It's *very* easy to knock off. (Within a year or two, people started selling software that helped you detect and copy successful affiliate campaigns.)
- *You own zero assets in a business like that.* A $1 million per year direct linking affiliate business is equivalent to building a mansion on the side of a hill in Sao Paulo, on rented land. The next rainstorm could wash that mansion away in a mud slide. You have nothing to show for it.

■ *Invisible affiliates often have no ethics.* Some of them promote horrible products.

■ *Thousands of affiliates all do exactly the same thing at the same time.* They have no advantage over each other; they just drive bid prices up.

■ *Affiliates cluttered the internet with all kinds of lousy offers.* Sometimes you'd search for something, and ten people were all promoting the same thing at the same time. It took a while for Google to eliminate duplicate offers from their search results, but they did.

■ *Content is king,* and most affiliates create no content.

■ *Click for click, the most profitable offers are generally overpriced, overpromised products.* In the short term, "edgy" offers with unrealistic claims, obnoxious websites with pop-ups and no back button, and abusive return policies make twice as much money as sane, honest offers.

■ *Websites like* The New York Times *don't like "edgy" advertisers.* Neither does Google nor Facebook. In the early days, edgy advertisers were all they had. They accepted the money for a while, but as soon as sites like Facebook or Google have enough legitimate advertisers, they kick out the edgy ones.

■ *From the perspective of Google—or Facebook—affiliates are disposable.* "Thank you, Mr. Affiliate, for your giving us so much money for these last few years. Now that you've helped us attract 'real' businesses, we're done with you. Happy trails, you poor, pathetic scumbag."

■ *Google and Facebook don't like affiliates all that much.* After a couple of years, Google started tightening the screws on affiliates. Facebook will, too. Eventually Facebook will be as affiliate-hostile as Google.

Please understand that some affiliates are really cool and very likeable. At the same time, average, unsophisticated, garden-variety affiliates are the trailer trash of the internet. Just tellin' it like it is.

So with that in mind, I'd like to offer you nine tips on how you build a robust, stable, long-term, internet business.

1. *Build a presence over time that's difficult or impossible to knock off.* Any business that can be replicated with "cut and paste" is the online equivalent of a shantytown. A trailer park in Tornado Alley. You want original content, extensive sales funnels, and a USP that's hard for others to attain.

2. *Build assets:* email lists, snail-mail lists, unique products, unique processes, unique experiences. You want your business to run on systems that you own, not rent. You want to build a brand. Better if there's more to those systems than meets the eye. By the way, you can do all of those things as an affiliate. You can build a website, and content, and systems. All those things are hard, tangible

assets. Intellectual property. Technology. Patents. Things that aren't easy to replicate. Amazon is nothing more than a sophisticated affiliate for probably 25 percent of the things they sell. All those product reviews on Amazon are a *huge* asset.

3. *Consider the value of your product.* Google's staff who manually review websites use this criteria: "Would I send my grandma to this site?" Your criteria should be: "Would I sell this to my grandma? Or my sister-in-law?"

4. *Use a different style than everyone else.* Use your personality. You are *always* developing and sharpening your USP.

5. *Sell different things than everyone else.*

6. *Create great content.* Those who live by gaming the system die by gaming the system.

7. *Make your product something other sites, including Facebook, would feel proud to advertise.* Every shopping mall in the country would be delighted to have Nordstrom as their anchor store; become Nordstrom for internet sites.

8. *Do not look like, taste like, or smell like an affiliate*—even if you are an affiliate. You should add value to the equation.

9. *Understand how media companies tighten the screws on affiliates and "thin" advertisers.* I shall explain this concept in the next section.

W-a-a-a-y back in 2004 (how many internet dog years has that been?) I recorded a now-famous teleseminar called *Jet Fuel for Google Cash*. Everything in it applies to Facebook advertisers, too. As an owner of this book you can get the seminar as a special free bonus at www.perrymarshall.com/fbtools/. I strongly suggest you listen to it.

The thrust of *Jet Fuel for Google Cash* is that affiliate marketing is just a way to test new markets. It's not a permanent place to camp out!

As pay per click grew more sophisticated, Google started erecting hoops for advertisers to jump through. It created something called a "Quality Score," which was both an automatic and manual index of your site's quality.

If your QS was 1, you had to bid a minimum of $10 per click for your ads to get shown. Which was just another way of saying "get lost." One day without warning, Google threw the switch, initiated quality scores, and instantly shut out tens of thousands of advertisers.

Google also made it impossible for more than one ad to show at one time in any search result for a single website. This eliminated duplicate affiliates. Only the highest paying one got a spot.

It even started penalizing AdWords accounts that had *at one time* promoted affiliate offers that Google now (not then) decided it didn't like.

Google didn't explain what it was doing; many times it did not warn people. Google representatives wouldn't accept phone calls, and even if you were spending $80,000 per month they wouldn't talk to you. You're just dead. End of story.

Facebook has done the same thing. Do you think Mark Zuckerberg is any more compassionate than Larry and Sergey?

Algorithm-based bans trigger a lot of collateral damage, but Facebook and Google seldom care. As long as they're right three-fourths of the time, they're happy.

Oh, and by the way they will also pay people in India and the Philippines $2 per hour to judge the quality of your $20,000 website, and you may have no recourse. One time Google banned my site. A Google rep from India sent me an email that said, "Also please stop scams."

Please understand, I'm not trying to discourage you. And if you run an honest, straightforward business you probably won't have any problems. But you must recognize these things can and do happen, and companies like Google and Facebook have no qualms about "thinning the herd."

Google and Facebook want their users to have the highest-quality experience possible. They do not ultimately consider their advertisers to be their customers. They consider their *users* to be their customers. Never forget that.

You need to study the above list of nine tips very closely. And here are some more:

- You need to make sure that you're absolutely straightforward with customers about things like recurring billing and charge amounts. Nothing will get you in hot water faster than charging peoples' credit cards without permission. That will get you thrown out of Facebook. It will get your merchant account canceled, too. It will also get you slapped with fines and lawsuits by the attorney general of some state somewhere.
- The claims on your site need to be true, they need to be verifiable, and they need to be reasonably realistic. No fake testimonials. Readers should be able to find the people or companies who say they liked doing business with you. Providing hard, verifiable proof isn't merely honest. It's good marketing.
- You need transparency. That's what social media is all about in the first place, right? You have a Facebook page where real people interact; you have an email address; you have a phone number. You have real people who can fog a mirror and answer questions.

  Some categories are automatically suspect: make-money opportunities, weight loss, medical products, alternative medicine, drugs, gambling, real estate, marketing techniques, stock trading, securities, and adult websites—all attract more than their share of riffraff and are heavily scrutinized. Some such sites are highly regulated. Some markets are filled with vermin. (These categories are also *very* profitable for ninjas.)

- "Boring" categories seldom have problems. If you sell barcode readers or packaging machines, if you own a local insurance agency, or if you market sewing supplies, you have little to worry about.

BID PRICES: THE TREND IS USUALLY UP

Let's say you're buying clicks for 60 cents and you're profiting an average of 40 cents on each click. Congratulations—you're a successful online marketer!

You need to expect that those clicks are going to get more expensive. 62 cents . . . 70 cents . . . 85 cents . . . a buck.

You need to test and track so that the following can happen:

- Your ads get better and better CTRs (thus counteracting the upward pressure of bid prices).
- You convert more and more visitors to buyers, pushing your profit margins up.
- You sell more in each transaction.
- You sell more after the first transaction.

In every market—and in every form of advertising—bid prices will tend to rise until most advertisers are breaking even acquiring a new customer. They're not making money on new customers, only on repeat business.

If you enter a market and find that you're making money hand over fist—and you don't even have a sophisticated sales funnel—then you need to stay ahead of the pack and build that sales funnel out. 'Cause the competitors are coming, I promise.

On the other hand, if you're building and cultivating an email list, if you sell products at a wide range of price points, if you have cross-sells and upsells, if you connect to your customers in multiple ways (email, chat, in person, live events, brick and mortar), you grow your roots deeper. Your business becomes stable.

Once you get ahead of the curve, your job of *staying* ahead becomes much less tiresome. It is frankly much easier to be number one in your market than to be number four or number five and fighting over the scraps. And once you get to number one, momentum is on your side, because you can test more things faster than your competitors.

I cannot tell you how much better it is to be number one than to be number four or five. In fact, this is a core of Richard Koch's concept of "The Star Principle," the formula he used to multiply a few million dollars to hundreds of millions in two decades. You can score your own business according to Richard's formula in just a few minutes at www.StarPrinciple.com.

YOU MUST DIVERSIFY

For years I've told my Google AdWords students: If one year from now you're still getting 100 percent of your traffic from Google, I have failed to do my job. Ditto with Facebook. You might get started on Facebook. For the next six months all your traffic may come exclusively from Facebook.

But once you start figuring out the formula, as soon as you start selling, you need to expand into other **paid** (not necessarily free) media, including:

- Google AdWords display network
- Google AdWords search
- Paid YouTube placements
- Yahoo!
- MS Bing
- LinkedIn
- Affiliates
- Banner ads
- Retargeting
- Paid insertions in email newsletters
- Print advertising
- Radio
- TV

Of course, there's also free media, such as the following:

- Search engine optimization
- Viral Facebook traffic
- Twitter
- YouTube
- Newspapers and magazines
- Blogs
- Publicity

Any business that works with *one* of these mediums will probably work with several of them. Your business begins to diversify as your traffic diversifies.

Your goal is for none of these to represent more than 20 percent of your business. Once you achieve that, it becomes very unlikely that any one disaster will tank you.

WHAT I LEARNED FROM INFOMERCIALS

Some people watch infomercials; some buy from them. Some don't.

I for one have never bought a single thing from an infomercial. I'm not "an infomercial buyer."

In general, I don't even care to watch them all that much, even though they are extremely educational for salespeople. (Tip: If you want to witness a sales pitch that has been scientifically proven to work, just watch an infomercial that's been on the air for three months. I can guarantee you, it's making money. Take notes and look for ideas you can borrow.)

But anyway, in 2002, when I first began using pay per click, I almost instantly knew how the entire AdWords market was going to develop. Even though it was virgin territory, it was undeveloped, and nobody understood it.

I knew that in ten years it would become a fiercely competitive, dog-eat-dog marketplace, and there would be certain things you HAD to do in order to win, and I knew that because I had studied infomercials.

You can make the exact same predictions about Facebook. What does Facebook have to do with infomercials?

Back in the '80s, broadcasting laws changed, and it suddenly became possible for TV stations to sell extended slots to advertisers. You may recall that 30 years ago most TV stations went off the air at 1 A.M. or 2 A.M., saying, "We'll be back at 6 A.M."

So people started making 30-minute commercials.

I remember when I was a kid, turning on the TV one night and seeing an infomercial shot at a Holiday Inn meeting room. It was a single camera pointed at an overhead projector, and some guy was pitching information on how to get rich in real estate.

When infomercials were new, the airtime was incredibly cheap. You could actually shoot a cheap video at a seminar, air it, and make money.

Then companies started discovering that this worked. And the bid prices went up. Today if you want to *test* an infomercial you're going to spend a minimum of $75,000 to $100,000 to put a show in the can and test it in a few markets. It's going to have to be professionally produced and superbly scripted; otherwise, it doesn't even stand a chance.

Most of the players in the infomercial biz are companies who specialize in this and do hundreds of millions of dollars of business. The largest such company is Guthy-Renker, whose sales are about $2 billion.

The barrier to entry is now very, very high.

I knew that pay per click would be a microbusiness version of the same thing, on the internet. And as online advertising matured, I always knew what was next. I knew history repeats itself so I had studied history.

Here are some factoids about the similarities between infomercials and Facebook that I would like you to think about:

It used to be said that infomercials were the most competitive place you could possibly sell anything, because the customer's hand is always on the remote control, and she can change channels if she gets bored for two seconds. That's even truer online: People have 12 windows open, and the entire internet is only a click away.

Sales funnels get more sophisticated as media prices rise. A few years ago, a simple long-form sales letter did the trick. Now, many products require a well-scripted, well-shot video. A few require a carefully engineered webinar.

Barriers to entry go up. Good for you if you're an insider, bad for you if you're an outsider.

One last comment about internet media companies:

They favor their existing advertisers over new ones. New advertisers are a "credit risk." If companies are going to take space away from an existing, profitable advertiser and give it to a newcomer, they're exposing both the customer and their bottom line. So they'll serve ads only a little bit at first.

You can expect the formulas Facebook uses to determine ad serving to become more sophisticated and more automated all the time.

The good news is, as you crawl inside the machine and experience it, you'll develop an intuitive feel. It will no longer be formula, it will be natural to you. That's how you will know you're achieving mastery.

Go to www.perrymarshall.com/fbtools for the latest updates & to get valuable resources for more clicks from Facebook for less money.

Chapter 21

Guard Your Stack

"ONE LONG SHOT AND THREE FISH IN A BARREL"

Every Friday for years, my late friend Tom Hoobyar and I (Perry) had a regular afternoon chat. Tom was a salty dog, old enough to be my father; me, a Gen X marketing punk. We coached each other. The two of us watching each other's backs made a good team.

A few years before, he'd left his post as CEO of a Silicon Valley bio-tech firm, exchanging small tech company entrepreneurship for lone-wolf entrepreneurship. Big shift. Suddenly, he found himself where I was when I started my present business; he'd also had about ten times as many careers as me.

> *"Hell, there are no rules here—we're trying to accomplish something."*
>
> —Thomas A. Edison

As he described one of his projects, I recalled a formula that helped me keep the income steady when I was getting started. But before I explain that formula, we've got to address the matter of taking risks and matching them to your risk tolerance.

Tom was describing the simultaneous launch of three or four different products and, in some cases, building a new prospect list from scratch in order to launch them. His plans were thorough, as they normally were with Tom.

Still, a little warning bell went off in my head: "Too many long shots at one time" feeling about launching that many products simultaneously.

When I went out on my own, the first order of business was to secure enough monthly retainer income from active consulting projects (*hunting*) to cover my nut. Then and only then would I embark on a much lengthier process of building a list, selling information, and being a published author (*farming*).

For several years I had three to four consulting clients who collectively more than paid the bills. So I could afford to invest in developing a robust information business. Once the consulting business was in place, I stopped taking new clients, tightened my belt a little, and invested in list-building and product development. The product income slowly matched and then replaced the consulting income, giving me more options.

The consulting was shooting fish in a barrel. For the most part, any particular project was a slam-dunk—writing a white paper or magazine article or press release or building an opt-in page, suddenly getting my client 15 leads a day instead of one or two—that, for me, was easy. (And sometimes a little boring.) My clients got the results they were after, and I got paid.

I said to Tom: "Tom, a real nice formula for building a prevailing business with minimal risk is **One Long Shot and Three Fish in a Barrel**. One big project that is long-term and speculative with huge upside potential and two or three or four small games you know you can easily win, that will definitely pay the bills, and eliminate the panic factor from your decisions."

When people are consumed with fear—and possibly shame because they're running out of money or whatever—they make bad decisions. Fear alone is *always* a bad foundation for decision making.

Every dollar and every minute you spend buying Facebook traffic or any other kind of traffic is a risk and an investment of your time.

Invest wisely, and your business will prosper. Invest poorly, and you'll be divorced and stocking shelves at Walmart. That's why the last chapter of this book is about *managing risk*.

It's difficult to imagine a career track with a higher failure rate than rock 'n' roll. Drummer Mike Portnoy is one of my personal fave musicians. Someone once asked Mike, "Did you have a backup plan (alternate career), just in case?"

His answer: "I never gave myself an option. As soon as you have a 'backup plan,' you will be likely to fall back on it the minute the times are tough. Succeeding requires 100 percent dedication and perseverance, which means you have no choice but to keep trying and moving forward. And to be honest, I never *thought* about making music my career . . . it kind of just happened because it is what I 'did.'"

When Mike was trying to make it, he was delivering Chinese food for a living and had no family to support. For me it was different—wife and three kids, a mortgage and car payment. Being "out on the street" was the number-one item on the "unacceptable outcomes" list. Destitution was more unacceptable than failing in business. I *had* to have a backup plan.

RISK, PARANOIA, AND THE BURNING OF BOATS

People have wildly different reactions to risk. For me, having a backup plan does *not* necessarily mean that I'm going to yank the parachute lever when the going gets tough. (If anything, I'm prone to taking a long, circuitous, "challenging" route when an easier way is sitting right there in plain sight.) Knowing that I *do* have a backup plan is reassuring because I'm less fearful. The trapeze artist takes bigger risks when she knows there's a net to catch her if she falls.

Other people may need to close off all exits. The famous story of Cortes burning his boats before conquering Mexico comes to mind . . . except I researched that story and found out it's a legend.

Cortes didn't burn his boats at all. He had 12, ran nine into the sand (to keep enemies from using them against him), and kept three—*and* a master shipbuilder among his crew. According to *Fast Company* and John Coatsworth, dean of the School of International and Public Affairs at Columbia University and an American scholar on Latin America, "Cortes beached the ships to prevent anyone from heading back to Cuba to report to the Spanish nobilities that he was engaged in an utterly unauthorized and illegal expedition. He was running for cover."

So much for Cortes motivating his men.

---

ser·en·dip·i·ty

1. The faculty of making fortunate discoveries by accident.

2. The fact or occurrence of such discoveries.

3. An instance of making such a discovery.

Serendipity will bring you from where you *thought* you wanted to be to where you *should* have been all along. I don't know about you, but very few things I've ever done turned out exactly the way I envisioned them at the beginning—sometimes much different.

It's usually just plain dumb to "burn the boats." I've long lived by the phrase "never burn a bridge," which normally means do NOT get all uppity and tell somebody off. Even if you're "sure" you'll never ever need anything from that person in the future because you probably will anyway.

I've rarely violated that rule and have never been sorry for *not* breaking it.

Why It's Hard to Hire a Good Marketing Consultant

Many marketing geniuses are on the rise, and the good ones do outstanding work. We've trained a whole bunch of 'em. Problem is, if they're really good, they're only available to do project work for a window of time, typically a couple of years. Here's why.

A gal does crackerjack consulting work—she's the "rainmaker" for her client. Eventually, she has the following conversation with herself:

"Self, you boosted your client's sales by $1.5 million this year."

"By golly I think you're right."

"They made $350,000 of additional profit, and they paid you $30,000 in fees. Oh, and the CEO's got heartburn about the $15,000 bonus he's supposed to pay you at year's end—you know, the 1 percent of sales growth thing. He wants to trim that back to 0.5 percent for next year. But he says we can easily expect another $3 million growth for next year, and he feels a $15,000 bonus is real good for a gal your age."

"You mean I futzed around with that 'marketing communications manager' for eight months and pounded all those changes through their bureaucracy, we *still* grew sales 1.5 million, and he's complaining? Self, I'll find a product someplace and we'll sell it all by ourselves, thank you very much, and I won't have to deal with these tight-fisted morons anymore."

"Gary Halbert was right, clients *do* suck."

She takes fewer and fewer clients at higher and higher fees, only accepting deals that match her growing list of requirements, and eventually she does no client work at all—because she went to a trade show and found a Korean tent manufacturer, and now she's distributing their stuff online and taking a 70 percent gross margin.

The Korean guys don't have the slightest idea how to replicate what she does, and she's got a little blue notebook with seven other promising projects a lot like this one. She can eventually have all of them running in tandem, if she wants. Suddenly those $15,000 bonuses are chump change. Not worthwhile if it takes a fight to get 'em.

The upshot of all this is that she's going to be available for two to three years and after that she's unavailable. She's doing her own thing.

Facebook ad consultants, take note.

One time I got into a tiff with a client, and I was feeling intimidated. I asked the legendary copywriter John Carlton for some advice; after I explained the situation to him, he said, "Perry, you're not just a mouth in the food chain, you *are* the food chain. Listen up—if the CEO's hand isn't shaking when he writes you the check, you're not charging enough."

If you know how to research markets, understand groups of people, buy clicks from Facebook and sell—then you can write your own checks.

"Three Fish in a Barrel" Can Take Many Forms

At my "Dilbert" cube job, we worked furiously for four years. Finally the owners sold the firm to a publicly traded company for $18 million. I left with a check. That happened because of the *long shot*—we'd invested $2 million (mostly borrowed from angel investors) in product development and created a digital communications chip that people in our industry needed.

But that long-shot chip was still not even selling yet, and the whole project was possible in the first place only because the company's bread and butter was something else. We were distributing communication boards from three European companies in the United States and Canada. Buying them, marking them up, and reselling them.

We gained great insights from selling and supporting these products, which helped us design our chip. The margins kept the lights on. It was a natural transition from one to the other—in fact, the new chip was designed to be interchangeable with the old computer boards.

Remember that when you buy a product from Germany or Sweden and resell it in the United States, you turn your money around a *lot* faster than if you've spent two years and $2 million designing a chip. But even that distribution business was bootstrapped by another business when it was new. At first *that* business was a long shot. So while we were getting that distribution business in place, with subdistributors and reps all over the country, a process that took a couple of years, we were doing hardware/software consulting projects.

A company would come to us and say, "Hey, can you write this software for us?" and we'd do it. Hand-to-mouth projects. Shooting fish in a barrel. Putting food on the table in the short term.

People sometimes think they're above doing simple things that pay the bills because they're enamored with the romance of their long-shot deal. Not only do they underestimate the task of making the long shot happen, they often don't recognize that the lesser, related business will teach them many important things they still need to know.

Again, all these situations come with a side benefit of giving you a view into situations you wouldn't otherwise be privy to. Sometimes we can be totally blind to things that are happening right in front of our eyes.

> A **long shot** is anything that involves building a list slowly from scratch, extensive and expensive product development, investment of big dollars, and slow accumulation of assets.
>
> **Shooting fish in a barrel** is anything where there's existing, pent-up demand for something you can easily assemble or convert from existing resources; "will-work-for-food" opportunities that pay on an hourly or per-job basis; affiliate or joint venture situations where an existing set of customers can be matched to a new offer.

One guy merely lays bricks; another builds a wall; another builds a cathedral. There are always easy opportunities sitting right in front of you that you haven't seized yet.

Multiple, Multiple Backup Plans in Your Shirt Pocket

Doing consulting work was at the top of my list of "shooting fish in a barrel" options, but it was by no means the only thing on that list. There were a bunch of other options on my "B" list, like writing content for industry magazines ("stringer work"); being a Chicago sales rep for one or more companies; actively soliciting consulting projects through direct mail, magazine publicity, and ads in trade magazines; and starting a new publishing venture with my buddy Heather in Toronto.

I was prepared to do any and all of these things.

When you've got a backup list that long, and you're in the middle of a tough negotiation, all you have to do is remind yourself that you've got that big, long "B" list to fall back on, and you can easily maintain your composure.

SELL EARLY, SELL OFTEN

 Many entrepreneurs are building start-ups from the ground up. An interesting question I (Tom) hear is "When should I start advertising?"

Most people wait waaaaaay too late.

Here is my suggestion. Start waaaaaay too early.

Start on day one.

On your first day, put up a simple web page with a description of what you are trying to do and a form for someone to give you their name and email so you can tell them when you are ready to launch.

Don't wait.

Each day you work on your start-up, add more to your web page, and add ways for people to send friends to your page.

Don't wait.

Every week or two, mail out to your list of prospects the progress you are making and how the idea is growing. Offer a forum for them to make suggestions.

Don't wait.

If you are building software and are unfunded, try to release a beta version of some minimal working functionality as soon as possible. Hopefully within two months of starting the business. Release software when it is too early and have people look at it and try to use it. Their feedback is priceless.

Don't wait.

If you are building software, or any service, try to get someone to pay for it while you are still embarrassed to ask for money. Someone paying for your product or service is the best indication you are not delusional in your start-up idea. Don't wait.

If you've never failed, you've probably never really pushed yourself hard enough. Fail at something. It is good for the soul.

Don't wait.

—Thomas Meloche

HORTON HEARS A WHO

Dr. Seuss wrote the story of Horton the elephant who, while splashing in a pool located in the Jungle of Nool, hears a small speck of dust speaking to him. Turns out the speck is a tiny planet, home to a city called Whoville. Microscopic inhabitants known as Whos are led by their courageous mayor.

Horton can't see them, but with his large ears he can hear them. The mayor asks Horton to protect them from harm. Horton happily agrees, proclaiming throughout the book that "even though you can't see or hear them at all, a person's a person, no matter how small."

The other animals force Horton into a cage for believing in something that they're unable to see or hear. Horton tells the Whos that, lest they end up being boiled in "Beezelnut Oil," they need to make themselves heard to the other animals.

The Whos orchestrate themselves and in the end a "very small shirker named JoJo" makes enough of a peep for the jungle animals to hear the sound. Finally everyone agrees, "A person's a person, no matter how small."

When you operate a small, online business you are a Who.

Large animals in the jungle can't hear you. Or if they do, they ignore you. Here's an example: In 2011, the state of Illinois created a new law. The law dictates that if an affiliate in Chicago generates a sale to a customer in Ohio, shipped and fulfilled by Amazon in Kansas, the customer in Ohio has to pay 8 percent Illinois sales tax.

How much sense does that make?

What if the buyer lives in Seattle where Amazon's headquarters are and buys through an affiliate link from the woman in Illinois? Does Amazon pay sales tax to both states? Well, the whole reason mail-order companies don't pay sales tax is to keep states from hindering interstate commerce with ridiculous tariffs. You can easily imagine how this could escalate out of hand.

It's probably unconstitutional, but that didn't keep Governor Patrick Quinn from signing it into law, which meant Amazon and Overstock and a bunch of other companies had to terminate their affiliate programs in the state of Illinois.

The hundreds or even thousands of letters and emails to the governor didn't help. A whole bunch of Whovilles, snuffed out.

I'm not telling you this to gripe. I'm just telling this so you know, there's pros *and* cons to being an invisible business. And one of the cons is that some huge beast can flick its tail and push you out of the way.

I started this chapter talking about managing risk, and this is just another example. Maybe you solve this problem by getting only a portion of your revenue from affiliates. Maybe you incorporate in a different state. Maybe you have multiple sources of traffic. Maybe you have a fallback position in case one of your product lines doesn't work out.

The other thing you need to do is band together with other Whos. Let me tell you how a different group of Whos escaped the wrath of the state of Illinois.

This picture on page 313 shows what happened in the Illinois state capitol when the state threatened home-schooling parents with regulation.

My friend, what you see here is only the *overflow*. This is the part of the crowd that spilled out of the main auditorium. Thousands of home-schooling parents took a day off work and drove down to Springfield, Illinois (that's 3.5 hours south of Chicago, a long, boring drive). Considerable inconvenience.

Then for hours, legislators heard about how home-schooled kids are in the 80th percentile and are courted by major universities, while kids in the Illinois public schools can't even read. *No thanks, State of Illinois, we don't need your "help" educating our children.*

The state legislature *quickly* backed down.

This is the second time I've seen this happen, by the way. Several years ago I went to a hearing about a similar bill. About 50 very resolute individuals spent 2.5 hours making

sure lawmakers heard loud and clear that we did not want them meddling in our affairs, and we do an excellent job without any of their red tape.

They heard it again, and again, and again. Finally the person running the meeting said, "Uh, OK, everyone, we get the point, and we realize that the original legislation will not achieve the objective it was originally intended to accomplish."

My friend, those guys will definitely think twice before trying again to regulate home schools.

My point is this: "Virtual" is great most of the time. But being REAL—in person, breathing and fogging a mirror, showing up and confronting a lawmaker—*that* is how you get counted in the affairs of the brick-and-mortar world, government, or otherwise. Being an invisible noncitizen won't get you any representation at all.

This brings up the whole issue of online marketers as a community vs. being a vast sea of invisible, faceless people hiding behind their computers. If you've been around Planet Perry for a few years, you'll notice I've stepped up my delivery of seminars in the last couple of years.

Why?

Because a community of people who never meet each other really isn't much of a community. Google advertisers had to band together when Google started "slapping" them left and right.

Facebook advertisers will likewise need a voice, because your friendly Facebook rep in the Philippines may be just another "Who" at Facebook.

Many, if not most, online marketers can find some way to physically connect with their customers *in person*. You included. Surely there's a way.

There certainly is such a thing in Planet Perry. I invite you to register for the free bonuses for this book at www.perrymarshall.com/fbtools and try our Mastermind club membership when you get there. You'll get email updates about Facebook's system and information about what other successful Facebook marketers are doing.

BIG CHALLENGES, DARK FEARS, AND THE S-T-R-E-T-C-H-I-N-G OF COMFORT ZONES

I just got back from the Upper Peninsula of Michigan, 450 miles north of Chicago, where my daughter and I went on a daddy-daughter camping trip.

No running water, no electricity, cabin in the woods, swimming in the river, and being close to nature. It was great. Good for our relationship too, and not a moment too soon. She's my oldest, and she's halfway grown up already. College years are approaching fast, and every minute is precious.

One of the things we did was pole climbing and rope climbing, with harnesses and mountain-climbing gear and all that stuff. One day we climbed this contraption of ladders and ropes, built on a tower 50 feet high.

I'm sure I appeared composed and seemed to be doing just fine, but halfway up that thing I was desperately wanting to be anywhere else. I'm struggling to get a toehold; I'm hanging by my fingers; my hands are sweaty; I'm 25 feet in the air swinging back and forth. And all of my normal instincts are screaming *Get us down from here right now, Perry! Like, Now!*

I don't know about you, but all my years of living on planet Earth have conditioned me to feel safe only when my feet are on ground. Especially ground that isn't moving. Even though I had a big cable attached to my chest, even though I could have let go and fallen only six inches—even though I was actually completely safe—I didn't *feel* safe.

At that point you can only do one of two things: Go up or go down. Finish the climb or quit. I took a ten-second break and collected my thoughts, and what ran through my mind was *Hey, Perry, this is just like every other significant thing you've ever done in your life—as scary as all get-out, risky, totally unnatural. And it made you nervous because . . . because it mattered.*

Insignificant things don't feel that way. Watching TV, eating pizza, and drinking beer—those things don't make you feel nervous and scared. They don't shove you out of your comfort zones.

I was talking to one of the girls at the camp and told her, "When you feel that nervous, 'let's get out of here right now' feeling, it either means a) you really shouldn't be doing this at all, so you'd best go right back down to the ground where you came from, or b) you feel nervous because it matters, because it *is* important, because you *should* be doing it."

Which is to say, if you don't feel scared every now and then, you're not doing anything important.

Life is too short to not go ahead and get totally terrified every now and then. It's a sign that your soul is still alive and kicking.

I'm guessing it took me five, six, maybe seven minutes to climb that 50-foot rope ladder. But then about a half-hour later I watched two of the camp counselors race to the top on a bet. First place, 40 seconds, second place 45 seconds. Young, wiry guys. They practically sprinted up that thing, better than a foot a second.

Watching them, I realized that people can get used to, and even quite comfortable with, climbing at dizzying heights and doing things that are totally abnormal and terrifying to most people.

Not only that, but everything I've gotten really good at—everything you've gotten really good at in life—was a lot like rope climbing or mountain climbing. Once you've acquired a certain level of skill, whether it's climbing a 10,000-foot peak or making a million dollars a year, it isn't such a big deal. On a good day, you might not even break a sweat.

It's usually the first 50 feet—making that first dollar of actual profit—that deters most people. Get past that point and the competition thins dramatically. Soon you find you're not only comfortable with it but enjoying it. That's how the serial entrepreneur is born—so addicted to the adventure he or she can't stop.

My friend, I've come to recognize that feeling of terror, that icy sensation of exposure and fright, is a signal that what I've just begun is important. That it *ought* to be done. The fear is a signal that it's worthwhile.

Yes, you might feel fear when you've begun something totally foolish. But you'll also feel that fear when you start a new enterprise, when you seek to repair a broken relationship, when you pick up the phone to make that important phone call. Nothing that matters happens until you do it.

The winner takes all, and the winner is you—when you decide to conquer fear and make it your ally.

—Perry Marshall

About the Authors

PERRY MARSHALL

Perry Marshall is the number-one author and world's most quoted authority on pay-per-click advertising. He is the author of the best-selling guide to Google advertising, the *Ultimate Guide to Google AdWords*, and the biggest-selling guide to Facebook advertising, the first edition of the *Ultimate Guide to Facebook Advertising*.

His company, Perry S. Marshall & Associates, consults with companies in over 300 industries on generating sales leads, web traffic, and maximizing advertising results.

Prior to his consulting career, he helped grow a tech company in Chicago from $200,000 to $4 million sales in four years, and the firm was sold to a public company for $18 million.

Like direct marketing pioneer Claude Hopkins, Perry has both an engineering degree and a love for persuasive copywriting.

He's led marketing seminars, spoken at conferences around the world, and consulted in hundreds of industries from computer hardware and software to high–end consulting, from health and fitness to corporate finance.

He's published hundreds of articles on sales, marketing, and technology, and his works include 80/20 Sales & Marketing (Entrepreneur Press, 2013), Ultimate Guide to Google AdWords (Entrepreneur Press, 2014), and a technical book, Industrial Ethernet (ISA, 2nd Edition).

He's spoken at conferences around the world and consulted in over 200 industries, from computer hardware and software to high–end consulting, from health and fitness to corporate finance.

KEITH KRANCE

After six years as an airline pilot for Horizon Air, a subsidiary of Alaska Airlines, and racking up over 4,000 flight hours, Keith's entrepreneur spirit finally took over. After leveraging some early real estate success, he started, owned, and operated several brick-and-mortar retail businesses as a part of two franchises. After a few years of "grinding" through managing these businesses he started diving into direct response online marketing.

He quickly fell in love with Facebook advertising, as he had never seen any other advertising medium like it in the offline world; similar to billboards and TV advertising yet cheaper to test and implement, and much more targeted.

Keith is now the founder and president of Dominate Web Media, a full service agency and consulting company specializing in helping businesses scale their marketing and reach by using strategic Facebook advertising, retargeting, and tapping into dozens of other online media channels and social media marketing platforms. His team has managed several million dollars in Facebook advertising, which has generated hundreds of thousands of new leads, and several million dollars in revenue generated directly from Facebook and other online media channels.

Dominate Web Media has worked with clients in dozens of different markets all over the world, helping both small and larger businesses. In addition to fully managing client campaigns, Keith has online learning programs and coaching programs where he works directly with entrepreneurs and business owners to help them scale their business and increase profits by setting up successful campaigns and sales processes optimized for online and social media traffic and maximum ROI.

THOMAS MELOCHE

At the age of 38, Meloche along with three partners founded Menlo Innovations, a software consultancy and development firm. The immediate challenges he and his partners faced were staggering: a software industry in a quality crisis, the collapse of the internet bubble, the beginning of the offshore movement, and an economy in free-fall after the terrorist attacks of 9/11. Most would not believe it possible to start up a software consultancy in the midst of such monumental turmoil. The circumstances, however, do reflect many of the same day-to-day struggles organizations face today—a world dominated by change. Meloche lead Menlo Innovations' marketing initiatives implementing techniques he learned from Perry Marshall.

Menlo is now world famous. Last year executives from over 200 corporations around the world traveled to Menlo to tour the facility and observe their operations first-hand. A book on Menlo, *Joy Inc. How We Built a Workplace People Love*, has become a best seller.

"Don't forget," Meloche reminds his audiences, "My success with Menlo and dozens of other companies is because of direct marketing fundamentals. The details of how to best leverage Facebook may change, but the direct marketing fundamentals never do."

Thomas Meloche is President and chief-dishwasher of Meloche Consulting Inc., consulting on Facebook advertising and organizational transformation.

Index